Metaphor, Analogy, and the Place of Places

Metaphor, Analogy, and the Place of Places

Where Religion and Philosophy Meet

Carl G. Vaught

Provost Series

Baylor University Press
Waco, Texas USA

Scripture quotations are from the New Revised Standard Version Bible, copyright 1989, Division of Christian Education of the National Council of the Churches of Christ in the United States of America. Used by permission. All rights reserved.

Book Design by Diane Smith
Cover Design by Joan Osth

Library of Congress Cataloging-in-Publication Data

Vaught, Carl G., 1939-
    Metaphor, analogy, and the place of places : where religion and philosophy meet / Carl G. Vaught.
        p. cm. -- (Provost series)
    Includes bibliographical references and index.
    ISBN 1-932792-07-4 (hardcover : alk. paper)
    1. Philosophy and religion.   I. Title. II. Series.
    B56.V38 2004
    210--dc22
                                                    2004015372

Printed in the United States of America on acid-free paper

For my colleagues in the

Department of Philosophy

at Baylor

Contents

Preface

This book addresses a cluster of questions about what happens when religion and philosophy meet. My thesis is that they stand together and apart in a rich variety of ways. As the first chapter of part one indicates, both domains focus on what is ultimate, however differently they express their concerns about its nature. It is also important to notice that both religion and philosophy begin with mythology and that this fact brings them together from the outset. Another way of expressing what binds religion and philosophy together is to point to mystery, power, and structure as irreducible conceptions within each realm and to the openness, otherness, and intelligibility to which they give us access. Finally, the language of religion and philosophy that will be discussed in this book begins with silence, power, and speech and involves an interplay among figurative, performative, and intelligible modes of discourse.

In chapter 2, I will argue that the history of theology and philosophy must make a place for the medieval thinkers, standing in between the ancients on the one hand and the moderns on the other. The conflict between these two contexts has overdetermined our attitude toward the history of religion and philosophy, but once a new conception of their relation to one another moves beyond this conflict, the religious and philosophical reflection that emerges from it can fill the vacuum between the ancient and the modern worlds. When we bring Jerusalem and Athens into relation with one another in chapter 3, this points to a confrontation between them that is irreducible, but it also points to a positive relation between them that we need to affirm. As a consequence, continuity and discontinuity emerge as central themes in the discussion of the relation between religion and philosophy.

Part two develops the theme that religion and philosophy belong together and apart in four chapters about Augustine, Hegel, Heidegger, and Jaspers. In chapter 4, the focus is on faith seeking understanding as the motto of Augustine's life, on auditory metaphors that give him access to

God, and on the language of the heart that the figurative discourse of
Augustine's *Confessions* expresses. Chapter 5 discusses the immanence and
the transcendence of God in Augustine's theological and philosophical enterprise; chapter 6 turns to the problem of difference in Hegel's philosophical
system; and chapter 7, considers the problems of Being and *Existenz* in
Heidegger and Jaspers.

In part three, the discussion turns to the concepts of metaphor, analogy,
and the Place of places as ways of giving access to God. Chapter 8 introduces
the concept of the quest for wholeness for the first time in this book.
However, there are analogues to it in some of the other chapters; and the
concepts of metaphor and analogy and of the Place of places developed here
are central elements in some of my earlier reflections. Chapter 9 returns to
the concepts of space, time, and eternity; to the categories of mystery, power,
and structure; and to the figurative, performative, and intelligible uses of
language that give us access to them.

The final chapter begins with the philosophical concern about the
nature of Truth and with the traditional philosophical theories that have
attempted to explicate it. In the process, I connect these theories with their
scientific and theological counterparts, seeking to do justice to the scientific
attempt to find the truth and to the theological concern with the highest
Truth. However, my ultimate aim in this book about the relation between
religion and philosophy is to develop an account of the nature of Truth that
will bring it into relation with God. As in some of the earlier chapters, this
relation is expressed in terms of the crucial role of metaphorical and analogical discourse in human experience.

Before I turn my attention to the three parts of the book and to the ten
chapters they contain, I should mention four final issues. The first consideration is that reflections about Augustine are often at the center of our attention as his appearance in chapters 4, 5, and 7 suggests. From historical,
theological, and philosophical points of view, it is what Augustine says to us
and what we need to say to him that motivates our inquiry. The second issue
to be emphasized is that the problem of difference appears as a fundamental
element of our inquiry. This becomes evident when we notice that it stands
at the center of the chapter about Hegel and is an essential part of the chapter about Heidegger and Jaspers. The third point to notice is that the concepts of space, time, and eternity are crucial categories in discussing the
nature of religion and philosophy and the relation between them. Space
opens up a region between one individual and another and between each
individual and the larger community of which it is a part. As a consequence,
it allows us to move outward toward the larger world and to turn inward

toward a world of our own. Time points to the developmental aspect of individuals and communities as they move from stage to stage to seek fulfillment and to the origins from which both individuals and communities emerge. Eternity points upward and downward, giving space and time a dimension of ultimate significance; and the Place of places holds space and time together, bringing them into relation with what is ultimate, whether we articulate it from a religious or a philosophical point of view. The final categories considered are metaphor, analogy, and the Place of places, which appear in many chapters. The fundamental thing to notice about these aspects of my system is that metaphors are a way of articulating the temporal dimension of experience, analogies are a way of expressing the spatial side of experience, and the Place of places is a way of unifying space, time, and eternity, all of which have emerged as crucial elements of our analysis.

There are a number of individuals and institutions that have made it possible for me to write this book. First, I express my gratitude to the students at Penn State and Baylor who have attended my lectures and seminars about many of these topics. Second, I thank the former Provost at Baylor, Donald Schmeltekopf, for initiating this series; and I am grateful to our current Provost, David Lyle Jeffery, who not only supports this project but has also written a book for it. Third, I want to express my appreciation to my colleagues in the philosophy department at Baylor for providing me with a supportive and exciting academic environment in which to write this book. I am pleased to dedicate this volume to them. Fourth, I thank the editor of Baylor Press, Carey Newman, for his help and encouragement about a variety of issues; he is the best editor I have ever had. I also want to thank Diane Smith, the production manager at the Press, for helping me put this book into final form. In addition, I am especially grateful to Amy Antoninka for entering many of my handwritten revisions into the manuscript, for finding and entering most of the notes into the text, and for preparing the index. I also thank one of the external the readers that the press commissioned to evaluate the manuscript for many helpful suggestions, nearly all of which I have incorporated in the final version of the text. Finally, my wife, Jane, recognized before I did what I was trying to accomplish in this book. One day at breakfast she asked me questions about what the book is about, and my initial replies were the typical abstract responses of a philosopher. Yet having listened carefully, she moved to the heart of the issue by saying, your title should be, "When Religion and Philosophy Meet." Because of the insight she displayed on this as on so many other occasions, I am happy to embody her suggestion in the title that finally emerged.

I have presented earlier versions of most of these chapters to many institutions and at a number of philosophical meetings. A version of chapter 1
was delivered to the Philosophical Society at Penn State, January 21, 1994
and in a series of lectures given at Georgetown College, Georgetown,
Kentucky, September 25, 2003. A previous version of chapter 2 was presented to the University Scholars Program at Penn State, November 17,
1992; and a version of chapter 3 was delivered to the department of philosophy, Vassar College, April 2, 1987 and to the department of philosophy,
Whittenburg University, Springfield, Ohio, April 30, 1987. Versions of
chapter 4 were given as the Keynote Address to the Baptist Association of
Philosophy Teachers at Baylor, November 16, 1989; to the department of
philosophy at the University of Amsterdam, April 26, 1991; to the Joseph
Butler Society in Oriel College, Oxford University, May 6, 1991; to The
Baptist Association of Philosophy Teachers at Baylor, September 23, 2000;
to the University of North Carolina in Asheville on April 23, 2004; to The
"D" Society, Faculty of Divinity, Cambridge University, November 16,
1990; to The Baptist Association of Philosophy Teachers at Georgetown
College, Georgetown, Kentucky, November 17, 1991; to The Society for
Phenomenology and Existential Philosophy, Georgetown University,
Washington, D.C., October 12, 1996 and was presented as the Keynote
address to the North Texas Philosophical Association at the University of
Dallas in Dallas, Texas, April 17, 2004.

A version of chapter 5 was delivered to the Philosophy Colloquium, at
Baylor, April 25, 2003; chapter 6 was presented to the Hegel Society of
America, Emory University, Atlanta, Georgia, October 9, 1986; part of
chapter 7 was given to the Philosophy Colloquium at Baylor, November 9,
2001; and chapter 8 was presented at a variety of places: The University of
Montana, April 17, 1974; Brigham Young University, October 6, 1976;
Western Carolina University, May 5, 1977; Iowa State University, March 30,
1978; and The Conference on Reality and Meaning, University of Toronto,
August 19, 1983. Finally, chapter 9 was delivered to the Graduate
Philosophy Club at Penn State on October 20, 1969.

List of Abbreviations

Barnes   Barnes, Jonathan, ed. *The Complete Works of Aristotle.* 2 vols. Rev. Oxford Translation. Princeton: Princeton University Press, 1984.

Brown   Hesiod, *Theogony.* Translated by Norman O. Brown. Indianapolis: Liberal Arts, 1953.

BT   Heidegger, Martin. *Being and Time.* Translated by John Macquarie and Edward Robinson. London: Blackwell, 2000.

C   Augustine, St. *Confessions.* References are given by book, chapter, and paragraph form in the text, permitting readers to find these references in any Latin edition and in any translation.

CD   Barth, Karl. *Church Dogmatics.* 5 vols. Translated by G. T. Thomas. Edinburgh: T&T Clark, 1936.

Cooper   Cooper, John M., ed. *Plato: Complete Works.* Indianapolis: Hackett, 1997.

CPR   Kant, Immanuel. *Critique of Pure Reason.* Translated by Norman Kemp Smith. New York: St. Martin's, 1965.

CT   Heidegger, Martin. *The Concept of Time.* Translated by William McNeill. Oxford: Blackwell, 1992.

Haldane   Hegel, G. W. F. *Lectures on the History of Philosophy.* Vol. 1. Edited and Translated by E. S. Haldane. London: Routledge and Kegan Paul, 1955.

Haldane and Simpson
>Hegel, G. W. F. *Lectures on the History of Philosophy*. Vol. 3. Edited and Translated by E. S. Haldane and Frances H. Simpson. London: Routledge and Kegan Paul, 1955.

ID   Heidegger, Martin. *Identity and Difference*. Translated by Joan Stambaugh. New York: Harper and Row, 1969.

IM   Heidegger, Martin. *An Introduction to Metaphysics*. Translated by Ralph Manheim. New Haven: Yale University Press, 1959.

M   Anselm, St. *Monologion*. References are given by chapter in the text, permitting readers to find these references in any Latin edition and in any translation.

OFCW   Augustine, St. *On Free Choice of the Will*. References are given by chapter and paragraph form in the text, permitting readers to find these references in any Latin edition and in any translation.

P   Anselm, St. *Proslogion*. References are given by chapter in the text, permitting readers to find these references in any Latin edition and in any translation.

Pegis   Pegis, Anton C., ed. *Basic Writings of St. Thomas Aquinas*. 2 vols. New York: Random House, 1945.

PM   Hegel, G. W. F. *Philosophy of Mind*. Translated by William Wallace. Oxford: Clarendon, , 1959.

PN   Hegel, G. W. F. *Philosophy of Nature*. Translated by A. V. Miller. Oxford: Clarendon, 1970.

PS   Hegel, G. W. F. *The Phenomenology of Spirit*. Translated by A. V. Miller. New York: Humanities, 1977.

QW   Vaught, Carl. G. *The Quest for Wholeness*. Albany: The State University of New York Press, 1982.

RE   Jaspers, Karl. *Reason and Existenz: Five Lectures.* Translated by William Earle. New York: Noonday, 1955.

S   Augustine, St. *Soliloquies.* References are given by chapter and paragraph form in the text, permitting readers to find these references in any Latin edition and in any translation.

SL   Hegel, G. W. F. *Science of Logic.* Translated by A. V. Miller. New York: Humanities, 1969.

ST   Tillich, Paul. *Systematic Theology.* 3 vols. Chicago: University of Chicago Press, 1951, 1957, 1963.

WP   Nietzsche, Fredrick. *Will to Power.* Edited by Walter Kaufmann. Translated by Walter Kaufmann and R. J. Hollingdale. New York: Vintage Books, 1968.

PART ONE

The Relation Between Religion and Philosophy

Chapter 1

The Origins, the Context, and the Language of Religion and Philosophy

Religion and philosophy begin with mythology; or in a more contemporary and conventional formulation, they begin with the stories that emerge from the deepest levels of our individual and collective experience. The clearest indication that this is so is that children are natural philosophers and theologians. The imaginative stories they tell, the provocative questions they ask, and the creative conceptions they frame forge an indissoluble link between the mythic dimension of childhood and the abstract discourse in which theologians and philosophers express themselves. One of the reasons that the questions they ask are so strange and unfamiliar is that they express a steadfast refusal to relinquish the imagination, the astonishment, and the creativity of a child who faces a world that often resists his attempt to come to terms with it. Nevertheless, the child, the theologian, and the philosopher try to make this world their own by spinning a web of words that expresses the mystery, the power, and the structure of experience to which they respond.

The problem with most professional philosophers and theologians is that we have forgotten the stories with which we began. Some of these stories are responses to our own experiences in childhood. Others are expressions of the collective wisdom of the culture in which we are embedded, receiving abiding formulation in legends, fairytales, dreams, and other expressions of the collective unconscious that bind us together. Still others mark our own self-conscious entry into religion and philosophy, providing the *mythos* that sustains our efforts to come to grips with later, more sophis-

3

ticated questions about the meaning and the structure of human existence. Yet the stories with which we begin usually remain in the background, and our reflections will be impoverished, theoretical truncations of experience unless we try to remember them and indicate something about how our mature reflections emerge from the ground they presuppose.

In my own case, three experiences stand at the gateway of my entrance into mythological consciousness and point to the philosophical reflections to which it often leads. The first expresses itself in the story of the comic book and the fig tree; the second, in the fable of the Golden boys and the goat; and the third, in the anecdote of the squirrel and the open cage. The events behind these stories occur in serial order, beginning at the age of two and moving to the age of four. The first episode may be a conflation of three events, the first two of which my mother has described to me on many occasions, while the other is one I can remember clearly. In any case, they merge for me now as a single event that unfolds in three stages. First, my mother and I walk to the corner drugstore. Then I take a comic book from the shelf while she is occupied in another part of the store. Finally, I leave without paying for it.

When my mother discovers what I have done, she takes me back to the store to return the book and to apologize to the owner for taking something that does not belong to me. After we return home, I run away, going back to the drugstore to look at the shelf where the comic book sits. This time I look at it without picking it up and return home as if nothing had occurred. However, my father who is working under a fig tree in the backyard calls me under it with him, strips off one of its branches, and switches my bare legs for running away from home. As I recall the episode, four impressions remain: I am fascinated with the comic book, unimpressed about apologizing without a clear concept of having stolen it, remember the second trip to the drugstore as an adventure rather than a way of running away from home, and feel both fear and disdain for being punished under the fig tree for doing something that had felt so natural and harmless. To this episode I trace philosophical and theological significance: my lack of respect for authority, my concept of original innocence, my fear of original sin, and my keen awareness of the reality of retribution.

The second episode occurs the next year and begins when the voice of my mother wakes me from an afternoon nap. I can still here her calling, "Son, wake up; the Golden boys have brought you a goat." I get up slowly from the bed, walk onto the back steps into the blinding light of Abilene, Texas in the middle of the afternoon, and rubbing my eyes from the sleep and the sun, see the goat on a rope being held by two friends from around the corner. A hasty conference ensues between my parents: My mother says, "They're trying to pawn off a goat they don't want on us"; my father asks, "What harm will it do"? I beg my parents to let me keep it; and the rope passes from the hands of the Golden boys to mine. For several weeks I play with the gift from my friends, tying him to a wagon and urging him to pull me around the yard. I also learn not to turn my back on him because he is a billy goat and butts me from behind at the slightest provocation.

One day, a farmer comes to the house, takes me for a walk in the grape vineyard behind our house, and offers me a fifty-cent piece for the goat, which I take because I realize that I don't have a choice. The denouement comes when my father brings home a package of meat several weeks later and announces, "Son, we are going to have some of your goat for dinner." No doubt he was teasing me; but at the time, I didn't realize it. I can scarcely decide which stage of this extended episode is the most memorable: "Son, the Golden boys have brought you a goat"; rubbing my eyes in the blinding sunlight and taking the rope; riding in my wagon as the goat pulls it across the backyard; remembering never to turn my back on him; the walk with Mr. Beaty in the vineyard; the fifty-cent piece in my hand; or the smile on my father's face as he tells me what we are about to have for dinner. Perhaps it is just as well that I continue to remember the episode as a whole, rather than breaking it apart into its constituents.

The third event is clearer and simpler. One day my father drives up to our house to say that someone down the street has a squirrel to give away. We get into the car together, find the address, go up to the door, and take the squirrel home in a cage. My father builds a house for the squirrel in the backyard, and every morning and afternoon I go out to feed it and talk to it as the summer days go by. Then one day my father tells me that the squirrel has escaped, and when I go into the yard to find the door of its house open, I begin to call it to come home. My father tells me that the situation is hopeless, but I continue to call without the slightest doubt that the squirrel will return. What I remember most clearly about this episode is looking up at the spreading branches of the trees, calling my squirrel to come back home, and beginning to forge the concept of an origin from which one can wander away.

If religion and philosophy begin with stories like these, it is also true that they originate in the kind of responses we make to them. It is possible to forget about them, to write them off as insignificant vestiges of childish immaturity, or to regard them as anecdotes of merely autobiographical or psychological interest. However, if we extend the reflection of childhood on such stories, we can make access to religion and philosophy in the richest possible terms. Stories like these generate wonder and the desire for wisdom; they mobilize faith and the search for understanding; they plunge us into doubt and produce the quest for certainty; and they demand interpretation and foster hope for an orientation that gives us a place to stand and to develop. Wonder, faith, doubt, and interpretation lead us to the context of theology and philosophy out of which a disciplined response to the stories with which we begin originates.

The unconscious psychological roots of our existence, the stories that are buried in childhood, the imaginative dimension of the soul they express, and the archetypal images they produce are the ground out of which religion and philosophy emerge. The love of wisdom is both a monstrous and a wondrous thing, releasing frightening and exhilarating responses from those who seek it because it speaks from both the heights and the depths of existence. It should not be surprising that most of us try to change the subject, transforming the love of wisdom into the phenomenology of experience, the analysis of ordinary language, the speculative attempt to frame a system of categories, or the deconstruction of previous philosophical efforts to think systematically. It is harder to embrace a context for thinking that remains true to its mythological origins, while it tries to elaborate the mysterious, the powerful, and the intelligible contours that theological and philosophical thinking exemplify.

The context of religion and philosophy involves an interplay among temporal, spatial, and eternal dimensions, each of which moves in two directions, and all of which come to focus on a dynamic and unfolding Place where they converge. Philosophical reflection moves forward and backward on a temporal axis, outward and inward on a spatial axis, and upward and downward on a vertical axis that intersects the horizontal dimension of experience to give it eternal significance. The temporal dimension of this context unfolds in a sequence of stages, the spatial dimension involves an interplay between the individual and the community, and the eternal dimension allows us to raise the perennial question about what it means to be human. Every mythological story worth telling implicates all three dimensions and becomes a Place of mystery, power, and structure that the theologian and the philosopher must face and try to understand.

The temporal, the spatial, and the eternal dimensions of experience both intersect and unfold in a Place that makes other places possible, that mirrors their structure at the distinctively reflective level, and that orients thinking with respect to them. This Place of places is both the condition for the possibility of the places out of which mythological stories emerge and the original of which these other places are the images. In this Place, the richness of experience, the profundity of reflection, and metaphorical and analogical language converge and interact to give us access to the meaning of human existence.

The richness of experience is its own justification; the initial purpose of the mythological stories we tell is to evoke this richness without apology, excuse, or antecedent categorial reflection. Nevertheless, philosophical categories are relevant to the experiences and stories with which we begin, pointing to the mystery, the power, and the structure they exemplify. The experiences that mobilize theological and philosophical reflection and the stories that express their significance first presuppose a place of silence, then involve a place of power, and finally generate a place of speech. The mystery, the power, and the structure of religion and philosophy interact with one another here.

These religious and philosophical categories articulate the content of the Place of places, both grounding and reflecting the mythological origins that the temporal, the spatial, and the eternal dimensions of experience express. They also demand three kinds of response from anyone who wishes to embrace these origins and articulate their significance. Mystery requires reflective openness; power demands an acknowledgment of otherness; and structure points to the possibility of philosophical intelligibility. At the human level, the intersection of mystery, power, and structure requires a corresponding intersection of openness, otherness, and intelligibility in the reflective consciousness to which the mythological stories with which we begin are addressed.

Philosophical categories and the human responses they evoke require a language appropriate to the experiences they generate and to the reflection they provoke. This language must be figurative, performative, and intelligible at the same time; for the mystery of experience requires figurative discourse; the power of existence demands performative discourse; and the intelligibility of life needs comprehensible discourse. Yet before we focus on the language of theology and philosophy, let us return to the temporal, the spatial, and the eternal dimensions of the framework that makes philosophy and theology possible and that mirrors their origins at the reflective level. This leads us back to the Place of places where time, space, and eternity interact, and where the mystery, the power, and the structure of experience are evoked.

One of the most obvious features about the concept of place is that it displays temporal, spatial, and eternal dimensions. Places are to be characterized in terms of the past they presuppose, the present they instantiate, and the future toward which they are oriented; they are to be distinguished from one another in terms of the spatial relations they bear to one another, and the dimension of depth they display points to the eternal dimension they exhibit. The dependence of the concept of place on time, space, and eternity implies that it is a concept only in an extended sense of the term, for space, time, and eternity make predication possible without being predicates themselves.[1] This does not mean that space, time, and eternity cannot be characterized, but simply that they are not categorical terms from which characterizations of objects or events can be made. These terms are the presuppositions of predication and the *termini ex quo* of religious and philosophical discourse rather than conceptual devices from which a categorical system either can or ought to be constructed.

Since space, time, and eternity are not categories, an adequate attempt to understand them involves a stretched use of language that transcends the limitations of ordinary discourse. It is also important to notice that time has taken precedence over space and eternity in modern and contemporary philosophy and that temporality has been the horizon in which the modern tradition has approached philosophical questions (*BT*, 39). There are at least three reasons for this. First, when modern and contemporary philosophers inherited the contrast between time and eternity from their Greek and medieval predecessors, and when they rebelled against eternity in the name of reason or experience, time became quite naturally the framework in which the liberation of the philosophical consciousness expressed itself. It is true that space also stands in contrast with eternity; but since the crucial distinction between eternity and the finite order is the contrast between permanence and change, space was subordinated to time for the purposes of developing a distinctively modern theological and philosophical consciousness (*BT*, 39). Second, eternity is more easily spatialized than temporalized because the concepts of permanence and stability can be represented more directly by spatial analogies than by symbols with a temporal connotation. In contemporary terms, onto-theological metaphysics represents the presence of eternity in spatial concepts; and the repudiation of it in the name of fundamental ontology carries with it the rejection of representational language as a primordial mode of discourse (*BT*, 43). Finally, the modern and contemporary preference for time instead of eternity is motivated by the belief that truth must be relativized and that historicism must be given its due if we are to express what is distinctive about the modern and the contemporary philosophical consciousness.

In modern and contemporary philosophy, time is the dominant conception; space is an abstract mathematical matrix that can be expressed in geometrical terms; eternity is timeless and generates a chasm between the finite and the infinite that can be transcended from a temporal point of view; and Place is the dynamic concatenation of space, time, and eternity, where time is the fundamental conception. Yet serious difficulties arise about a position of this kind, the first of which is that the original term in a theological and philosophical system need not always be abstract, except from the standpoint of the knower who tries to grasp its significance. When we begin with space in making the transition from time to place, we may be able to understand the spatial element only after this transition has been affected. Yet what is abstract for the intellect may be concrete, and what is last in the order of knowing might be first in the order of being.[2] I believe that this is true of the concept of space, for unless we were first positioned in space, we would not be able to make a transition from space and time to place. Space is the abstract possibility of spatial location and of synthetic activity, but it is also the aspect of place in which I can locate and orient myself in contrast with whatever else there is. Spatial location should not be reduced to an abstract facet of a larger temporal context, but is the condition in which we can stand in radical contrast with other things and persons and with the larger community. Place also presupposes eternity, as well as being a concatenation of space and time. Eternity is needed to give significance to any spatiotemporal nexus, and Place is the mysterious, the powerful, and the intelligible reflection of the places it makes possible. Eternity is mysterious, time is powerful, and space is intelligible; it is the interplay among these dimensions that makes the concept of Place both the ground and the reflection of the places to which the stories with which we began give us access.

The second difficulty with an account of the concept of place that makes temporality the essential element in religion and philosophy is that it assumes that the inverse transition from place and time to space is merely an analytical reflection of the synthetic development that moves in the opposite direction. The claim that time is more important than space in generating the concept of place gives pride of place to the termination of inquiry in contrast with its *arche*. However, the quest for a beginning and for a sense of place that gives us access to it is not merely the analytical reversal of a synthetic act, but a way of uncovering a dimension of depth in human experience, the weight of which can only be borne by an adequate concept of eternity. Place is a necessary condition for originating something new by permitting us to engage in a sequence of synthetic acts, but it is also the origin from which these acts of origination spring. To uncover an origin in this sense is not simply to engage in an analytical reversal of synthetic activity, but to give an account of the mystery, the power, and the structure of time, space, and eternity from which an adequate concept of the context of philosophy emerges.

The language required to do justice to the stories with which we began and to the Place where theological and philosophical reflection occurs must be sensitive to the mystery, the power, and the intelligibility of both contexts. Thus, the language of religion and philosophy must be both an intersection and an interaction of figurative, performative, and intelligible discourse to respond to the richness of the contexts that evoke it. As a first approximation, mystery corresponds to eternity, temporality to power, and spatial configuration to intelligibility. This implies that figurative discourse is required by the eternal dimension of experience, that its temporal aspect evokes performative discourse, and that its spatial side demands intelligible speech. There is something to this suggestion; for the mystery of eternity strains religious and philosophical language to the breaking point, the power of time requires a way of speaking that mobilizes and reflects the actions we perform, and the structure of space provides the mathematical stability that intelligible discourse tries to articulate. However, the difficulty with this approach to religious and philosophical language is the literalistic mentality that it reflects. Proceeding in this way presupposes a simple correlation between time, space, and eternity; power, structure, and mystery; performative, intelligible, and figurative language. The dimensions of experience that make mythological stories possible, the philosophical categories that frame the context of religion and philosophy, and the modes of discourse that make it possible for us to speak about them are too complex for any correlation of this kind to be more than a clue about how to proceed.

Yet with this clue in mind, we can begin to generate a more subtle account of theological and philosophical language by noticing that time, space, and eternity have a mystery, a power, and a structure of their own and that the three kinds of discourse that we have distinguished have a role in describing each of these dimensions of experience. The mystery of time is reflected in our incapacity to answer the question, "What is it?," provoking us to use figurative discourse in trying to describe and come to grips with it. Its power is revealed in its irrepressible movement and in the omnivorousness with which it devours its children,[3] making it necessary for us to express both the movement and the negativity of time rather than describing the passage of time as it unfolds before us. And the structure of time becomes evident in our capacity to distinguish among the past, the present, and the future, and to locate ourselves in it by using intelligible language that presupposes temporal coordinates.

In contrast with both time and eternity, the mystery of space is its capacity to bind things together and to hold them apart, not only metrically, but also physically as parts of a spatial continuum. Understanding this requires a figurative use of language that speaks about an abstract spatial medium as if it were a concrete domain in which finite things can stand side by side. The power of space is its ability to provide an orientation for things in space without which we would be unable to distinguish left from right and inside from outside. This power requires a corresponding use of performative discourse, for we can express what the orientation of something is only by speaking as if it were setting out to do something as opposed to describing the context in which it finds itself. Finally, the intelligibility of space is its status as an abstract medium in which the things space can display determinate dimensions that enable us to enumerate, to measure, and to weigh them. The precise mathematical language that we can bring to bear on things enables us to perform these operations.

The mystery, the power, and the intelligibility of eternity cannot be approached directly as we have done in reflecting on space and time. Rather, its mystery is revealed indirectly by our incapacity to capture it conceptually. Hints about its power manifest themselves when it makes an impact on us at a level of feeling that lies beneath the level of theological and philosophical reflection. Yet we are constrained to speak about it if we want to understand the significance of life, thought, and action, where this dimension of meaning would be impossible without the presence and the absence of eternity. If we answer the call to speak about what remains hidden even when it reveals itself, we must speak in a fashion that brings figurative, performative, and intelligible language together. The use of figurative discourse acknowledges that what we try to speak about can never be comprehended adequately; performative language permits us to respond to what reveals itself beneath the level of cognition; and intelligible discourse forces us to admit that life, thought, and action would be meaningless apart from the presence and the absence of eternity.

I began this chapter with the language of myth to suggest that religion and philosophy begin with figurative, performative, and intelligible discourse. The stories about the comic book and the fig tree, the Golden boys and the goat, and the squirrel and the cage express my own sense of wonder, faith, doubt, and interpretation that the experiences of childhood generate in the prolonged adolescence of the philosopher. Then I developed the context of theology and philosophy by pointing to the interplay among the temporal, the spatial, and the eternal dimensions that make experience possible, and to the mystery, the power, and the structure that make theology and philosophy relevant to it. I also spoke about the language of religion and philosophy and about the need to bring figurative, performative, and intelligible discourse into relation with time, space, and eternity and with the mystery, the power, and the structure that they presuppose. The final thing to be done is to indicate that the dimensions of experience, the categories of theology and philosophy, and the modes of language appropriate to them not only make experience, religion, philosophy, and discourse possible, but also reflect what they ground in their own internal constitution. This task involves something like the transition from the middle to the later Platonic dialogues,[4] where the questions that arise drive the problems of rest and motion, permanence and change, and identity and difference up into the context that serves as the condition for the possibility of experience and cognition at the lower levels of experience.[5]

When we move in this direction, we find four features about the categories and the language of theology and philosophy that mirror the stories with which we began. First, the categories of mystery, power, and structure that make experience and reflection possible have a mystery, a power, and a structure of their own. Second, these categories are not only self-referential, but also have a time, a space, and an eternity appropriate to them. Third, language about the categories and about the time, space, and eternity in which we can locate them must be figurative, performative, and intelligible in ways that image the corresponding features of the stories with which we began and the pre-reflective experience they presuppose. Finally, the categories, the temporal, spatial, and eternal dimensions that they exhibit, and the figurative, performative, and intelligible discourse that they make necessary display an openness, an otherness, and a demand for intelligibility that mobilize metaphor and analogy as the most important features of the language of theology and philosophy.

The language that this inexhaustible domain requires is figurative, performative, and intelligible at the same time. It is figurative because the space, time, and eternity that it presupposes are spatial, temporal, and eternal in extended senses of these terms. The transition from time, space, and eternity in pre-reflective experience and in the mythological stories it generates to the temporal, spatial, and eternal dimensions of the categories transforms the phenomenology of experience and the stories that emerge from it into a temporal, spatial, and eternal logic of reflection. The language we must use about this philosophical domain is performative because the categories it includes move as if they had a will of their own. Speaking about them not only forces us to stretch language beyond its ordinary uses but also requires us to acknowledge that the categories unfold of their own accord as if they were instantiating an internal verbal demand. Finally, the language we use in this context is intelligible because there are analogies between the ways in which the categories are related to one another and the ways they behave in relation to a concrete subject matter. These analogies, with the similarities and the differences to which they call our attention, enable us to find our way around within this rarified domain.

The analogies that bind and separate time, space, and eternity in their ordinary senses from these same categories as they apply to themselves points to the openness, the otherness, and the demand for intelligibility that call our attention to metaphor and analogy as the most important aspects of the language of religion and philosophy. Because the relation among the categories is open-ended, the demand for openness in religion and philosophy is appropriate; and we can respond to it by learning to use metaphorical language in philosophical contexts. One of the most important features of a metaphor is its open texture that prevents us from paraphrasing it.[6] The fact that the categories are not only related to one another, but also stand in contrast with one another, points to the presence of radical otherness within theology and philosophy as autonomous activities. Yet the autonomy of theology and philosophy does not imply that it is a self-contained enterprise in which thought thinks about its own conditions. The analogical language that theological and philosophical reflection requires points to a moment of difference that holds the categories apart.[7] Finally, the relation of these categories to one another generates a demand for intelligibility that the use of analogical discourse is intended to satisfy. Analogical language not only holds its terms apart, but also binds them together in a community where both identity and difference are preserved.[8] In this case, the Place of places is the nexus that orients our approach to time, space, and eternity, not only as a way of understanding the Being of beings, but as a way of glimpsing the Being of Being as well.

Chapter 2

A New Conception of the History of Philosophy

Since the beginning of the nineteenth century, two antithetical views of the history of philosophy have dominated the interpretation of the Western philosophical tradition. On the one hand, philosophy has been understood as the progressive unfolding of the truth, beginning with the initial glimpses of it by the Greeks and culminating with the comprehensive elaboration of it in Hegel's philosophical system.[1] This view both generates and is sustained by the idea of progress, is supported by the conviction that science as an unfolding quest for truth is the proper model for philosophy, and is substantiated by Hegel's capacity to bring his own scientific system to progressive articulation (*PS*, 51–52, 485–93).[2] According to this conception of the nature of philosophy, the end toward which philosophy is directed is more important than the beginning, and the goal of absolute comprehension is the standard in terms of which all previous stages of the history of philosophy are to be assessed (*PS*, 11). On the other hand, this same process has been regarded as a radical degeneration, falling away from a primordial beginning that was infinitely rich and calling for a recovery of the authentic Voice of Being as it once spoke to the Presocratic philosophers (*IM*, 13–15, 52–74, 91–108, and 127–52). This view is expressed most clearly in Heidegger's claim that what is truly great always begins in greatness and in his assertion that subsequent philosophers have dichotomized and represented what will always transcend analytical abstraction (*IM*, 12–15; *BT*, 21–28). According to this alternative, the beginning of philosophy is more fundamental than the end, and the origin to which it calls our attention must be recovered by the destruction of the intervening ontological tradition.[3]

Despite their radical differences, the role of medieval philosophy on both views is the same. In each case, the medieval period stands in between the beginning and the end of philosophical reflection, appearing either as a halfway house to progress or as a degenerate mode of reflection that must be overcome. Perhaps it would be more accurate to say that what is distinctive about medieval philosophy is absent as a decisive influence, creating a vacuum in which a conflict has occurred between the ancient and the modern worlds (*IM*, 13–14).[4] This vacuum forces contemporary philosophers to take a stand in what has often been called the "war between the ancients and the moderns." And if most of our contemporaries have settled this confrontation from the side of the modern tradition, the fact remains that it has developed in the space generated by the absence of medieval philosophy as a viable philosophical alternative.

There is an especially poignant passage in Hegel's *Phenomenology* in which the negative role of the medieval era is formulated explicitly. After his discussion of Stoicism and Skepticism as the culmination of the ancient world, Hegel speaks about the unhappy consciousness, separated from the ground of its existence by an infinite chasm. He refers in this connection to the burning of incense and to the ringing of bells, as if this were all that existed in the medieval world to mediate the contrast between the finite and the infinite (*PS*, 126–38). As this contrast becomes infinite, and as the soul becomes unhappier still, there is little wonder that Hegel should have flanked the unhappy consciousness with Stoicism and Skepticism (*PS*, 119–26), on the one hand, and with Reason (*PS*, 139–262) on the other, moving forward into a less arid region where the modern spirit could finally come to itself. As Hegel understands the history of philosophy, the medieval consciousness yearns for what it can never understand; and having contracted into the unhappiness of philosophical unintelligibility, it becomes the negative condition for his own decisive resolution of the controversy between the ancient and the modern worlds.

Whatever the merits of this negative characterization of the role of medieval philosophy in the history of thought, I find it especially ironical that the period of philosophical history that is founded on a doctrine of creation *ex nihilo* should have become so brittle and desiccated that it scarcely seems to exist except as a collection of relics and of historical curiosities. This is not to say that the scholars who have labored to preserve what is of philosophical significance in the medieval period have labored in vain.[5] However, it is to acknowledge the fact that the contemporary philosophical situation is overdetermined by a conception of the history of philosophy in which medieval philosophy does not play a significant role.

In response to this situation, I am proposing an alternative interpretation of the history of philosophy that fills the chasm between the ancient and the modern worlds and that allows medieval philosophy to become a world of its own, rich enough to sustain philosophical reflection. Despite the obvious dependence of the medieval thinkers on their Greek predecessors and the tendency of some of the modern thinkers to reject the philosophical tradition, I am convinced that the mutual independence of the established periods of the history of philosophy ought to be acknowledged. As a result, I will defend the thesis that ancient, medieval, and modern philosophy are autonomous regions and that an understanding of this fact can lead to a reappraisal of the structure of the history of philosophy from the standpoint of the medieval tradition. In what follows, I will first characterize the similarities and the differences among the traditional periods of the history of philosophy, attempting to establish what is unique about each era. I will then suggest how the uniqueness of the medieval period can resolve the conflict between the ancient and the modern worlds and allow us to reestablish a harmony between the origins from which philosophy begins and the end toward which it develops. Finally, I will argue that the contemporary philosophical interest in language can give us a fruitful mode of access to what is central in the medieval world and that language is the key for reinterpreting the philosophical tradition from a point of view that transcends the metaphor of war.

Perhaps the most obvious way to formulate the similarities that bind the periods of the history of philosophy together is to say that in every era, the concepts of nature and art, God and religion, and human beings and science are the pivotal conceptions. No historical period is indifferent to any of these conceptions, and these concepts provide the descriptive and categorial structure in terms of which the history of philosophy can be understood. It should go without saying that the meaning of each of these concepts undergoes modification from period to period and that what binds these transformations together is at best a series of family resemblances. For example, *physis* for the Greeks, *natura* for the medieval thinkers, and nature as it was understood in modern philosophy are vastly different conceptions,[6] to say nothing of the modifications in the concepts of God and man that occur in the course of their historical development. Yet even the possibility of a history of any of these concepts presupposes that some common threads are to be discerned, and that the use of the same word in more than one era has more than a merely nominal significance. If this were not the case, the history of philosophy would be impossible, and we would be unable to understand its development because of our imprisonment within a limited historical perspective. That we bring our own presuppositions to our philosophical task ought to be admitted, but that these presuppositions make responsible inquiry impossible is a philosophical thesis that must be rejected.

If we are to avoid the difficulties of historicism without ignoring the fact that the history of philosophy is not a seamless fabric, it is important to emphasize the differences that hold its respective periods apart and to give an explanation of these differences in terms of the fundamental concepts to be found in each era. This can be done by suggesting that though the concepts of nature and art, God and religion, and human beings and science are significant conceptions throughout the entire history of philosophy, a different pair of concepts dominates each period. In the ancient world, art and nature are the pivotal conceptions; in the medieval period, religion and God are the central themes; and in the modern era, science and the human realm are the crucial concepts in terms of which the significance of human existence is to be articulated. As a consequence, the meaning of existence and the place of life in the cosmos differ from one period to the next, depending on which concepts provide the framework through which the world is to be understood.

To understand the dimension of difference that separates these frameworks properly, we must not assume that each of them is merely a variation on a set of underlying conceptions, all of which are equally fundamental. If this were so, the periods of the history of philosophy would all rotate on a common axis, and we might be tempted to approach them as though they were alternative ways of rearranging a set of common categories. We should therefore notice that each period of the history of philosophy presupposes that the pair of concepts to which it is committed dominates the others, introducing within each world a radical asymmetry. This asymmetry might tempt us to assume that each historical period is cut off from the others and that a coherent account of the history of philosophy is impossible without dissolving the radical differences between one period and the others.

In the ancient world, nature, understood in mythical terms, gives birth to human beings and the gods; and it serves as the standard in terms of which both concepts are to be measured. For the medieval thinkers, the God of Judaism, Christianity, and Islam creates both nature and the human realm, and is the source of power and meaning that human beings and nature are required to imitate. And in the modern world, the human being attempts to comprehend and to subordinate the other pivotal conceptions through science, mathematics, and technology, fashioning a conceptual net within which both nature and God can be incorporated. From a systematic point of view, the most important fact about these radical asymmetries is that they are the explanation for the differences of meaning that each of the fundamental conceptions displays as we move from one period to another. To formulate the point in terms of our earlier example, *physis* is transformed into *natura* because its generative powers are subordinated to God as a more fundamental principle of emergence, and *natura* is transformed into matter in motion because the qualitative characteristics, in virtue of which it imitates its creative source, are subordinated to the mathematical dimensions that allow it to become accessible to scientific inquiry (*IM*, 11–13). Thus, the periods of the history of philosophy are not only bound together because the same concepts appear in each era, but are also held apart by the fact that the dominance of different concepts in each world produces semantical changes in these concepts and in the ones that are subordinated to them.

Yet how are these asymmetries to be articulated in more strictly philosophical terms, and how do they sustain the thesis that the respective periods of the history of philosophy are related but autonomous regions? In attempting to answer this question with respect to the ancient world, it is important to emphasize the fact that nature understood as *physis* is not merely a collection of entities, but is the generative process from which these entities come into existence. As Hesiod formulates the point in the *Theogony*: Chaos, Earth, and Eros came into existence out of a primordial process of emergence; and after Sky was born, the gods were produced from the union of Earth and Sky. In Hesiod's account, each stage of this process opens up a different strain of Becoming, and the process before us can be articulated adequately only in aesthetic terms.[7] On the other hand, "nature" as it is used in the phrase, the "nature of things," points to a conception of nature as an intelligible structure through which things in the world are to be understood. These structures are the genera or the species of typical Aristotelian propositions and are the structural counterparts of the entities that come into existence from an original process of emergence.[8]

The word "genus" points to a connection between both senses of the concept of nature; for the term not only means a "principle of order or classification," but also the "first principle from which a thing originates." Some thinkers have concluded from this fact that the concept of origination is the more fundamental conception and that the concept of nature as intelligible structure is derivative (*IM*, 13–14, 159, 161–75). However, it does not follow from the etymology of the term that structure is to be subordinated to process, but simply that they belong together as two distinguishable but related conceptions of nature. In fact, the most obvious aspect of the development of ancient philosophy is the interplay between these two conceptions, culminating in the Platonic and the Aristotelian attempts to unify them. Being and Becoming, development and order, process and structure are bound together for all the significant thinkers of the ancient world, and one dimension becomes the fundamental element only in degenerate interpretations of their original intentions.

The crucial role of the intelligible dimension in ancient philosophy is reflected in the ancient philosophers' insistence on the primacy of the real order and on the belief that natural objects, the structures in terms of which they are ordered, and the process of emergence through which they come into existence are accessible. This is expressed in the Greek conviction that sight is the most important of the senses, for it is through vision that we are able to gain access both to things and structures, as well as to the process from which things emerge in an ordered pattern.[9] The aesthetic dimension of the Greek consciousness is also visual, beginning with the mosaic pattern of the *Iliad* and the *Odyssey* and culminating in the statues in which both human beings and the gods are represented (*PS*, 439–53).[10] In both cases, what is conveyed is the need to subordinate human consciousness to a process or a pattern more fundamental than itself to which the human realm owes both its existence and its order.

This same point can be expressed in logical terms by considering the form of proposition mentioned earlier; for the subject, the predicate, and the copula aim at fundamental aspects of the cosmos to which the human being must respond. In the declarative sentence, "Socrates is a man," the subject, the intelligible structure, and the process of emergence are represented by the subject, the predicate, and the copula; and it is these distinctions as expressed both logically and aesthetically that are the source of the claim that nature and art are the fundamental conceptions in the ancient world.

By contrast with this approach to the problems before us, philosophers in the modern world focus their attention on human beings and science as the definitive philosophical conceptions. They do this primarily because nature loses its character as a process of emergence or as a set of intelligible structures, issuing in a conception of the natural order as matter in motion. If the intelligible process of the Greek tradition is to be incorporated, it must be located in the human subject, where the recalcitrance of the object is to be overcome by an autonomous quest for complete comprehension. This familiar project begins with Descartes's attempt to transpose the objective concepts of process and structure by a mathematical method of scientific and technological conquest. Descartes shifts process and structure to the side of the subject by inaugurating a project of radical doubt in which the objectivity of the given is undermined, and where all that survives is God, the soul, and the mathematical method in terms of which cognitions are to be ordered and developed. In fact, it might even be argued that he claims divinity for himself by suggesting that though he has an infinite will and a merely finite intellect, and though error arises because the will outruns the intellect, a mathematical method is available to him in terms of which these errors can be overcome. It is this mathematical method and its accessibility to the finite intellect that displaces nature and God and brings human beings and science to the center of the modern world, launching a project of absolute comprehension that defines the modern philosophical consciousness.[11]

This project was brought to completion in the nineteenth century by Hegel's explicit transformation of substance into subject and by his insistence that the traditional form of proposition can be transformed into a speculative proposition. He claims that in the statement that Socrates is a man, we not only find the substance, the structure, and the process of the Greek tradition, but also the subject who utters the sentence and the speechact that issues in the comprehension of the substance in terms of the structure that is appropriate to it. In fact, the copula of the original statement is not so much the process from which the substance comes into existence as the process of reflection in terms of which the subject is able to comprehend the substance as it develops its concrete content (*PS*, 36–37). As Hegel formulates the point in *Phenomenology*, this concrete development moves from stage to stage toward an increasingly adequate articulation; and the structures in terms of which the substance was characterized initially become stages in its self-development. The mathematical dimension of Descartes's original project is subordinated to a process of emergence; and as Hegel understands it, this process is the reflective journey in which the scientific quest for absolute comprehension is brought to completion (*PS*, 36–41).

The quest for comprehension expresses itself in human terms by displacing the sense of sight with the sense of touch as our basic mode of access to the world. Absolute comprehension presupposes that we are able to lay hands on the world, overcoming the noetic distance of the Greeks with the kind of practical immediacy that is characteristic of the scientific and the technological revolutions (*PS*, 439–53).[12] It is no accident that philosophy in the aftermath of Hegel has focused so insistently on the problem of theory and practice and has suggested that theory must be subordinated to practice if we are to comprehend the cosmos from a scientific point of view.[13] If nature and art are the central concepts in the ancient world, and if the human realm and science are the pivotal conceptions in the modern era, God and religion are at the center of the medieval philosophical tradition.

From its own point of view, and formulated anachronistically, the medieval era stands in between a world in which the subject is subordinated to objects, to a process of emergence, and to a set of structures that stand over against it and a world in which the object is subordinated to the subject and to the process of reflection that makes it accessible. The medieval world also heightens the discontinuity between its basic concepts and the other central notions that we have been considering. This heightened sense of discontinuity is grounded in the transcendence of God and in a doctrine of creation *ex nihilo*. In the other two eras, a pair of concepts is more fundamental than the others but an underlying continuity also connects them. By contrast, discontinuity comes to the forefront in the medieval commitment to creation, according to which God and the world are really distinct, not standing in a merely logical relation that binds them together.[14] It is this fact that underlies the scandal of religion that sometimes seems to threaten philosophical rationality and that sets the medieval period off from the others as a world of its own.

In approaching the medieval world, we might be tempted to ignore the problem of God and to focus on secondary issues; for to concentrate on this problem is to place an apparently non-philosophical issue at the center of our reflections. As a result, we might discuss the logic, the science, or the philosophical anthropology of the Middle Ages, seeking to avoid the problem of God within a philosophical context. However, if we are to be true to our subject matter, this will not suffice; for we must admit that a divine self-disclosure is central to it and must take our philosophical bearings from this fact. In human terms, this means that the sense of sight that was so important in the ancient world, and the sense of touch that animates the modern tradition are replaced by the sense of hearing, requiring the medieval thinker to listen to the Voice of God as the foundation on which his reflections are grounded. Because he is separated from the world by an infinite chasm that only creation can mediate, God cannot present himself as an objective content of cognition; and because of this infinite distance, we are unable to reach across it to touch God directly. Instead, the Creator must speak if we are to have access to his nature, and it is this fact that accounts for the dependence of the medieval philosophers on a speaking Word.[15]

When God speaks, he addresses his creatures at the center of their being; and a clear indication that this is so is to be found in the primacy of existential propositions for the medieval thinkers. The form of proposition that is central in the medieval world is not "Socrates is a man," understood in either Aristotelian or Hegelian terms, but "Socrates exists," understood as calling our attention to the real distinction between God and the world and to the relation of creation that binds them together.[16] The process of emergence, the objective standards of the ancient world, and the quest for absolute comprehension on the part of modern philosophy are counterbalanced by an existential situation in which man stands before God and listens to what he reveals about his nature and existence.

The rebirth of an autonomous conception of medieval philosophy can overcome the conflict between the ancient and the modern worlds and enable us to transcend the warfare that has defined the traditional conceptions of the history of philosophy. In logical terms, this is made possible by introducing the concept of God as a third term, standing over against both nature and the human realm as the definitive concepts in terms of which philosophical reflection can be developed. When these two concepts confront one another, a conflict arises about which is primary, for there is no intervening element to prevent either of them from attempting to subordinate the other. As C. S. Peirce claimed, a dyadic relation is always defined by resistance, recalcitrance, and opposition; and it is precisely this kind of relation that has produced the conflict we have been considering.[17] Yet when the medieval period is placed between the other two, the conflict between them can be mediated by referring the central concepts of each era to their creative ground. According to the medieval account of the role of both concepts, nature and the human being stand in contrast with the ground of their existence; and it is their absolute dependence on a common source that binds them together in polar interaction and mutual dependence.

God as a creative source does not constitute a larger whole of which both nature and the human realm are subordinate elements. If this were so, the doctrine of creation would be indistinguishable from the modern quest for comprehension, and God could be equated with Absolute Spirit as the fundamental term of the modern philosophical enterprise. As the ground of existence, God remains distinct from his creatures; and it is this irreducible dimension of difference that allows each of them to retain a certain measure of independence. The grounding relation also binds the terms it grounds together, allowing them to be related reciprocally because of their mutual dependence on the same creative source. The doctrine of creation *ex nihilo* allows both nature and the human realm to stand over against their creative ground and in contrast with one another, and it also permits them to be related to the other terms from which they remain substantially distinct.

There are two problems with this response to the conflict between ancient and modern philosophy that must be dealt with if the orientation reflected in this chapter is to be embraced. First, the introduction of the doctrine of creation *ex nihilo* might suggest that the conflict before us is being mediated by a term that is absolutely unintelligible and that the warfare to be outflanked is being exchanged for a theological standpoint that can never be articulated. The night in which all cows are black (*PS*, 65) is no solution to a problem as central as the one we have been considering, and it is therefore necessary to consider in more detail how the position being developed here is to be understood philosophically. In the second place, the terms in which we have characterized the periods of the history of philosophy might appear to be unfruitful ways of engaging in contemporary philosophical reflection; for there is a sense in which nature, human beings, and God no longer form the horizons in which most of us live. The development of contemporary philosophy from analysis, to structuralism, to hermeneutics, to deconstruction suggests that language is the new horizon of philosophical reflection and that the task of philosophy is to turn away from the past in order to develop the linguistic resources of the contemporary situation. However, the paradox of the contemporary fascination with language is that language can become a vehicle for recovering the concepts of nature, the human realm, and God and for developing the suggestion that medieval philosophy is the key to overcoming the conflict between the ancient and the modern worlds. Let me illustrate this point by turning to a linguistic analysis of the doctrine of creation *ex nihilo* and by using this analysis to develop some of the most important implications of our earlier discussion.

The first step in developing our account from a linguistic point of view is to notice that the act of creation is an act of speaking and that the medieval tradition is founded on the performative utterance through which it claims that human beings and nature came into existence.[18] God speaks, and the world comes into being, not out of God himself, nor as a determinate product fashioned from preexisting material, but from absolute nothingness simply through the power of primordial language. This speaking Word is an intersection of mystery, power, and structure; for the act of creation is both unprecedented and unpredictable, is the active process that brings the world into existence, and is the primordial source in terms of which the human realm and nature are to be made intelligible. The mystery and the power of the Greek conception of *physis*, and the power and the structure of the modern quest for comprehension are reflected in creation; for this single act binds together the mysterious background of things, the powerful ground of things, and the intelligible meaning of things into a primordial unity.

It is important to emphasize the fact that creation *ex nihilo* is not strictly speaking a relation, for the second term in this "relation" is dependent on the source from which it comes into existence. To the extent that creation has been accomplished, a relation obtains between the ground and its product, but the absolute priority of the ground suggests that creation itself is not a relation, either symmetrical or asymmetrical. This crucial point also implies that the way in which creation *ex nihilo* unifies God and the world cannot be the sense of unity in which both terms are included within a larger whole. The unity in question derives from an act of speaking, understood as a linguistic performance, and this performance generates a product that is both non-linguistic and distinct from its creative ground. The sense in which creation unifies God and the world must be interpreted in such a way that the real distinction between God and the world is both preserved and made intelligible in appropriately linguistic terms.

We can elaborate our understanding of the relation between God and the world by analyzing a second crucial context of linguistic interaction on which the medieval tradition focused its attention. The episode I have in mind is recorded in the third chapter of Exodus where Moses encounters God at the burning bush. When he stands before God, Moses says, "I am here," and when Moses asks God to reveal his name, God responds, "I AM."[19] As I have argued in another context, the content of these utterances is intelligible, for Moses identifies his location and God identifies himself as a mysterious center of power that has, is, and will be present throughout the entire range of nature and history (*QW*, 82–89). Yet the most important point to notice is that both utterances are performative acts and that they enable Moses and God to present themselves to one another across a space that both binds them together and holds them apart.

The performative dimension of discourse creates the linguistic space in which Moses and God encounter one another, and it enables Moses to recover the meaning of his existence in the light of God's promise to be present throughout all the modes of time. Moses has been alienated from his origins and has been exiled in the desert for forty years, uncertain about the future and about whether there is a future in which the meaning of his life could be developed (Acts 7:30). Yet when God reveals himself as the one who is present in power, and as the one who has, is, and will be present as the sustaining ground of Moses' existence, the temporal modes of Moses' life are gathered up into a unity that reflects the primordial unity of God (*QW*, 76–77).

Moses' claim that I am here, and God's response that I AM are both existential propositions, and this fact serves to secure the real distinction between them as they stand over against one another. Two centers of mystery, power, and structure confront one another; and though the second is dependent on the first, it stands in contrast with the ground of its existence as a distinct entity. These two participants in the conversation are also unified by their interaction at the burning bush, but the unity in question does not include them both within a larger context. Moses is related to God as an image to an original, and it is because his own mystery, power, and structure can be brought into an imagistic relation with the mystery, power, and intelligibility of God that he is able to recover the meaning of his life.

As the medieval period develops, it provides a further linguistic articulation of these original linguistic acts, and it does so by considering some of the ways in which language can be used to characterize God and his relations to the world. The language in question is either ascriptive or relational and returns us to the traditional Aristotelian form of proposition we have considered already. As a consequence, the focus of our attention comes to rest either on the subject, the predicate, the copula, or the relations that can be expressed in propositions of this kind. For example, in the claims that God is wise or that God is the Creator, we can focus either on God himself, on the property of wisdom, on the copula that connects them, or on the relation in which God stands to his created products. The most familiar analysis of these terms suggests that they should be understood as either negative, eminent, or analogical, where the first preserves the transcendence of God, the second preserves the perfection of God, and the third makes God cognitively accessible while it preserves the radical difference between God and the world.[20]

In terms of our earlier analysis, the subject of an Aristotelian proposition that ascribes properties or relations to God points to his power, the predicates of the proposition point to his intelligible structure, and the copula or the relation that binds them together point to the mystery of creation in which power and structure are united. It is this mystery that is preserved by negative theology, but it is also the power and the structure to be found there that the positive side of eminent and analogical discourse attempt to make accessible. As Aquinas was perhaps the first to recognize, these modes of predication presuppose the prior existential context of a performative utterance, for standing behind the claims that God is wise or that God is the Creator is the existential proposition that God *is*, uttered on a particular occasion.[21] The mystery, the power, and the structure of propositional discourse about God, and the attempts of negative, eminent, and analogical discourse to preserve the mystery and the intelligibility of God are grounded in the performative utterance in which all three of these dimensions are expressed. As a result, the elaborate theories of predication developed in medieval philosophy presuppose the performative context in which God reveals himself as the mysterious, powerful, and intelligible ground of the created order.[22]

The claim that God created the world and the subsequent claim to Moses at the burning bush that I AM WHO I AM can be approached from a merely propositional point of view. When we proceed in this way, the utterances in question can be placed in quotation marks, enabling the subsequent discussion to preserve a certain measure of theoretical detachment. For purposes of scholarly analysis, this is perfectly appropriate; and indeed, a bracketing device of this kind is necessary if we are to entertain the medieval view of the world as one possibility among others. However, we must not forget that the original versions of both statements were formulated without quotation marks and that they were first expressed as performative utterances. The most serious question to be raised about the medieval period pertains to the relation between the theoretical formulation of these utterances and their performative expression. When we confront this question, we can choose to maintain our theoretical distance, discussing the history of philosophy by distinguishing its periods in descriptive or categorial terms. However, the possibility always exists that the quotation marks might drop away, and that the content of the statements about creation and about the existence of God might begin to speak creatively and existentially. This is the threat to be confronted by any serious attempt to study medieval philosophy, and indeed, the ground of both the fear and the disdain for a philosophical inquiry that takes its bearings from the primacy of religion and God. Could it perhaps be the case that in the utterances, "Let there be light," and "I AM WHO I AM," light might still appear and God might still reveal himself? If this should occur, medieval philosophy would not only be an autonomous realm in contrast with others, but "faith seeking understanding" might become once more the philosophical reflection of an existential enterprise.

Chapter 3

Athens and Jerusalem

What does Athens have to do with Jerusalem? This familiar question often arises when we ask about the relation between religion and philosophy, and it points to an initial discontinuity that resists philosophical mediation. Waiting off stage is the equally familiar distinction between the God of the philosophers and the God of Abraham, Isaac, and Jacob.[1] Both the question and the distinction point to an unbridgeable chasm between two realms that stand in radical contrast. Socrates formulates the crucial issue in his question to Euthyphro: "Do the gods love what is holy because it is holy, or is it holy because they love it?"[2] The history of the relation between religion and philosophy is a series of competing answers to this question.

I faced this question for the first time as an undergraduate in my dormitory room, and as I paced back and forth in my room at Baylor University, it reverberated in what I later discovered are the two sides of my consciousness. The God of the philosophers and the philosophical systems it presupposes are theoretical constructs, and philosophical gods are philosophers writ large. They explain, ground, sustain, and fill in the cracks in our attempts to understand the cosmos. Aristotle illustrates what I have in mind by describing the God of the philosophers as thought thinking itself,[3] and Hegel deifies himself when he claims that his *Logic* is what God is thinking before the creation of the world (*SL*, 50).

By contrast, the God of Abraham, Isaac, and Jacob takes us by surprise. He demands that Abraham sacrifice his son on Mount Moriah (Gen 22:1-2).

He is present when Isaac violates the tradition of the ancient family by giving the birthright and the blessing to his younger son (Gen 27:18–29). He speaks when Jacob wrestles with the angel, transforming him from a trickster into one who strives with God (Gen 32:28). The God of faith appears in dreams and visions; he speaks to the non-discursive side of our consciousness in commands and promises; he demands faith and obedience; and he leaves only traces of his presence in images and symbols.

The contrast between religion and philosophy might simply seem to be part of a philosopher's quarrel, since it is one of the tasks of the philosopher to distinguish autonomous regions and to point to the roles appropriate to them. However, a Christian theologian was the first to raise the question about the relation between Athens and Jerusalem when he claimed that we must believe because belief is absurd.[4] The truth of the matter is that the distinction between religion and philosophy arises in both contexts, and it points to a radical discontinuity between two sides of ourselves.

When we suggest that religion and philosophy are autonomous activities, they come into conflict inevitably. Mutual claims to autonomy about the most important questions mask conflicting claims to cover the whole ground. The inescapable question arises: How can we avoid taking a stand about which realm is fundamental? When Jerusalem looks at Athens and when Athens gazes at Jerusalem, this moment of mutual recognition hides incompatible responses to the question about which realm is fundamental. The opposition between Athens and Jerusalem expresses itself most forcefully as a contrast between Eros and belief without evidence; and as a consequence, philosophical desire stands opposed to religious commitment.

Most traditional accounts of the origin of philosophy take their bearings from Plato's story of the birth of Eros. Eros is the offspring of Poverty and Invention, and it stands in between absolute lack and absolute fulfillment.[5] Eros also has a directional orientation, struggling to move away from what it lacks to what it seeks and attempting to come to rest in an aesthetic and cognitive grasp of what is higher than itself.[6] The usual interpretation of this myth concludes that philosophy is an erotic activity,[7] that it is the desire for understanding, and that it sometimes expresses itself as the quest for absolute comprehension.[8]

The discontinuity of faith stands in radical contrast with the desire for comprehension. This opposition expresses itself in the scandal of particularity that often characterizes the religious consciousness. This scandal suggests three things. First, the religious consciousness is individual. Second, it stands alone before the ground of its existence. Finally, the isolated individual is unable to communicate the intelligible content of its encounter with God.

As Kierkegaard formulates the point,

> [We cannot mediate] faith into the universal, for [we] would thereby [destroy it.] Faith is this paradox, and the individual absolutely cannot make himself intelligible to anybody. People imagine maybe that the individual can make himself intelligible to another individual in the same case. Such a notion would be unthinkable if in our time people did not in so many ways seek to creep slyly into greatness. The one knight of faith can render no aid to the other. Either the individual becomes a knight of faith by assuming the burden of the paradox, or he never becomes one. In these regions partnership is unthinkable.[9]

Somewhat surprisingly, we find this same appraisal of the nature of faith in the great thinker that Kierkegaard was most determined to refute. In his *Lectures on the Philosophy of Religion*, Hegel claims that Hebrew religion accentuates the opposition between the human being and God. This is manifest by the fact that God reveals himself to his people in a series of external relations that they can never understand.[10] First, he expresses himself as the power of creation. Then he claims that he is the absolute Lord and Master.[11] Finally, he becomes the arbitrary will that chooses a particular nation as his own, confirming this choice through a merely contractual agreement. Hegel concludes that God remains external to his own people and that he does not disclose his mystery, even to the patriarchs with whom he chooses to speak.[12] Again we face the questions, "What does Athens have to do with Jerusalem?," and "What does the God of the philosophers have to do with the God of Abraham, Isaac, and Jacob?"

In one of his early essays, Paul Tillich distinguishes between two types of philosophy of religion. He says,

> One can distinguish two ways of approaching God: the way of overcoming estrangement and the way of meeting a stranger. In the first way man discovers himself when he discovers God. He discovers something that is identical with himself although it transcends him infinitely, something from which he is estranged, but from which he never can be separated. In the second way man meets a stranger when he meets God. The meeting is accidental. Essentially they do not belong to each other. They may become friends on a tentative and conjectural basis. [Yet] there is no certainty about the stranger man has met. He may disappear, and [we can make] only probable statements about his nature.[13]

The types of philosophy of religion are ontological and cosmological: the first is the way of overcoming estrangement, and the second is the way of meeting a stranger. Tillich prefers the ontological approach because it suggests that faith and philosophy belong together, where both are ways of overcoming estrangement rather than ways of meeting a stranger.

The ontological path in religion and philosophy binds the fragments of the fragmented soul together. The etymology of the word "religion" points in this direction. *Religio* derives from two verbal roots that mean "to gather, bind, tie, or fasten."[14] In its original form, religion binds the members of an ancient family together, requiring its participants to engage in ritualistic behavior. Religion exists before theology, and it is a region where we can live before it becomes a domain about which we can raise theological questions.

In the ancient family, religion defines the meaning of human existence. To have a place within a family is to participate in rites and rituals with other family members. A person is who he is because of the role he plays within this larger context. This role comes to focus when the family gathers around a hearth fire. The family clustered at the hearth celebrates its traditions, and the meaning of one's being is the unity that emerges from participation in them.[15]

The unity of philosophy reflects the unity of religion. *Philosophia* derives from two Greek nouns that together mean "love of wisdom." However, we often fail to notice that love transcends desire and that wisdom is not identical with knowledge. The love to which *philia* points is the love of friendship, and wisdom is both practical and theoretical. Both *philia* and *sophia* call our attention to a way of life in which the philosopher attempts to live on friendly terms with wisdom. Philosophical friendship fulfills desire by pointing to the unity of the philosophical life.[16]

What prevents us from understanding this conclusion is the mistaken belief that we must define philosophy as an exclusively erotic activity. *Eros* is always in the background as a necessary condition for philosophical reflection. However, it is a mistake to reduce the love of wisdom to the desire for understanding. Philosophy is an erotic activity, but this is not its essence. If it were, it would be an unending and hopeless attempt to attain the satisfaction it seeks. If we define philosophy as an erotic desire for what it is not, it can never be a realm that sustains itself. The love of wisdom points to a domain that transcends desire and is a region of reciprocity for which *Eros* is a necessary but not a sufficient condition.

Because of a preference for discontinuity, we might reject the definition of philosophy as friendship with wisdom, substituting a definition of it as an erotic longing for what we lack. If philosophy were the desire for what we lack rather than friendship with wisdom, many of us could be philosophers. However, if philosophy is the love of wisdom, a serious question arises about whether there are any philosophers. How many philosophers are there?

Three? Seven? Twelve? Can wisdom have many friends? The temptation for every friend of wisdom is to believe that he or she is wisdom's only friend. Can the friends of wisdom generate a community? Is it possible for us not only to be friends of wisdom, but also friends with one another? If so, philosophy might become a realm that can sustain human existence.

To believe that this is so requires us to shake off our cynicism and to embrace a life of faith. The belief that philosophy is possible and that it can occur in a community does not depend on reason. Rather, faith is the condition that makes it possible for philosophers to be reasonable. If philosophy were simply an erotic activity, it would be an expression of our natural consciousness. Since most discussions of its nature assume that this is so, the problem of faith and philosophy usually arises as a problem of radical discontinuity. Yet when we define philosophy as the love of wisdom, we discover that it has a hidden religious dimension. This hidden dimension is faith in the possibility of philosophy, understood as friendship with wisdom.

The Anselmian phrase, "faith seeking understanding," is one expression of the possibility to which I am referring (*P*, Prologue). Anselm's philosophical "ancestor," Augustine, equates God with Truth (*C*, 10.24.35); and he also claims that the quest for Truth is the quest for Wisdom (*C*, 2.6.7). In doing so, he attempts to bring us into a positive relation with the religious and the philosophical absolutes simultaneously. For Augustine, the tasks of theology and philosophy are identical; for faith in God is faith in the Wisdom that makes philosophy possible. What faith seeks to understand is Wisdom as the ground of philosophical friendship. As a result, the Wisdom that makes friendship possible is the God faith seeks to understand.

The faith Augustine has in mind is not simply a belief that certain propositions about God's nature and existence are true. Rather, faith involves an existential commitment in which our hearts stretch out toward God in trust and obedience (*C*, 10.17.26). Augustine believes that God exists (*C*, 7.10.16), and he defends his claim that God is identical with Truth (*C*, 10.24.35). Nevertheless, faith involves more than this. It is an act of the will that enables us to reach beyond ourselves toward the sustaining ground of our existence. The understanding to which Augustine refers is not simply a matter of clarifying and defending beliefs about God that one possesses already. Since Augustine identifies understanding with Wisdom (*C*, 1.1.1), he attempts to grasp the truth about God in both theoretical and practical terms. Faith seeks understanding (*intellectum*) to deepen its relation to God, and it is a way of developing trust in God at the distinctively reflective level (*C*, 10.17.26). The Augustinian claim that faith and philosophy belong together reflects the ontological approach to the philosophy of religion. However, there is another strand in the philosophical tradition that emphasizes the differences between religion and philosophy. Tillich calls this strand cosmological, where the thought of Thomas Aquinas illustrates this approach in an arresting way.[17] In doing so, Aquinas points to the importance of the problem of difference in both faith and philosophy. As a consequence, difference is present, not only in the contrast between faith and philosophy, but also in each realm taken separately, where the presence of radical otherness counterbalances the Augustinian quest for ontological mediation.

The distinction that Aquinas draws between Truth and the Highest Truth emphasizes the role of difference in both realms. From an ontological point of view, God and Truth are identical. However, when Aquinas identifies God with the Highest Truth rather than with Truth itself, God the Creator stands in radical contrast with us.[18] According to the ontological approach, God is closer to us than we are to ourselves; for the cosmological approach, there is an infinite distance between God and the soul.[19]

Formulated anachronistically, Augustine attempts to integrate what Aquinas tries to separate. In doing so, he merges philosophy and theology so skillfully that it is hard to distinguish them. Aquinas, by contrast, insists that faith and philosophy play different roles. In the sublunar realm, philosophy attempts to demonstrate what God could have revealed, but has not. It also demonstrates certain truths about God that faith apprehends. However, it is unable to demonstrate other truths about the highest being that only faith can embrace. This tripartite division establishes a distinction between the logical and the real orders; and since God transcends us infinitely, no transcendental term like Truth or Wisdom can span the chasm that separates us (Pegis, 1:118–19).

The history of the relation between faith and philosophy pulls them in opposite directions. What begins as a contrast between faith and philosophy becomes an opposition between two separate realms. The nominalism of Ockham and his followers reflects the consequences of abandoning the ontological tradition.[20] It is here that Tillich's description of the cosmological approach to God as a way of meeting a stranger is compelling. The God of the philosophers and the God of Abraham, Isaac, and Jacob merge in a *deus absconditus*. This God transcends both Truth and Wisdom, standing in contrast with us as an unmediated center of power and mystery.

When the chasm between God and the world becomes infinite, faith seeking understanding comes to a standstill. There is no longer an ontological substratum connecting God and the soul that allows us to find God at the center of our being. This leads some thinkers to replace faith seeking understanding with revelation requiring interpretation. Karl Barth defends this position in his commentary on Paul's epistle to the Romans. For example, he translates verses sixteen and seventeen of the first chapter of Romans in the following way:

> I am not ashamed of the gospel. It is the power of God unto salvation to every one that believes, to the Jew first, and also to the Greek. [It reveals] the righteousness of God from faithfulness unto faith. As it is written, "But the righteous shall live from my faithfulness."[21]

Barth rejects the ontological tradition, but he also believes that no cosmological or natural relation connects God and the soul. As a consequence, he concludes that the analogy of being, which Aquinas elaborates,[22] is not able to bind the knower and the known together.[23]

Barth's remedy for the human predicament is to appeal to a revelation that spans the chasm between God and the world, where this revelation expresses the grace and faithfulness of God. It also requires faith in God as an appropriate response. If there is any analogy here, it is not the analogy of being, but the analogy of faith. The analogy of faith rests on the belief that faith is analogous to and depends on the faithfulness of God (CD, 1:279–83). Because we are not only finite, but also fallen, this ground no longer bears a natural relation to us. Rather, our relation to God presupposes a gratuitous act for which there is no systematic explanation. Barth suggests that apart from the faithfulness of God, the unity of religion and friendship with Wisdom is an unreachable ideal (CD, 1:279–83).

The radical discontinuity between God and the world emerges most clearly in the story of Abraham and Isaac. The midrashic commentaries call the sacrifice of Isaac "the Binding." In this way, they transmute the binding that unifies the ancient family into a binding that expresses the discontinuity between God and the soul (QW, 58–64). The book of Genesis tells us that after Abraham and Isaac take a three-day journey, they finally reach the top of Mount Moriah. The father builds an altar, arranges the wood, and binds his son on it to offer him to God. The Binding takes three forms. First, Abraham binds Isaac to the altar. Second, he binds Isaac to God. Finally, when the father raises his knife and God intervenes, God binds Abraham and Isaac together as members of a new kind of community (QW, 63). When God demands that Abraham sacrifice his son, and when Abraham obeys in silence, a chasm opens up between them. This chasm reflects the primacy of God as the Creator of the world. The discontinuity that defines the original relation between Creator and creature reappears in the contrast between Abraham and God. When Abraham raises his knife, God speaks to restore the son to his father. However, this act not only binds them together, but also separates them. Though Abraham and Isaac climb the mountain together, they go down separately. They do so because each has faced God for himself and has experienced the individuation that such a radical encounter always brings. The Binding on the mountain is also a separating, and it presupposes the moment of difference that defines God's original relation to the world (QW, 63).

When Abraham and Isaac climb the mountain, the unity of the ancient family and the power of genetic succession bind them together (QW, 63). However, when they come down, what binds them is the much more profound fact that they have stood alone before God in a moment of annihilation. As a result, they now stand before God as two individuals, sharing the separation and the unity reflected in the familiar litany, "I am [. . .] the God of Abraham, the God of Isaac, and the God of Jacob" (Exod 3:6). On Mount Moriah, the faithfulness of God both grounds and expresses itself in the faith of Abraham and Isaac. This faith reaches across a chasm that God has crossed already, and it emerges from the depths of their being as a response to the grace of God.

When Abraham binds his son to the altar, the Binding does not generate a larger whole of which Abraham, Isaac, and God are parts. What prevents unification from occurring in this form is the specter of death. Abraham binds Isaac to the altar, not to play a religious role in an ancient family, but to offer him as a sacrifice; and when he contemplates the death of his son, he faces the loss of the family that God has promised to give him. When Abraham sacrifices his son, he also sacrifices himself. To lose one's son is to lose the family that gives meaning to human existence. Nevertheless, God demands that he do it; Abraham prepares himself to do it; he begins to do it; and it is as though he had already done it. Only after all these preliminary stages does God intervene (Gen 22:1-12).

The question arises naturally: What does Abraham receive when he gets his son back? He does not recover the ancient family with which he goes up the mountain. When Abraham raises the knife to sacrifice his son, the unity of the ancient family explodes. The Binding on Mount Moriah is radically different from the binding of rite and ritual around a hearth fire. In this case, the dominance of absolute difference transmutes the meaning of unity. Radical discontinuity expresses itself in God's demand that Abraham sacrifice his son. It reverberates in Abraham's willingness to obey, even though God never gives him a reason for doing so. Yet when Abraham looks down into the abyss, God generates a transformed conception of unity (QW, 58–64).

In the ancient family, binding tilts in the direction of identity, while the more radical act of the Binding on Mount Moriah tilts in the direction of difference. When Isaac climbs down from the altar, his relation with his father can never be the same; for he can no longer simply play a role within a larger community. From this moment on, Abraham can also never define the meaning of his life as having a child. The meaning of Abraham's life is now a function of his bondage to a source of mystery and power that has difference at its center. If Isaac is to understand the meaning of his life, he must also work it out in relation to this same ground. In both cases, the knight of faith stands alone. Kierkegaard's profound analysis of this episode is correct about this.[24] Yet what he fails to emphasize is that the father and his son also stand together. What binds them together is that they both confront the same God, and the willingness of Abraham and Isaac to face radical otherness unites them in a community that the moment of difference generates.[25]

The dominance of difference in the Hebrew tradition is a fact that even the most causal observer must acknowledge. Its presence in our collective consciousness is responsible for the distinction between the God of the philosophers and the God of Abraham, Isaac, and Jacob. Yet what can we say about the moment of difference in philosophy? How can we comprehend it, not only as an irreducible element of religion, but also as a definitive aspect of philosophy understood as the love of wisdom?

The clearest way to answer this question is to remember that the love of wisdom is the love of friendship. Friendship involves reciprocity, and it presupposes difference within the larger unity to which friendship gives us access. Friendship is a relation of reciprocity rather than a relation of inclusion. This is true of friendship between persons, and it is no less true when we understand philosophy as friendship with wisdom. In this special case the philosopher loves wisdom as a term with which he stands in contrast. As a consequence, the moment of difference within philosophy undermines any attempt to interpret the binding of philosophy as an example of identity.

In his discussion of friendship in the *Nicomachean Ethics*, Aristotle insists that friendship is always friendship among equals. He also characterizes the contemplation of wisdom as a divine activity.[26] In both cases, it might seem that friendship with wisdom entails that the philosopher must be wise. It might also seem that the divinity of the philosopher as a lover of wisdom reflects the divinity of wisdom as a divine activity. Perhaps this will prove to be the case. Yet even if it does, the dimension of difference will be present nonetheless. In the relation between the philosopher and the object of philosophical friendship, the philosopher is not the primary term. Rather, he seeks wisdom as both more original and originative than himself.

In our earlier discussion of the ontological and the cosmological approaches to God, a distinction emerged between faith seeking understanding and revelation requiring interpretation. Faith seeking understanding presupposes that God is identical with Truth and Wisdom; and in stretching out toward God, it seeks understanding as a way of deepening its relation to him. In this way, faith overcomes estrangement at both the existential and reflective levels (*CD*, 1:11–16). By contrast, revelation presupposes that God stands over against the world and that a dimension of irreducible difference defines his relation to it. If we are to bridge this chasm, we must respond to the grace of God that reaches across it, where faith presupposes the faithfulness of God and requires us to interpret what God has done already (*P*, 1).

We must not assume that the relative dominance of identity and difference in these two concepts of faith merely holds them apart. A dimension of difference exists in faith seeking understanding. Unity is also present in the response of faith to revelation. Understanding is not merely an extension of faith that takes its existential dimension into a reflective context. Rather, it is an ecstatic activity that reflects the dynamism of faith at the distinctively reflective level. Revelation also does not address a natural consciousness that remains alienated from it, but expresses the faithfulness of God that evokes the faith of the believer, bringing it into a reflective relation with God in the analogy of faith.

Anselm's discovery of the ontological argument is an example of the interplay of identity and difference in both kinds of faith. As an Augustinian, Anselm begins with faith seeking understanding (*P*, 1). However, the faith he expresses is not a response to existential fragmentation of the kind we find in Augustine's *Confessions* (*C*, 10.28.39), but to the reflective fragmentation generated by the many arguments for God's existence that he develops in the *Monologion* (*M*, 1–4). Against this background, Anselm asks whether there is a single argument that will demonstrate both that God is and who he is (*P*, Prologue). He struggles to find it and almost succeeds. Yet it continues to elude him, and he concludes in desperation that he will never find it. Yet when he decides to give up looking, he says,

> In spite of my unwillingness and my resistance to it, it began to force itself on me more and more pressingly. So it was that one day when I was quite worn out there came to me, in the very conflict of my thoughts, what I

had despaired of finding. I eagerly grasped the notion which in my distraction I had been rejecting. (*P*, Prologue)

The understanding that Anselm achieves in this moment of insight brings unity to his reflections (*P*, Prologue), and it is an image of the unity that Augustine finds at the culmination of his existential journey (*P*, 9). Faith seeking understanding does not merely stretch toward it, but is the existential original of which understanding is the reflective image. The understanding that Anselm achieves is not only an extension of faith that takes experience up into a reflective context, but is also an ecstatic activity that reflects the dynamism of faith. This generates an analogy between experience and reflection that binds them together and holds them apart. Thus, a dimension of difference appears at the heart of *fides quaerens intellectum* (*P*, 1). Yet difference emerges in a sharper sense when Anselm finds the solution to his problem in a moment of insight. Amidst conflict and despair, God appears in the guise of the ontological argument; and in this moment, difference generates identity (*P*, Prologue). In Anselm's *Proslogion*, the cosmological and the ontological traditions meet, and the God of Abraham, Isaac, and Jacob becomes the God of the philosophers.

Anselm sustains his insight by claiming that God is a being a greater than which cannot be conceived. This characterization of God reverberates with the same internal dynamism that faith in God expresses. In fact, the dynamism of Anselm's discourse about God is analogous both to faith as an existential enterprise and to understanding as a reflective activity. In both cases, analogy binds God and the soul together while it also holds them apart.[27] The arguments of *Proslogion* 2–4 move us from the nature to the existence of God, and they challenge us to make an inference that spans the chasm between the real and the logical orders (*P*, 3). Yet when the argument is complete, Anselm also says that God is beyond comprehension (*P*, 15). In this way, he points to the abysmal ground of difference out of which his original insight emerges. As a consequence, irreducible difference undergirds the unity of the ontological argument.

The two sides of human consciousness correspond to the distinction between the ontological and the cosmological traditions. While one side of our consciousness seeks ontological mediation, the other is open to cosmic interruptions. However, each side participates in the interests of the other. Though the ontological approach often becomes a philosophical system, it also attempts to overcome estrangement at the non-verbal level.[28] The cosmological approach presupposes a chasm across which God must address us if we are to come to ourselves. Yet we often respond to this chasm by generating a cluster of arguments intended to connect God and the world.[29]

The participation of the two sides of us in one another points to a place where they meet. In a physiological formulation, this place is the *corpus callosum*. In religious language, it is the Holy of Holies. In philosophical terms, it is the Place of places. This Place is first a place of silence. Then it is a place of power. Finally, it is a place of speech. Mystery, power, and structure intersect there. In this Place both the love of wisdom and the structure of God are born. The love of wisdom is ontological; the structure of God is cosmological; but in the mysterious Place from which they emerge, each attempts to respond to the needs of the other. The philosopher spins his system to overcome an estrangement that he can feel more easily than he can describe, and the theologian speaks about God to make God's power and mystery accessible to the cognitive consciousness.

In the distinctions I have been drawing, I have been describing the Trinity from a philosophical point of view. The Father is the intersection of power and mystery, the Son is the convergence of mystery and structure, and the Spirit is the interaction of structure and power. In the Gospel of John, Jesus says, "The Father loves the Son and shows him all that he himself is doing" (5:20a). In this case, the word "love" is a translation of *philia*. The interplay between the Father and the Son that the Spirit mediates is the supreme example of friendship. In this case, the Father, the Son, and the Spirit converge as a community of friends.

Both the philosophical interplay of mystery, power, and structure and the community of persons in the Trinity could remain self-contained. There is no reason for either of these realms to break beyond itself. Nevertheless, this occurs when the Voice of Being speaks;[30] and it also occurs when we hear the Voice of God (*P*, 10). The Voice of Being is ontological, and it draws us into the circle of reflection made possible by philosophy as the love of wisdom. In this circle, mystery, power, and structure intersect. Our initial response is erotic, but *Eros* finally seeks to lead us to a place where philosophical friendship flourishes.[31] By contrast, the Voice of God spans a cosmological chasm. Its first word is a word of love, and the love it expresses is *agape*. However, God's last word is not *agape* but *philia*. The purpose of *agape* is to lead us into the Holy of Holies, where, at the mercy seat, the act of atonement transforms God's enemies into his friends (cf. Rom 5:6-11).

What does the first epistle of John mean when it tells us that God is love? (4:8). It means that God chooses to respond to the world with *agape*. John's point is not that God loves us because of his nature, but that he loves us because of a choice. He makes this choice when he crosses the chasm that separates us from him. John speaks to little children, and the words he speaks are "God is love" (1 John 4:8). The Old Testament uses many names for God. But when God responds to these names, or even names himself, he preserves his mystery. In the same way, there is mystery at the heart of the claim that God is love. God chooses to express himself as love. There is no reason for it in the hidden depths of God. The furthest we can reach is to the Place where God speaks. Having chosen to speak, he says, "God is love."

Love of this kind leads to *philia*. Unlike *Eros*, *philia* does not lack something and seek fulfillment. Nor does it simply give itself away gratuitously. Rather, it points to a communion between one person and another that transcends giving and receiving. Jesus often uses this word when he describes his relationship with his father. God loves the son in *philia*, and he wants to love us in a way that transcends both *Eros* and *agape*. It is at this point that faith and philosophy meet.

The love that makes faith and friendship possible presupposes the mystery and power of God. This mystery and power first express themselves in an act of speaking. God speaks, and the world comes into being, not from preexisting material, but simply through the power of primordial language (Gen 1:1-3). The act of creation is unprecedented and unpredictable, but it is also the primordial source that makes human beings and nature intelligible. The act of creation binds the mysterious background of things, the powerful ground of things, and the intelligible meaning of things into a unity.

We can understand the life of faith only from the standpoint of speaking and hearing as primordial phenomena. An infinite chasm separates God from the world; as a consequence, God cannot present himself as an objective content of cognition. Because of the infinite distance between God and the world, we are also unable to reach across it to touch him directly. Yet God mediates this chasm when he speaks and the soul listens. As Augustine expresses the point in the *Confessions*:

> Let me learn from you, and put the ear of my heart to your mouth. Do not let the tumult of [my] vanity deafen the ear of [my] heart. The Word itself calls [me] to return. With him is a place of unperturbed rest, where love is not forsaken unless it first forsakes. (*C*, 4.5.10)

At this juncture, what Augustine needs to hear and seeks to understand is that God will transform his fragmented heart. On the basis of God's original act of speaking, Augustine can speak; and he responds to the original utterances of God with performative discourse. Augustine's request to let him respond is a way of presenting himself to God as a being who has something to say. The resulting conversation is a reflection of the depth of creation and redemption that makes discourse possible. A conversation with God does not give us a theory about him, but God himself; and it does not generate a theoretical account of the soul, but points to the possibility of divine transformation. The most serious question for the Christian philosopher is the proper relation between theoretical discourse about God and the performative dimension it presupposes. Our deepest problem is not cognitive, but personal. As a result, a theoretical response to our fragmented condition is not sufficient. The central question becomes: What power can allow us to respond to the problem before us as active participants?

Let me answer this final question in personal terms, describing the stages that have led me to embrace both faith and philosophy. Faith and philosophy begin in childhood and with the power of imagination to which almost every child responds. Imagination always precedes reflection; and before we can understand reflective discourse, we must listen to mythology. Storytelling often points to the discord of the human soul and to the development that leads beyond it; but it also suggests that wholeness sometimes comes, not as the result of human achievement, but simply as a gift.

The stories of our collective consciousness are richly human, and they contain expressive uses of language. They also display a reflective dimension that is indispensable if they are to be coherent expressions of the wholeness they suggest. Both faith and philosophy should reflect the richness of experience to which stories give us access. They must also find a way of speaking about the most fundamental issues that combines the concreteness of storytelling with the clarity of reflective discourse. As I suggested in chapter 1, religion and philosophy begin with mythology; and structure as a reasoned account presupposes mythology as a dramatic narrative.

Wholeness in experience differs from the quest for wholeness as a theoretical problem. Our teachers often refuse to acknowledge the integrity of the mythic world from which we come; and they demand instead, clarity of thought and precision of linguistic expression. I can still remember the familiar litany of the typically analytical questions: What do you mean? How do you know? What are your presuppositions? Analytical reflection stands in radical contrast with the stories we once understood, and abstract discourse often cuts us off from the expressive uses of language we once were able to affirm. As a result, a tension emerges between the stories with which we begin and the reflection we sometimes embrace. This tension transforms experience into a theological and philosophical problem.

Abstract reflection is of enormous significance because it enables us to grasp the form of experience and to articulate the structure of human existence. Yet stories that reflect the richness of experience and reflection that captures its structure generate different worlds. The contrast between imagination and reflection launches the quest for wholeness in faith and philosophy, and it also leads to reflective attempts to deal with the problems of fragmentation and unity. However, the central problem we face is this: When abstract reflection has done its work, how can we recover the texture of direct experience that even children understand?

Asking "What does X mean?" does not guarantee that we are asking questions in non-sophistical ways. One way to make our analytical questions genuine is to formulate them with clarity and precision. However, another remedy for sophistry is to place our inquiries within a systematic context. We might even become convinced that we must find a framework rich enough to encompass the world as a whole and our place in it. Having abandoned our imaginative access to the world by embracing abstract reflection, we might turn back toward the world in a richer sense altogether. When this occurs, our quest for wholeness can become an attempt to understand the Whole.

When we attempt to do this, the Voice of God sometimes interrupts our reflections. It asks: Suppose you construct a philosophical system? How does it relate to the concrete situation from which you come and to which your reflections must return? Does the whole that you are attempting to understand contain the richness of your origins? Or do they resist inclusion in a larger unity? Can the quest for wholeness come to completion in a system? Or does it point to a ground that you can never include within a wider context? In your own case, what is the relation between faith and philosophy?

Both faith and philosophy seek unity. In both cases, the unity in question emerges in an act of binding. Unity not only appears within each region, but also between the two realms as a dimension of identity that binds them together. Because an act of binding occurs in both faith and philosophy, these separate realms participate in a higher level of unity, where the finite and the infinite intersect. However, they also differ because their origins point in different directions. Faith begins with what lies beyond the world and moves through an obedient response to the binding of a larger community. Philosophy begins with desire and moves through reflection toward the binding reciprocity of friendship with wisdom. The relation between faith and philosophy involves both identity and difference. These two dimensions appear, not only within each region, but also at the higher level where they unite.

In a final formulation that is both conceptual and imagistic at the same time, faith and philosophy are mirror images. They begin from different origins, move in different directions, and culminate in a twofold unity that allows each realm to be a universal nexus. This mirroring relation defines the identity and difference of faith and philosophy, and it permits us to bind them together and to hold them apart. Yet three final questions remain: Who can hold the mirror in his hand? Who can participate in the acts of binding on either side? And who can refrain from standing on both sides at once, embracing the ground from which both religion and philosophy emerge?

PART TWO

Augustine, Hegel, Heidegger, and Jaspers

Chapter 4

The Rhetoric of Augustine's
Confessions

The distinguishing trait of the Augustinian philosophical tradition is that it binds religion and philosophy together by claiming that faith makes understanding possible. Unlike every other tradition, its adherents refuse to make a radical separation between faith and reason, claiming that both are necessary to give us philosophical access to God. In his book about the freedom of the will, Augustine points to his conception of the proper relation between faith and reason by quoting the claim of the prophet Isaiah that unless we believe, we shall not understand (*OFCW*, 5, 39).[1] This sentence is the motto of Augustine's reflective life; and as a consequence, faith seeking understanding becomes the rhetorical pattern of his quest for wisdom.

Though it can scarcely be denied that Augustine proceeds in this way, it is less clear what the Augustinian formula means and whether it is true. In this chapter, I will address these issues, first by pointing to contexts to which the Augustinian dictum applies, then by discussing the interpretation of them to be found in remarks by Alvin Plantinga[2] and Nicholas Wolterstorff,[3] and finally by showing how Augustine's motto undergirds the structure of his *Confessions* as an experiential and reflective journey toward God.

Augustine sometimes illustrates the claim that understanding presupposes faith by focusing on how we know which people are our parents. Since we cannot remember our infancy and have no direct awareness of our temporal origins, we must depend on what others tell us to know who was responsible for bringing us into existence (*C*, 1.6.7–1.6.8). In this case, faith and belief are synonymous terms, and the understanding to which it leads is knowledge about the epistemic content of our original belief.

Augustine mentions other examples of faith seeking understanding, where faith and belief, on the one hand, and understanding and knowledge on the other are interchangeable. For example, there are many events in human history, many facts about places and cities, and many things about people that we have not seen that we must believe if we are to know anything about them (*C*, 1.6.10). In all these cases, faith is a necessary condition for what we need to know about the world.

The most important context to which Augustine's maxim applies is the one in which the knowledge of God is at stake. In this context, the understanding (*intellectum*) that faith is seeking is an understanding of God, where the quest for understanding can be understood as a quest for wisdom. One of the central questions that arises about this context is whether faith seeking understanding is to be reduced to belief seeking knowledge, or whether more than this is involved in the conception that undergirds the Augustinian tradition.[4]

In a recent paper about his place in this tradition, Alvin Plantinga suggests that faith, on the one hand, and understanding on the other are to be equated with belief and knowledge. He claims that the deliverances of faith are propositions that imply other propositions about various philosophical issues, suggesting that to the extent that we can move from one set of propositions to the other, we make the transition from faith to understanding.[5] Plantinga also claims that the conditional sentences that connect what we believe with what we know are deliverances of reason rather than faith. He concludes that one of the distinctive tasks of the Christian philosopher is to look for statements of this kind, where the statements in question give us indispensable tools to make the transition from belief to knowledge.

Plantinga not only believes that he is being true to the Augustinian tradition by making these proposals, but he also believes that Augustine was correct when he claimed that unless we believe, we will not understand. As he formulates the point, "My sympathies lie with the Augustinian view; I am at best suspicious of the epistemic benefits claimed on behalf of philosophy or science untainted by theology."[6] Plantinga's reason for making this claim is that all of us believe many things within every field of inquiry that we have never verified and that to the extent that this is so, most of our knowledge depends on faith.

If faith is equated with belief, and if understanding is reduced to knowledge, Plantinga's explication and defense of Augustine's formula are persuasive, pointing to the fact that belief is prior to knowledge both temporally and logically. However, Augustine often suggests that Plantinga's conviction is susceptible of another interpretation, where faith is to be equated with trust, and where understanding (*intellectum*) is a way of deepening the trust with which we begin (*C,* 1.1.1). If this is so, faith seeking understanding points to a transition from trust to understanding, which is not reducible to the more familiar transition from belief to knowledge (*C,* 1.1.1).

In his book about the relation between reason and religion, Nick Wolterstorff expresses part of what I have in mind about Augustine's rhetoric by equating religion with authentic commitment rather than with propositional assent.[7] This leaves open the possibility that the transition from faith to understanding might be a way of deepening our initial religious commitment at the distinctively reflective level. However, Wolterstorff looses the thread of his insight by implying that Augustine's philosophy can be reduced to epistemic terms, claiming that it is a way of relating the "belief-content" of one's commitment to a "comprehensive, coherent, consistent, and true body of theories in the sciences."[8]

There is something to be said for this interpretation, for Augustine's formula clearly has an epistemic dimension. However, it is equally important to notice that Augustine plunges deeper than this and that in the final analysis, faith seeking understanding is to be equated with trust seeking wisdom (*C,* 10.17.26). At the most fundamental level, the transition from faith to understanding is a way of deepening the trust with which we begin rather than a way of moving from one epistemic condition to another (*C,* 1.1.1).

In discussing Augustine's rhetoric, I will approach his commitment to the primacy of faith in existential terms, focusing my attention on the *Confessions* as the *locus classicus* in which the journey from faith to understanding unfolds. First, I will indicate how the concept of faith seeking understanding emerges at the beginning of his inquiry. Second, I will turn to his discussion of memory, time, and creation as ways of pointing to the proper relation between faith and understanding. Third, I will suggest how the exclusively epistemic interpretation of Augustine's intentions misses the basic thrust of his philosophical position. Fourth, I will discuss Augustine's use of auditory metaphors in the *Confessions.* Finally, I will focus my attention on the ways Augustine's rhetoric expresses itself in his use of the language of the heart.

When we turn to the *Confessions,* the first point to notice about Augustine's conception of faith is that he places it within a larger context, beginning with the greatness of God, moving to the claim that we are restless until we find our rest in him, and concluding with a question about which comes first, knowing God or calling on him. The first option

expressed by this question points to the permanent truth of the platonic tradition that faith in God presupposes an initial understanding of the concept
of God. Otherwise, we might call on God as other than he is (*C*, 1.1.1). On
the other hand, Augustine claims that we might embrace the view that we
must call on God in order to know him, where faith expresses itself as a way
of stretching out toward the one we want to understand (*C*, 10.1.1).

On the other hand, Augustine seems to move in a different direction
from this by suggesting that faith is to be equated with belief. In quoting a
passage from the book of Romans, he asks, "How shall they call on him in
whom they have not believed? Or how shall they believe without a
preacher?" (*C*, 1.1.1). Augustine answers Paul's questions by claiming that
preaching comes before believing, that believing leads to calling and seeking,
and that on this basis, it is possible to move to finding and praising
(*C*, 1.1.1). In this way, he introduces the motto that guides the *Confessions*,
where faith is equated with belief, and where faith seeking understanding
can be explicated as a way of making the transitions from believing to seeking and from seeking to finding.

It is important to make two emendations to this way of understanding
Augustine's rhetorical intentions, one which points to the platonic dimension in his thinking, and the other which calls our attention to an existential
way of comprehending the transition from faith to understanding.
Augustine never abandons the view that we must understand the concept of
God in order to believe in him (*C*, 7.18.24); and in this crucial respect,
knowledge of God is always prior to belief in him.[9] However, it is also
important to notice that when Augustine begins with belief, it is not to be
equated simply with acknowledging the fact that certain propositions about
God are true. Augustine makes this clear when he suggests that believing in
God is a way of bringing ourselves into relation with him, where faith is an
act of calling on God in trust and obedience (*C*, 10.17.26). Belief in the
truth of propositions is only an abstract dimension of faith in this existential
sense, and the transition from faith to understanding can be interpreted existentially as well.

How are we to understand Augustine's rhetoric in existential terms, and
how are we to make the transition from faith to understanding in a fashion
that takes this dimension of the issue into account? Augustine answers these
questions in the last four books of the *Confessions* when he turns to the problem of memory, the nature of time, and the hermeneutics of creation. He
makes the transition from faith to understanding at the beginning of his discussion of memory when he exclaims, "Let me know you, I shall know you,
even as I am known" (*C*, 10.1.1). The present subjunctive expresses a wish

to move from faith to understanding, and the future indicative expresses confidence that he will be able to find the understanding he seeks. Our central question becomes: How shall we understand this transition in terms that are more fundamental than the propositional analysis that we have been considering?

The nature of memory, the problem of time, and the hermeneutics of creation are related in two distinguishable ways to faith as ways of calling on God. First, memory, time, and creation *ex nihilo* are conditions that make Augustine's positive orientation toward God possible. Second, their intelligible structure is a mirror image of his journey toward God in distinctively reflective terms. In the last four books of the *Confessions*, Augustine attempts to deepen his relation to God, first by understanding how memory, time, and creation *ex nihilo* make faith in God possible, and then by understanding how each of these conditions is an image of faith at the reflective level.

Augustine's analysis of the nature of memory grounds and images the journey of faith he undertakes in the first nine books of the *Confessions*. Memory serves as the ground of this experiential journey, first because it is infinitely rich, then because it is self-transcendent, and finally because it can become a window that opens out toward God (*C*, 10.17.26). The infinite richness of memory manifests itself in the fact that it is virtually unlimited, and Augustine expresses awe and wonder about this dimension of it in the following way:

> Great is the power of memory, exceeding great is it, O God, an inner chamber, vast and unbounded! Who has penetrated to its very bottom? Yet it is a power of my mind and it belongs to my nature, and thus I do not comprehend all that I am. (*C*, 10.17.26)

The self-transcendence of memory is not only infinitely rich, but also expresses itself in the fact that it is able to remember itself (*C*, 10.17.26). In addition, it can reach toward God because forgetfulness can become a window through which God manifests himself.

In Augustine's existential journey toward God, he is a finite individual; but he also displays an infinite dimension. This makes it possible for him to stretch out toward God in faith, where faith is not only belief in the truth of certain propositions, but also a way of bringing himself into an existential relation with the ground of his existence. The infinite richness, the self-transcendence, and the forgetfulness of memory make faith possible, where the first expresses the fact that we have been made in the image of God, the second permits us to reach toward God by calling on him, and the third makes it necessary for God to manifest himself if we are ever to have a positive relation with him (*C*, 10.25.36).

Memory is not only a condition that makes faith possible, but also an image of faith at the reflective level. The infinite richness, the self-transcendence, and the openness of memory to what lies beyond itself are reflective images of faith, where the existential dimension of the act of faith appears in theoretical terms. The infinite richness of memory reflects the infinite richness of the person who has been created in the image of God; the self-transcendence of memory reflects the way in which we reach for God in experiential terms; and the forgetfulness of memory that makes it necessary for God to manifest himself reflects the way in which Augustine turns away from God and then is finally able to go back home (*C*, 10.26.37). As he summarizes the point at the end of his discussion of the nature of memory,

> Too late have I loved you, O beauty so ancient and so new, too late have I loved you! Behold, you were within me, while I was outside: it was there that I sought you, and, a deformed creature, rushed headlong on these things of beauty which you made. You were with me, but I was not with you. They kept me far from you, those fair things which, if they were not in you, would not exist at all. You have called to me, and cried out, and shattered my deafness. You have blazed forth with light, and have shone on me, and you have put my blindness to flight! You have sent forth fragrance, and I have drawn in my breath, and I pant after you. I have tasted you, and I hunger and thirst after you. You have touched me, and I have burned for your peace. (*C*, 10.27.38)

A second context in which Augustine indicates what faith seeking understanding means is to be found in his discussion of the problem of time. When Augustine asks, "What is time?," he does not know the answer to his own question, even though he uses the concept of time in ordinary discourse without any difficulty (*C*, 11.14.17). Part of Augustine's point is that a radical distinction obtains between philosophy and ordinary life, where a chasm opens up between what we know experientially and what we can articulate at the reflective level. Yet if this were all that Augustine had in mind, his point would parallel the epistemic distinction between faith, on the one hand, and understanding on the other. From an epistemic point of view, the difficulty about the problem of time is that we cannot explain theoretically what we know pre-reflectively. If this dimension of the issue exhausted the problem, Augustine's discussion of the nature of time would be an epistemic attempt to understand the temporal matrix in which his journey toward God unfolds.

However, a careful reading of the way in which Augustine formulates the problem of time indicates that there is more to the problem than this; and this dimension of the issue expresses itself first in the fact that Augustine asks the question, "What is time?" more than once (*C*, 11.14.17). When he asks "What is time?" on this second occasion, the emphasis falls on the "is," pointing to the fact that Augustine wants to bring stability to the temporal flux in which his life is embedded. Augustine's theory of time is not a subjective account of temporality that stands in contrast with the flux with which he begins, but a way of bringing stability to what would otherwise dissolve in a process of coming to be and passing away.

It is a well-known fact that Augustine equates the past with memory, the present with intuition, and the future with expectation and that he holds these three modes of temporality together in a synthetic unity (*C*, 11.15.18). However, it is easy to overlook the fact that this way of understanding the nature of time is an attempt to understand how faith in God can bring stability to the soul (*C*, 11.20.26). Faith in God is a positive orientation of the soul toward the ground of its existence, where this positive orientation is made possible and is reflected imagistically by the nature of time as Augustine understands it.

Time makes faith possible because it is the ecstatic context in which expectation, intuition, and memory are gathered together and are oriented toward God at the vertical level of experience. However, Augustine not only points to the past, the present, and the future that can be unified synthetically from the standpoint of the present, but also indicates how time moves from the future toward the past through the present, where this dynamic dimension of the nature of time is presupposed in claiming that faith orients us toward God (*C*, 11.25.32). This dimension of temporality does not merely come to be and pass away within the temporal flux, but can be retained, stabilized, and projected onto eternity from the standpoint of the present (*C*, 11.26.33).

To the extent that time can be analyzed in terms of memory, intuition, and expectation, it provides the context in which faith in God unfolds. The act of faith expresses itself in temporal terms, first as a recollection of God, then as an encounter with God, and finally as an expectation about God. Time is also an image of the existential journey toward God; for its distention, synthesis, and self-transcendence reflect the transition from Augustine's fallen condition to the transformation and fulfillment he is seeking (C, 11.29.39). As he expresses the point in bringing his analysis of the nature of time to a conclusion:

Behold, my life is a distention or distraction. But "your right hand has upheld me" so that [I] may be gathered together again from my former days, to follow the One; "forgetting the things that are behind" and not distended but extended, not to things that shall be and shall pass away, but "to those things which are before"; not purposely but purposively, "I follow on for the prize of my supernal vocation," where "I may hear the voice of your praise," and "contemplate your delights," which neither come nor go. (*C*, 11.29.39)

The final place in which we find a condition for and an image of Augustine's existential journey is in his analysis of the hermeneutics of creation. In the last two books of the *Confessions*, Augustine does three things. First, he gives a cosmological account of creation *ex nihilo* in which he attempts to understand the most universal conditions that make his journey toward God possible (*C*, 12.3.3). Then he shows how these conditions are imagistic reflections of his journey at the reflective level. Finally, he moves beyond these two dimensions of his inquiry by giving an allegorical interpretation of the first chapter of Genesis (*C*, 13.8.9). The allegorical language he uses in giving this account stands in between the cosmological language of creation and the existential language of his journey toward God; and in doing so, it binds these two dimensions of his journey together.

Augustine's account of creation *ex nihilo* presupposes that the creation, the fall, conversion, and fulfillment are distinguishable moments within creation itself. Creation first expresses itself in bringing unformed material into existence (*C*, 12.3.3), and the problem of the fall emerges in reflecting on what this material would have become unless it had been "converted to form" (*C*, 12.3.3). Augustine then makes the transition from conversion to fulfillment by claiming that the *telos* of creation is an orientation toward God that never turns away from him (*C*, 12.15.20).

The cosmological situation to which Augustine points is contrary to fact (*C*, 12.30.41); but in attempting to envisage it, he describes the universal context that his existential situation presupposes and illustrates. Augustine's experiential journey toward God is a particular instance of the relation of the cosmos to the ground of its existence, where this relation brings his journey into connection with its cosmological conditions (*C*, 13.7.8). These conditions are also images of the journey of faith at the reflective level, where creation, fall, conversion, and fulfillment are expressed in cosmological terms.

Augustine's rhetoric brings faith and understanding together, not only by suggesting that the second term is the condition for and a mirror image of the first, but also by developing a language in which faith and understanding are present together. The allegorical language that Augustine introduces is existential and theoretical simultaneously, and both his journey toward God and the cosmological context that grounds and reflects it are held together by a set of symbols that express the quest of faith for understanding in allegorical terms. The first of these symbols is the Church, where light and darkness can be distinguished and where "conversion to form" can be understood as a way of coming to the light (*C*, 13.3.4, 13.12.13). The second is the gathering of the waters into one place and the distinction between the land and the waters as a way of depicting the contrast between the City of God and the city of men (*C*, 13.17.20). The third is the creation of the living soul, which points to conversion as a way of turning away from affection for the world (*C*, 13.20.26). The fourth is the fulfillment of the soul that will result when it increases and multiplies, which occurs when faith is interpreted in many ways and when a single interpretation is understood in many ways as well (*C*, 13.20.27).

In all these ways, faith seeking understanding not only discovers propositions that the epistemic dimension of faith entails, but also uncovers conditions that make faith possible at the experiential level. In doing so, it points to ways in which these conditions express the act of faith in theoretical terms. As our reflections unfold, allegorical language permits us to focus our attention on both levels as we try to understand the ways of thinking that sustain the Augustinian tradition.

One of the most important ways to elaborate Augustine's rhetorical strategy in the *Confessions* is to approach his most personal book from an auditory point of view. In doing so, I make two assumptions: the first is about the relation between literal and figurative discourse; and the second is about the history of philosophy. The clearest way to discuss the first assumption is to recall the pattern of Augustine's philosophical development. After Cicero's *Hortensius* leads him to embrace philosophy as the love of wisdom (*C*, 3.4.7), he tries to become a professional philosopher, where this is the most accurate description of his nine-year bondage to Manichaeism (*C*, 4.1.1). During this period of his life, Augustine embraces the law of excluded middle and the part–whole logic of literal discourse, seeing the world as a dualistic opposition between good and evil and picturing God as a material entity in which the parts are less than the whole (*C*, 4.11.17). This philosophical literalism is the primary reason that he could not make progress as a Manichaean.

Augustine could never have written the *Confessions* without transcending literal discourse. On more than one occasion, he claims that what impedes his intellectual progress is his incapacity to conceive of a spiritual substance (*C*, 5.14.26, 6.3.4). "Substance" points toward solidity and is the sustaining power that undergirds an entity. By contrast, "spiritual" points to what is insubstantial, precisely because it is immaterial. To conceive of a spiritual substance, we must reconstrue it in metaphorical terms. The constituents of this metaphor are in tension with one another, and their unity emerges from their opposition. The fluidity of Augustine's language reflects his willingness to embrace metaphorical discourse; and he not only does so in this isolated case, but also in the auditory metaphors that he uses throughout the *Confessions*.

My second assumption is about the history of philosophy, where I assume that visual, auditory, and tactile dimensions are central in its development. In the ancient world, the sense of sight is the most important of the senses. When Aristotle says that all of us desire knowledge, he appeals to our capacity to see to illustrate his point; for he knows that it is through vision that we grasp the form or structure of a thing.[10] In modernity, the sense of touch replaces the sense of sight as the basic mode of access to the world. Modern philosophy presupposes that we can lay hands on the world, and it attempts to overcome the noetic distance of the Greeks with the practical immediacy of the scientific and the technological revolutions. Praxis presupposes immediacy, and the sense of touch gives the modern philosopher immediate access to things.[11]

By contrast with both the ancient and the modern worlds, we can understand Augustine's world only from the standpoint of speaking and hearing as primordial phenomena. An infinite distance separates God from the soul, and as a consequence, God cannot present himself as a visible content of cognition. We are also unable to reach across the space that separates us from him to touch him directly, but God crosses the chasm between the soul and himself when he speaks. As Augustine says:

> I call thee into my soul. Do not forsake me when I call on thee. [Thou] didst repeatedly urge with manifold calling that I should hear thee afar off and be turned and call on thee, who callest me. Do not let the tumult of [my] vanity deafen the ear of [my] heart. The Word itself calls [me] to return. With him is a place of unperturbed rest, where love is not forsaken unless it first forsakes. (*C*, 13.1.1, 4.11.16)

The responses that Augustine makes to God often take the form of auditory metaphors. For example, he says, "Let me learn from thee, who art Truth, and put the ear of my heart to thy mouth." Then he exclaims:

> Accept this sacrifice of my confessions from the hand of my tongue. Thou didst form it and hast prompted it to praise thy name. Thou didst cry to

me from afar, "I am that I am." And I heard this [as we hear things] in the heart, and there was no room for doubt. (*C*, 5.1.5; 7.10.16)

Finally, he says:

I renounce myself and choose thee. I do not do it with the words and sounds of the flesh, but with the words of the soul, and with the sound of my thoughts. I long to serve the cause of love. Trim away from my lips, inwardly and outwardly, all rashness and lying. Harken to my soul and hear it crying from the depths. Unless thy ears attend us even in the depths, where should we go? [And] to whom should we cry? I love a certain kind of sound in loving my God. [He] is the sound of my inner man. (*C*, 10.2.2; 11.2.3; 10.6.8)

It is to the structure of these auditory metaphors that we now turn.

Let me enumerate the crucial statements to which I wish to call your attention.

1. "Let me put the ear of my heart to thy mouth" (*C*, 4.5.10).
2. "Accept this sacrifice from the hand of my tongue" (*C*, 5.1.1).
3. "Thou didst cry to me from afar, and I heard this [as we hear things] in the heart" (*C*, 7.10.16).
4. "I choose thee with the words of the soul and with the sound of my thoughts" (*C*, 10.2.2).
5. "Trim away from my lips all rashness and lying" (*C*, 11.2.3).
6. "Harken to my soul and hear it crying from the depths" (*C*, 11.2.3).
7. "Unless thy ears attend us even in the depths, where should we go?" (*C*, 11.2.3).
8. Finally, Augustine says, "God is the sound of my inner man" (*C*, 10.6.8).

Several of the figurative uses of language in these statements seem to be synecdoches rather than metaphors. For example, instead of "my ear" and "my hand," we find the "ear of my heart" and the "hand of my tongue" (*C*, 5.1.1). And instead of a "rash and lying person," we find "rash and lying lips" (*C*, 11.2.3). In these two cases, Augustine speaks about a part of the body as if it were a person. We also have a substitution of a part for a whole in two other cases. Augustine says, the "words of the soul" instead of the "words of a man"; and he says, "Hear my soul crying from the depths" instead of "hear me crying from the depths" (*C*, 11.2.3). Should we speak

about auditory synecdoches rather than auditory metaphors in Augustine's
Confessions?

Other factors complicate the situation. When Augustine says that God
has a mouth and ears, he speaks about him as if he were a man. These
metaphors about God apparently reduce to anthropomorphisms. In the
eight statements that I have listed, one also seems to be a simile. Augustine
says, "I heard this [as we hear things] in the heart" (*C,* 7.10.16). In doing so,
he is comparing how he hears something with the way his heart hears it,
where this is not a metaphor, auditory or otherwise. Only one statement in
the list is metaphorical in the canonical way, where the metaphor in question is "God is the sound of my inner man" (*C,* 10.6.8). However, this
apparently straightforward metaphor raises problems of its own to which we
must return.

Even if there are five synecdoches among our examples, it is important
to notice that the contexts that include them are metaphorical. Consider one
of Augustine's favorite phrases, the "ear of my heart." Even if "heart" is
standing proxy for the person, what is metaphorical about the expression in
question is the entire utterance. It is the interaction between ear and heart
that produces the metaphor. This is also true of the other examples. The
"hand of my tongue," "rash and lying lips," and the "words of the soul"
involve metaphorical interactions. In each case, the tension and the interaction between the components of the utterance and the new meaning that
emerges from them constitute the metaphor.[12]

The same point holds true for the anthropomorphic examples. All
metaphors about God attribute finite characteristics to him, and it is the tension between these characteristics and God that makes these metaphors
dynamic centers of interaction. The simile is also merely apparent and does
not raise a serious problem. Augustine says, "I heard this [as we hear things]
in the heart." Yet he is not comparing how he hears with how his heart hears.
Rather, he is specifying the way he hears in this case by mentioning the heart.
Paradoxically, the statement that is most clearly metaphorical raises the most
difficult problem. Augustine's claim that God is the voice of his "inner man"
tempts us to identify God with Augustine's own voice. Yet if we do this, how
can we free him from the charge of pantheistic ontologism?

We must plunge more deeply into the rhetorical dimension of
Augustine's enterprise if the details of the discussion are not to obscure our
fundamental thesis. One way to do this is to notice that all the auditory
metaphors that we have been considering point to the unity and the separation between God and the soul. Consider the first example, "Let me put the
ear of my heart to thy mouth." The ear of the heart and the mouth of God

stand over against one another; otherwise, it would not be necessary for Augustine to bring the ear of his heart closer to God. Yet unity also emerges when the ear and the mouth coincide, allowing God to transform Augustine's fragmented heart.

In the statement before us, we find two auditory metaphors, both of which point in two directions. The "ear of my heart" points toward the center of Augustine's being and opens out to listen to the voice of God, while the "mouth of God" points to the depth of God's being and to his willingness to reveal himself to Augustine. In both cases, there is a tensional element internal to the metaphor. Augustine's heart is far away from God, and it is difficult for him to listen to God's voice. He has a natural tendency to turn back on himself and to seal off his heart so nothing can penetrate it. In a similar way, God as he is in himself is a perfect unity, with no inherent motivation to speak; and when he does so, it is in spite of his impassivity.

According to the interaction theory of metaphor that I have been presupposing, a metaphor displays three characteristics. First, its elements have antecedent meanings that stand in tension with one another. Second, these meanings interact to generate a new meaning that unifies the first two. Finally, the new meaning has an indefinite number of implications, opening out on an unlimited horizon of future interpretations.[13] Both the "ear of the heart" and the "mouth of God" are metaphors in this sense. "Ear," "heart," "mouth," and "God" have antecedent meanings; these meanings interact with one another to generate new meanings for the "ear of the heart" and the "mouth of God"; and these meanings generate an indefinite number of interpretations.

The auditory dimension of these metaphors adds an additional element to them. An auditory metaphor points beyond itself, not only by having an indefinite number of implications, but also because it displays a bidirectional structure. The constituents of an auditory metaphor point both outward and inward. This gives auditory metaphors a dimension of self-transcendence. The unity of an auditory metaphor also differs from the unity of metaphors of other kinds. The two directions in which they points are not a whole of which these directions are parts, but are an open space in which the directions in question become mirror images of one another.

In the "ear of my heart," the "ear" and the "heart" point in opposite directions. As Augustine plunges down into his heart, he turns inward. As he opens his ears to the voice of God, he turns outward. The auditory metaphor that emerges is a unity of these two directions, binding them together as mirror images that remain distinct from one another. Difference rather than identity is the dominant dimension in a metaphor of this kind. Furthermore, the statement, "Put the ear of my heart to your mouth," contains two auditory metaphors, both of which have difference as the primary element. In the "mouth of God," the direction that moves toward God and the one that moves away from him are mirror images that never blend into an identity; in this respect, the "ear of my heart" and the "mouth of God" reflect one another.

When Augustine says, "Let me put the ear of my heart to your mouth," the entire statement expresses a mirror-image relation. God speaks first, moving from passivity to activity. Then Augustine listens, moving from the discord of his fragmented heart to receptivity to the voice of God. The two directions of this double movement hold the metaphorical constituents of the statement before us both together and apart. This statement contains two auditory metaphors that we can analyze as a pair of mirror-image relations. However, the most important point to notice is that the entire statement is a unity of identity and difference. The sentential unity of the mirror images is an image that preserves the unity and the separation between God and the soul. The imagistic structure of the statement that unifies these auditory metaphors provides a place of interaction between God and the soul, where God speaks and Augustine listens in the space this image generates.

After Augustine hears God speak, he becomes active and God becomes receptive. Augustine says, "Accept this sacrifice from the hand of my tongue" (*C*, 5.1.1). Then he adds, "I choose thee with the words of the soul and with the sound of my thoughts" (*C*, 10.2.2). "Harken to my soul and hear it crying from the depths" (*C*, 11.2.3). "Unless thy ears attend us even in the depths, where should we go?" (*C*, 11.2.3) In all these cases, Augustine and God reverse roles and move in opposite directions. The God that speaks to the ear of Augustine's heart now listens with ears of his own. The hand of Augustine's tongue and the sound of his thoughts reach toward God and implore him to respond. On this occasion, the mirror-image of this double movement generates a space in which the *Confessions* becomes a conversation between God and the soul.

There is also a double direction in the auditory metaphors that Augustine uses. If the hand of Augustine's tongue is to make a sacrifice, he must turn away from what he is to what he wishes to become. If he chooses God with the words of his soul, he must renounce the words of his flesh; and if he chooses him with the sound of his thoughts, he must transcend the sound of his voice. When God harkens to Augustine's soul and hears it crying from the depths (*C*, 11.2.3), God hears a voice that has fallen away from him. Augustine cries from the depths because he has fallen so far away from God and because he longs to reverse the direction in which his soul has been moving. Yet he implores God to respond in the depths because he cannot rise to a higher place where he can hear God's voice. The two directions in which Augustine moves are internal to his soul and to the auditory metaphors that express his predicament.

Augustine finds what he seeks when he says, "Thou didst cry to me from afar. I heard this [as we hear things] in the heart" (*C*, 7.10.16). Augustine cannot bridge the chasm between God and the soul by using language that reverses the direction of his heart. Rather, God must speak so Augustine can hear, and he must hear so he can respond with a sacrifice from the hand of his tongue. Augustine can choose God only because God chooses him, and he can hear God speaking in the depths, only if God descends to meet him there. When this occurs, Augustine hears God in his heart and asks him to trim away rashness and lying from his lips.

God inverts the divine impassivity and reaches toward Augustine, and Augustine responds by inverting his tendency to turn away from God and by reaching toward the ground of his existence. In both cases, there is a double movement in the auditory metaphors that bring God and Augustine together. Yet the moment of transformation does not come when God reaches out for Augustine and Augustine reaches out for him. Salvation occurs only when God cries from afar and Augustine hears, and it comes to completion only when Augustine is willing to allow God to transform his lips.

This transaction requires a double reversal on the part of both Augustine and God. God must shift from impassivity to activity when he first addresses Augustine, and he must shift from activity to receptivity when Augustine asks him to listen. Finally, he must shift from receptivity to divine intervention to transform Augustine's soul. In a similar way, Augustine shifts from activity to receptivity when God first addresses him. Then he shifts from passivity to activity when he addresses God. Finally, he shifts from activity to receptivity when he hears God's voice and permits him to heal the lips with which he speaks.

The first auditory utterance that makes this transformation possible contains a pair of auditory metaphors. God cries from afar; Augustine hears in his heart; and taken together, these two metaphors generate a transaction between God and the soul. The second auditory utterance presupposes that God has crossed the chasm that separates him from Augustine. What God begins now comes to fruition; for when he touches Augustine's heart, we find a shift to the tactile dimension. God begins to trim away the rashness and the lying from Augustine's lips; and lest we think that God has come too close, we must not misinterpret the final auditory metaphor in the list with which we began. At this juncture Augustine says that God is the sound of his "inner man."

When God has trimmed away rashness and lying from his lips, does Augustine intend to say that he can speak in God's place? When his transformation moves toward completion, does God become a sound that emerges from Augustine's "inner man"? This would be an embarrassing consequence for a position that presupposes creation *ex nihilo* and that begins with a radical contrast between God and the soul. We must surely try to avoid it, especially if our thesis about the primacy of difference in Augustine's auditory metaphors is to survive critical scrutiny.

We can resolve this difficulty by noticing that Augustine's "inner man" is the object rather than the subject of God's voice; in this case, the "inner man" is an objective rather than a subjective genitive. God is the sound of Augustine's "inner man" only when he speaks to him to bring redemption. Yet there is this much truth in our difficulty: Once God's voice has spoken, Augustine begins to speak in a new way. He speaks with more authority, and he speaks under the impact of grace. With transformed lips, Augustine begins to speak God's words rather than words of his own; and in doing so, he becomes a vehicle for a source of power that remains beyond him.

Auditory rather than visual metaphors are at the heart of the *Confessions*, and this is so because Augustine never eradicates the space between God and the soul. Like their visual counterparts, auditory metaphors are interactions between distinct elements that generate new meanings. However, auditory metaphors differ from other kinds of metaphors in being inherently bidirectional. When they are about God and the soul, they point to the depth of our being and to what lies beyond the human realm. They also point to the hiddenness of God and to his willingness to reveal himself, even though nothing constrains him to do so. When auditory metaphors about God and the soul are present in the same sentence, they generate a space in which a transaction between time and eternity occurs. This rhetorical transaction takes us to the center of the *Confessions* and stands at the center of the faith that Augustine seeks to understand.

Another way to deal with the rhetoric of Augustine's enterprise is to focus our attention on the linguistic richness of the *Confessions*, which expresses itself in its rhetorical power and issues in its problematic textuality. I begin with the assumption that Augustine is more a Christian rhetorician than a Neoplatonist and that the intricate textuality of his religious and philosophical enterprise emerges from his attempt to think about the problems of death and eternity. My thesis is that the language of the heart at the center of the *Confessions* is reflected in figurative discourse and that the text can be understood only when metaphor and analogy are recognized as Augustine's principal ways of achieving his existential and reflective intentions.

Augustine's use of language is both performative and figurative, where the most familiar examples of these phenomena are visual metaphors that express the role of the intellect in the soul's search for God. For example, he speaks about the "light of truth" (*C*, 12.30.41, 13.18.23), "inner vision" (*C*, 6.16.26),[14] "seeing with the eye of the soul rather than with the eye of the flesh" (*C*, 7.10.16), and of the "trembling glance" (*C*, 7.17.23) that finally gives him access to God in the first stage of his Neoplatonic vision (*C*, 7.10.16). However, as I have suggested in the previous chapter, the great rhetorician uses equally powerful auditory metaphors to express his longing for existential transformation. First he asks, "Let me learn from thee, who art Truth, and put the ear of my heart to thy mouth" (*C*, 4.5.10). Then he writes: "Accept this sacrifice of my confessions from the hand of my tongue. Thou didst form it and hast prompted it to praise thy name" (*C*, 5.1.1). Finally, he implores God to "trim away" all "rashness and lying" from his lips, to harken to his soul, and to "hear it crying from the depths" (*C*, 1.2.3). In all these cases, Augustine uses figurative discourse, not as a rhetorical ornament, but as a linguistic way of stretching toward God, and as an ecstatic way of expressing what Margaret Miles has described as "desire and delight."[15]

The language of the heart, the figurative discourse that expresses it, and the visual and auditory metaphors in which they are embodied often come to focus in language about God and the soul. In the *Soliloquies*, Reason asks Augustine, "What do you wish to know?" When he answers that he wants to know God and the soul, and when his interlocutor asks, "Nothing more?" Augustine replies decisively, "Nothing whatever" (*S*, 25.4). In this single sentence, he identifies the crucial issues around which the language of the heart revolves.

In the *Confessions*, the language of God and the soul expresses itself in four stages: first, Augustine speaks about creation *ex nihilo* and about the act of speaking that creates the world (*C*, 4.10.15, 5.3.5, 11.6.8, 11.9.11); second, he speaks about the linguistic deception that leads us away from God to embrace our fallen condition (*C*, 2.6.12); third, he speaks about the voice of a child that points to the incarnation of the Word and to the conversion that a positive response to it makes possible (*C*, 8.12.28); and finally, he speaks about fulfillment that points beyond the language of desire and delight to satiety without satiation (*C*, 13.26.39), and to the language of praise that never comes to an end (*C*, 1.1.1). In all these cases, the figurative language that Augustine speaks not only attempts to bridge the otherwise unbridgeable chasm between God and the soul, but also points to metaphorical ways of describing the soul, and to analogical ways of bringing the soul into relation with God.

The four metaphors suggested by our transition from creation and fallenness to conversion and fulfillment involve four ways of bringing the finite and the infinite dimensions of the person together as it develops its relation with God. As an image of God that has been created *ex nihilo*, the person is a (finite–infinite being), limited as it stands in contrast with others, but unlimited as it stretches out toward the creative ground of its existence. As a creature that falls away from God, this same person is a (finite–infinite) being that seeks to deny its limitations, to break the hyphen that defines its original condition, and to become infinite in its own right as the master of nature and as the product of an act of self-deification. When he is converted, the (finite–infinite) being comes to itself and affirms its finitude through the power of the incarnation, where the infinite Word manifests itself in a finite form that fallen beings are commanded to imitate. Finally, this converted being moves toward fulfillment (finite–infinite) when its infinite richness begins to express itself fully through the finite limitations it embraces as it attempts to recover its original condition.[16]

In attempting to develop the language of God and the soul, I call the four modifications of the (finite–infinite) nexus that defines the human condition "metaphors" because a metaphor involves a tensional relation between two terms, the infinite richness of which can never be exhausted in a finite sequence of interpretations.[17] The (finite–infinite) metaphor that expresses our created condition points to the tension between limited and unlimited dimensions of our nature that place us in between God and the world and on the basis of which a dynamic relation between God and the soul can unfold. By contrast, the (finite–infinite) metaphor that expresses human fragmentation points to the fact that this tension sometimes ruptures, generating a virtually unlimited number of ways of breaking beyond the middle ground in which we are related to the creative source from which we emerge. Finally, when fallenness seeks conversion and conversion seeks fulfillment, the (finite–infinite) metaphors corresponding to both conditions continue to display the tension between competing dimensions of the soul. In the first case, this tension is expressed but delimited by an act in which the (finite–infinite) accepts its finitude (8.7.18); and in the second, it is developed in an indefinite number of ways as the (finite–infinite) being begins to learn how to express its infinite richness without losing its integrity (8.10.22).

Four analogies correspond to the four metaphors that define the human condition, and in all four cases, they bring these metaphors into relation with God. The (finite–infinite) being is created in the image of God, where this image is both a finite and an infinite reflection of the creative ground on which it depends. When a (finite–infinite) being falls away from God, it becomes a negative reflection of the ground on which it depends and a counterfeit image of the infinitude it was meant to express (*C*, 2.8.16). When it is converted, the (finite–infinite) being puts on a new garment, where the acceptance of its finitude becomes an image of the incarnation that makes transformation possible (*C*, 8.12.28). Finally, when this (finite–infinite) being moves toward fulfillment, it becomes an infinite expression in a finite context of the infinite source from which it emerges and to which it seeks to return (*C*, 9.10.23). The four metaphors that Augustine presupposes in describing the human condition can be brought into relation with God by introducing four corresponding analogies, where learning how to speak the language of God and the soul involves learning how to use the metaphors and the analogies in which they stand to give us access to the ground of our existence.[18]

Augustine's systematic use of metaphors and analogies not only gives us access to the language of the heart, and to the figurative discourse in which it expresses itself, but also enables us to call into question the familiar reading of Augustine as a Neoplatonic thinker who is committed to a radical dualism between the soul and the body.[19] According to this interpretation of his intentions, Augustine believes that the soul is the "true man" (*C*, 7.19.25) and that the body should be understood as a detriment to spiritual and philosophical progress (*C*, 7.19.25). It is true that there are a number of dualistic passages in the *Confessions*, where Augustine sometimes identifies himself with the soul, especially on those occasions in which he says that the soul can remember God and can be brought into an intelligible relation with him (*C*, 10.16.26). However, on most occasions, Augustine suggests that a man is a composite of a soul and a body and that an adequate response to the human predicament must take both dimensions of the human being into account (*C*, 10.27.38). Indeed, his identification of himself with the rational soul is only one aspect of a complex semantics in which metaphorical openness and analogical otherness converge to account for both the separation and the unity of the soul and the body, both of which are elements at the center of the confessional enterprise.

Let me illustrate this complex semantics, where the unity and the separation of Augustine's language about the soul and the body are concrete expressions of the language of the heart and of the figurative discourse in which it is embodied. In developing his account of the relation between the soul and the body, Augustine sometimes speaks as if he were a man who binds his soul and his body together as distinguishable elements (*C*, 7.19.25, 10.6.9); he sometimes suggests that he is to be identified with a soul (*anima*) using a body (*C*, 7.20.26, 10.27.38); he sometimes claims that he becomes so identified with his body that it places a weight on the soul that it is almost unable to bear (*C*, 7.21.27, 8.5.12, 10.28.39); and he sometimes says that he is a soul (*animus*) that not only transcends its body, but also transcends itself as it rises toward God (*C*, 10.8.15). In the first two cases, the soul and the body are bound together in a metaphorical unity; in the second two, they are held apart in analogical separation.

Metaphorical unity is an open-ended relation between two terms that is capable of endless articulation; and analogical separation is a relation between two terms that binds them together and holds them apart. In this case, the metaphors with which we begin and the similarities that bind them together and hold them apart cannot be reduced to the identities and differences to which they point.[20] Metaphorical unity differs from its dialectical surrogate in not positing a third term in which the articulation of the unity in question can ever come to rest, and analogical unity and separation differ from their mathematical ancestor in not being the logical product of identity and difference understood as more fundamental ontological categories.[21] Part of what I mean by speaking about metaphorical openness and analogical otherness can be expressed in the thesis that the unity of both concepts stands over against dialectical articulation, on the one hand, and univocity and equivocity on the other.

With these concepts before us, let me illustrate how Augustine uses them to develop a semantical account of the unity and the separation of the soul and the body, sliding back and forth between the need to bind them together and the wish to hold them apart. First, he says that his soul carries its body with it as he moves from conversion to fulfillment, pointing to the metaphorical unity of the human being as it stands before God in the resurrection (*C*, 10.8.12). Second, he claims that sensation occurs when the soul uses its body as an instrument to place itself in contact with the external world, suggesting that the soul and the body are bound together in an open-ended unity between the soul understood as an artisan and the body understood as a tool he uses as an extension of himself. Third, he suggests that the soul is borne downward by its own weight, where this weight points to the earth from which Augustine is made and to which he tries to return (*C*, 7.17.23, 10.8.14). Finally, in his quest for God, Augustine moves from the metaphorical unity of the soul and the body to their analogical separation, where he becomes identical with the rational soul as it moves up the ontological ladder toward God (*C*, 7.17.23, 10.8.15). Ultimately, it transcends itself to find God, who is beyond the mind, and who stands over against it (*C*, 7.17.23, 10.8.15).

This complex semantics makes it clear that Augustine is not a philosophical dualist, but a thinker who moves back and forth between the unity and the separation of the soul from the body in terms of which he defines the human being as a composite (*C*, 7.18.24). Without mobilizing the subtlety of figurative discourse, he would have been unable to do this, where either univocal or equivocal language would lose the analogical otherness between the soul and the body on the one hand, or the metaphorical unity of these same two elements on the other. Augustine speaks the language of the heart and the figurative discourse in which he expresses it from the point of intersection between metaphorical unity and analogical separation; it is because of his willingness to use language of this kind that he is able to address his readers from the center of his being.

The final issue we need to consider is the relation between the complex semantics that Augustine develops and the meaning of Being that he presupposes as he learns to speak the language of the heart. The most familiar interpretation of the ontology that underlies the *Confessions* claims that it is exclusively Neoplatonic, not only in its origins, but also in its essence, and that God is the upper bound of an ontological continuum that stretches downward from the One to the many.[22] According to this view, God is to be identified with *Vere Esse*, and everything other than God is to be understood by participation in God, who is to be understood, in turn, as Truth itself (*C*, 7.20.26). If we move in this direction, we might be able to do justice to the dimension of metaphorical openness in Augustine's thinking, but we will not be able to take account of his equally clear commitment to radical discontinuity as it expresses itself in the doctrine of creation *ex nihilo*.

According to this doctrine, God creates the world from absolute Nonbeing, where the speaking Word calls something into existence from nothing, not as an ontological extension of itself, or as a product fashioned from antecedently existing material, but as an image of an eternal original. The image-original relation that the doctrine of creation presupposes points beyond the continuum of Being in which God is identical with *Vere Esse* to the ground of this continuum in which God is to be identified with *Ipsum Esse*. If the open-ended unity of metaphorical discourse allows us to do justice to the ontological continuum in which all beings participate, the unity and separation of analogical discourse permits us to acknowledge the chasm between God and the world that is established by the act of creation. The relation between image and original that arises from creation preserves a greater degree of separation between God and the world than could have been acknowledged if Augustine had committed himself to a Neoplatonic doctrine of emanation that an unbroken continuum between God and the world illustrates.

If we take metaphorical openness and analogical otherness together, it is possible to develop an ontology that speaks about God as *Vere Esse* and as *Ipsum Esse* simultaneously, allowing Augustine to stand in between Neoplatonic continuity, on the one hand, and the radical discontinuity that emerges later as the defining theme of the Thomistic tradition. The complex semantics that Augustine develops is more subtle than the semantics presupposed by the doctrine of emanation[23] or the analogical discourse of Aquinas[24] that collapses eventually into the radical equivocity of his Ockhamist successors.[25] Just as Augustine slides back and forth between the unity and the separation of the soul and the body, so he moves back and forth between the unity and the separation of two meanings of Being. The first calls our attention to the continuity between God and the world; the second points to the radical discontinuity that holds them apart; and both together point not only to the Being of beings, but also to the Being of Being. The Being of beings presupposes a relation between God and the world that places them together in an ontological continuum in which God is the measure of the world as the Truth of being. By contrast, the Being of Being presupposes that God stands over against the world as he is in himself and that the world comes into existence through an act of creation in which Being manifests itself gratuitously by revealing itself as the Being of the beings that exist over against it.

The figurative discourse that Augustine uses, the complex semantics that he develops, the relation between the soul and the body that this semantical framework allows him to articulate, and the distinction that it permits him to draw between the Truth of Being and the Ground of Being intersect in the language of the heart that Augustine learns to speak as he writes the *Confessions*. Augustine addresses God from the center of his being, but he is able to do this only because the language he speaks does not bifurcate in the process and does not separate God into the standard of Truth, on the one hand, and the ground of existence on the other. To speak from the heart is to use a language that opens us up to what is closer to us than we are to ourselves and also over against us as the ground that creates us (*C*, 10.43.69), making it possible for us to express the mystery of being, to participate in the power of being, and to attempt to articulate the structure of being. The language of the heart, and the figurative discourse in which it expresses itself binds the mystery, the power, and the structure of Being together while it also holds them apart, allowing Augustine to move from creation to the fall and from conversion to fulfillment. In doing so, he not only addresses God from the center of his being, but also invites those who overhear the conversation to participate in it by speaking from the heart in existential and philosophical reflections of their own.

Chapter 5

Transcendence and Immanence in Augustine's *Confessions*

Genuine religion always involves the worship of what is genuinely ultimate; and as a consequence, religion, worship, and ultimate reality are related indissolubly. The task of reflective thought is to distinguish what is sound from what is spurious in religion, to characterize the meaning of religious devotion, and to attempt to articulate the nature of the ultimate reality to which worship is directed. As Augustine understood so clearly, all the perennial attempts to accomplish these purposes begin with the recognition that worship is legitimate only if it is directed toward a reality that is not only immanent, but that also stands beyond the realm of finite things (*C*, 1.1.1). We are able to distinguish genuine religion from idolatry in terms of this requirement. However, against this background, basic differences exist about the meaning of worship and about the nature of the extraordinary "object" toward which worship is directed.

We sometimes understand worship in terms of unconditional respect, love, and devotion, where the "object" of worship must be worthy of worship in this threefold guise. Accordingly, we claim that that we should regard the supreme religious "object" as a perfect being. Only what is perfect is worthy of unconditional respect and devotion, and only a being that manifests its perfection in perfect love is worthy of love that is equally unconditional.[1] On the other hand, sometimes worship involves a component that is not articulated adequately in the previous way. This component comprises what Rudolf Otto called the "non-rational" side of religion.[2] This aspect of religious experience involves the transcendence to which Augustine responds and the response of the worshiper to the mystery and the holiness of what is unconditioned (*C*, 1.2.2). These facts entail that we should distinguish two strands of interpretation in the philosophy of religion.[3] Against the background of agreement about the extraordinary character of the "object" of worship, some insist that the "object" in question must be characterized in terms of perfection and immanence. Others claim that the concepts of mystery and holiness are more adequate categories in terms of which this "object" ought to be understood.

These strands of interpretation have often existed in open conflict; but, the conflict has been uneasy, since the antagonists have usually recognized some measure of truth in the alternative account. Accordingly, the opposition between these alternatives has often consisted in the attempts of each to accommodate the definitive insights of the other, giving them a legitimate, if subordinate place, within a larger scheme of interpretation. In this chapter, I examine the opposition between these alternatives from the standpoint that seeks to interpret the "object" of worship in terms of mystery and holiness. From this standpoint, I will set forth the ground of its opposition to the concepts of perfection and immanence as the definitive categories in terms of which what is ultimate is to be understood. I will also indicate the way in which we can give these categories a subordinate role within the mode of interpretation in question. In developing the opposition, I will argue that the attempt to subordinate the concepts of perfection and immanence are illegitimate. However, I will attempt to show that they must not be used to replace the concepts of mystery and transcendence and that each of the four categories has a fundamental role to play in the attempt to understand the nature of the supreme religious "object." In characterizing these roles, I will consider certain problems that arise when we attempt to hold them together in terms of traditional dialectical conceptions; I will indicate the consequences of dialectical failure for the concrete context of religion.

From the standpoint of mystery and transcendence, we are tempted to reject the concept of a perfect being as an adequate description of the "object" of religious devotion. We can call this account into question by analyzing the concept of a being. Beings of whatever kind are finite, and their finitude is revealed in the fact that every being stands in contrast with others as a distinct and distinguishable individual. As Augustine argues, to be distinct and distinguishable is to be delimited, to be delimited is to be subject to limitation by negation, and to be subject to limitation is to be a finite thing (*C*, 2.8.16). Since worship is directed beyond the finite order to an ultimate reality that transcends finite limitations, the characterization of what is ultimate in terms of the concept of a being seems to be inadequate to the "object" that it seeks to represent. On the other hand, we must not overlook the fact that a reference to the concept of perfection is intended to remove the finitude of the being to which we ascribe it. When we claim that the "object" of worship is a perfect being, that "object" is unlimited; and as a consequence, not a being in an ordinary sense. Though we must admit that ordinary things are finite and that they manifest their finitude in imperfection, perfection negates the finitude usually ascribed to individuality.

Yet a question remains about the sense in which we can regard a perfect being as an individual. Individuality implies determination, and determination implies delimitation. If the claim that a perfect being is not a being in the customary sense negates delimitation, the perfection of what is ultimate is incompatible with the concept of individuality as we understand it ordinarily. Since the negation of delimitation is the negation of individuality, perfection is incompatible with the concept of individuality. On the other hand, if we ascribe perfection and immanence to what is ultimate, and if perfection does not imply the negation of delimitation, the concept of a perfect being is the concept of a being that is both perfect and finite. Finitude follows from delimitation, since delimitation is a mode of limitation. Yet if what is ultimate is also finite, worship is inappropriate. The worshiper seeks to orient himself to what is unconditioned; but in a perfect being, he finds something merely perfect of its kind—a being that stands in contrast with other finite things.

In attempting to overcome this dilemma, we might repudiate the concept of individuality as applicable to the ultimate "object" of religion. Accordingly, we could reinterpret the claim that the "object" of worship is a perfect being by claiming that the "object" in question is perfect, though not an individual that stands in contrast with other concrete things. We might then claim that the elimination of individuality involves the elimination of delimitation and that it removes the finitude of the otherwise unconditioned "object" of worship. It is important to notice that perfection is not a being; but a mode of Being in terms of which all finite things are measured. If we identify ultimate reality with perfection, it becomes the standard of value, and hence the standard of evaluation. On the other hand, if perfection is the measure of all things, it must be determinate. Otherwise, determinate ascriptions of value would never be possible. Yet determinations entail delimitation, delimitation implies finitude, and finitude is incompatible with the concept of ultimate reality. The identification of perfection with what is ultimate thus proves to be impossible, even when perfection is considered in itself.

Suppose we grant that a perfect being is the ultimate "object" of worship, contrary to the foregoing conclusions. As individuated and standing in contrast with finite things, the perfect being is the highest good. The worshiper attempts to relate himself to the good, where his fundamental aim expresses the wish to overcome his limitations. However, as Hegel claimed, the distance between the finite and the infinite is infinite (*PS*, 106–7). The following consequences follow from this insight: first, the perfect being with which the worshiper seeks identification functions as merely an ideal; second, since any finite progress toward perfection falls infinitely short of its goal, progress is impossible; finally, since the worshiper seeks fulfillment in identity, and since identity would obliterate his limitations, he cannot attain fulfillment. Perfection, for him, is the perfection of finitude, not its negation. Otherwise, the aim of the worshiper is revealed, not as the wish for fulfillment in God, but as the wish to become identical with God. The worshiper turns away in horror from the implications of his wish, for he sought identity with God that preserved some measure of difference. Instead, he finds that he in fact wishes to be divine himself.

If we begin with the concepts of immanence and perfection as attempts to articulate the nature of what is ultimate and unconditioned, we find that we progress from the concept of a being as an object unworthy of worship, to a perfect being as a contradictory "object" of worship, to perfection as less than ultimate and unconditioned. And if we posit a perfect being as ultimate in spite of these contradictions, it becomes an unreachable ideal, where our attempts to reach it reveal our *hubris*. The worshiper is thus thrown back on himself, where in order to preserve his "distance" from what is transcendent, he must live apart from God.

In spite of the difficulties that we have considered, we are not altogether at a loss in dealing with the foregoing issues. We must not forget that the categories of perfection and immanence comprise but a single mode of categorial interpretation. They stand in contrast with the concepts of mystery and transcendence, which provide an alternative account of the meaning of ultimate reality. Suppose we regard perfection and immanence, not as characterizing the ultimate as it is in itself, but as symbols that point to what is mysterious, holy, and unapproachable. We might then regard perfection and immanence as finite categories that give us access to what is transcendent. As finite, their content is inadequate to their object, issuing at points in contradiction. Yet this inadequacy suggests that their intended "object" is mysterious, and that it stands beyond the finite realm. Accordingly, we might give the concepts of perfection and immanence a subordinate place within a more fundamental scheme of interpretation, where they serve as symbols for the God beyond the gods.[4]

When we describe God as mysterious and transcendent, these concepts suggest that finite notions cannot circumscribe him. In fact, the concepts of mystery and transcendence provide successful characterizations, precisely because they imply that delimiting concepts are inadequate in this domain. It is also important to notice that when we construe these concepts as fundamental, we can preserve and enhance the infinite distance between the finite and the infinite. Worship ceases to consist in the quest for the absolute and becomes the adoration of the mystery and transcendence of what is ultimate and unconditioned; and the human task ceases to be the transcendence of finitude and becomes the problem of accepting one's finitude in the light of openness to mystery. When we understand ultimate reality in terms of mystery and holiness, we can remove the difficulties that beset the alternative interpretation. According to this conception of ultimate reality, we understand God in terms of non-objectifying speech,[5] and as a consequence, the infinite distance between the worshiper and the "object" of worship can be maintained and brought to focus.

It might seem that we should adopt the concepts of mystery and transcendence as the basic way of characterizing the meaning of ultimate reality. However, before we embrace this view we must ask a crucial question. If mystery and transcendence point to what is ultimate as a non-delimited and non-circumscribable "object" of religious devotion, and if we give perfection and immanence a subordinate role within this context as symbols for what is ultimate and unconditioned, how can the "object" to which these concepts direct our attention be intelligible to the finite understanding? Intelligibility rests on delimitation. Yet since perfection and immanence are symbolic concepts precisely because their referent is non-circumscribable, it would seem that we cannot understand the ultimate "object" of worship. Accordingly, the contradictions that follow from our earlier interpretation of the nature of God are replaced by the unintelligibility that the alternative account implies. In addition, the worshiper who stands open to mystery gives his devotion to an unknown God; and our frustration in the face of *hubris* is replaced by a total lack of understanding. Thus we might ask: How can the worshiper undertake the task of accepting his finitude in contrast with God, when the God in question has vanished from his horizon altogether?

We might suggest that though mystery implies a lack of determination in its "object," the concept of a holy mystery reintroduces the delimitation necessary for finite understanding. We can contrast what is sacred with what is profane, reintroducing determination; and determination, however minimal, provides the ground for an intelligible account of God as unconditioned. Yet we must not overlook the fact that if the holy stands in contrast with what is secular, what is holy then ceases to be simply unconditioned. It is opposed to the secular, regenerating the difficulties that beset the alternative conception of God. According to that interpretation, we conjoined the finite and delimited concept of a being with the concept of perfection in the attempt to articulate the nature of an unconditioned "object." However, the resulting concept led to difficulties of its own that undermined its value. As a consequence, it suggested an alternative approach to the problem of God in terms of non-objectifying speech. We find, however, that non-delimiting concepts fail to make the intelligibility of their "object" possible. We conjoined the concept of mystery with the concept of holiness, where the end in view was to reintroduce determination. Yet the God that such a concept represents is not the ultimate and unconditioned "object" of religion. What then shall we say in light of this?

When we contrast the categories of perfection and immanence with the concepts of mystery and transcendence, alternative and apparently incompatible views of the nature of God emerge, demanding in each case that we take account of the fundamental insights of the other. If God is worthy of unconditional respect and devotion, he must be a perfect being; for were he less than perfect, the unconditional nature of the act of worship would be inconsistent with the nature of its "object." And were he not a being, at least in the sense that he is delimited and determinate, worship would be directed toward an unknown God. On the other hand, we can scarcely identify God with perfection *simpliciter*, where we reject the reference to concreteness altogether. Perfection is worthy of unconditional respect and devotion only if it is actualized. Unless perfection is perfect, unconditional respect and devotion are misdirected; and unless perfection is actual, it is an "object" of hope rather than a "content" for worship.

On the other hand, we must understand God as mysterious and transcendent. Otherwise, the awe and wonder of the act of worship would not be intelligible within the context of religious experience. That mode of experience always involves a non-rational dimension, and this non-rational dimension evokes a reference to the mystery and the holiness of God. Respect, devotion, awe, and wonder thus comprise the meaning of the act of worship. As a consequence, we ought to characterize the "object" of worship in terms of perfection, mystery, concreteness, and holiness. If a dialectical position is to be possible within this context, we must discover a term that lies beyond the distinction between concreteness and mystery, perfection on the one hand and holiness on the other. Once we have discovered it, this term must fulfill the following conditions:

1. It must be intelligible.

2. It must preserve the transcendence of its referent.

3. It must not negate the unconditional nature of the "object" of worship.

4. It must unify the categories of immanence, transcendence, perfection, and holiness in a larger whole.

In the Western tradition, two concepts have emerged that seem to fulfill the foregoing conditions: on the one hand, the concept of Being-Itself (*ST*, 1:235); on the other hand, the concept of Spirit (*PS*, 323). However, I believe that we must acknowledge that both suggestions prove to be defective as attempts to achieve the reconciliation we seek.

For example, if God is identical with Being, we can preserve the mystery and the transcendence of what is ultimate. Being is mysterious because we cannot circumscribe it without reducing it to a delimited being, and Being is transcendent because it evokes awe and wonder in response to the existence of beings (*BT*, 82). On the other hand, Being is neutral to the distinction between the concrete and the abstract and to the contrast between the perfect and the imperfect. In transcending both conceptions, it seems to lose its intelligibility and fails to provide the unification of mystery, transcendence, perfection, and immanence. However, as I will argue in chapter 9, Being can supply the unity we seek if we adopt a somewhat unorthodox conception of the meaning of Being.

Spirit is just as inappropriate as the concept of Being in providing the unification of perfection, transcendence, immanence, and holiness. As in process, Spirit is immanent and mysterious—immanent because it develops through time, and mysterious because we cannot make it intelligible in terms of static forms under which we can subsume it (*PS*, 412; *BT*, 82). Yet Spirit is neither perfect nor transcendent. As in process, it aims for a *telos* that has not been reached; and as a consequence, it falls short of perfection. As dynamic and ultimate, it encompasses both the holy and the profane and cannot be reduced to either term of this polarity. As they are interpreted traditionally, Being and Spirit are inadequate as terms that can provide unification. Unless we can reinterpret these terms, or unless we can find another unifying concept, the two strands of the religious tradition will remain in conflict. On the surface, at least, the unification of perfection, concreteness, mystery, and holiness is impossible. If this proves to be the case, the religious consciousness would consist in an irreconcilable dyad: on the one hand, it displays respect and devotion for what is perfect and immanent; on the other hand; it exhibits awe and wonder in the face of mystery and transcendence.

The crucial question becomes: How can the religious consciousness survive the diremption implicit in this contradiction?

Part of the answer to this question is this: If each of the categories before us manifests itself as part of the meaning of ultimate reality, and if these categories remain in irresolvable conflict, we must accept the opposition between them as part of the meaning of ultimate reality. As a consequence, discord would be present at the heart of the nature of things, and we could only unify this discord in our willingness to accept the tension of what might appear to be an irreconcilable contradiction. We should expect that the worshiper would seek to avoid this. Accordingly, he might attempt to reduce the "object" of worship to something utterly mysterious or to something totally intelligible. By contrast, and as Augustine argued so forcibly in his account of the mind's journey toward God (C, 10.26.37), the religious consciousness ceases to be diremped only when it manifests its willingness to hold together the immanent and the transcendent strands of its religious commitment.

The transcendent dimension of Augustine's journey toward God emerges in the soul's attempt to move toward the knowledge of God through memory understood as a pathway (C, 10.17.26). As he understands its structure, memory is the mind's way to God; and forgetfulness is a cognitive and volitional reflection of the fall from paradise that separates our souls from God (C, 10.16.24–10.16.25). When God speaks to overcome our forgetfulness, he is immanent within the soul (C, 10.27.38); and when we listen, our temporal and reflective presents not only coincide in time, but are also brought together in relation to eternity.

The purpose of Augustine's discussion of the nature of memory is to retrace the pathway to God that he has traveled in his own experience. It is important for him to do this because memory is both an ontological condition and an imagistic reflection of his experiential journey. As a consequence, one of our most important tasks is to indicate how Augustine's discussion of the nature of memory is not simply a theoretical examination of a philosophical problem, but a way of instantiating his journey toward God in distinctively reflective terms.

Augustine begins his account of the mind's way to God by claiming that he knows that he loves God (C, 10.6.8). Yet having begun in this way, he turns abruptly from what he knows to what he does not know by asking, "What is it that I love when I love God?" (C, 10.6.8). This transition from confidence in the existence of God to a lack of confidence about the nature of God is typical of Augustine; for even at relatively early stages of his development, he believes in God's existence without understanding God's nature (C, 1.11.17).

Augustine attempts to answer the question before us by moving through a series of negations, claiming first that God is not bodily beauty, temporal glory, or the radiance of the light (*C*, 10.6.8). Then he says that God is not the melody of songs, the fragrance of flowers, the taste of honey, or the limbs that we embrace in physical love (*C*, 10.6.8). Yet having begun with negations, he moves to symbols that point beyond themselves by saying that he loves "a certain light, a certain voice, a certain odor, a certain food, and a certain embrace when [he loves] God"; for God is "a light, a voice, an odor, a food, [and] an embrace for the man within me" (*C*, 10.6.8). As a consequence, Augustine says that our senses give us access to God by pointing to light that "no place can contain," to words that "time does not speed away," to an aroma "that no wind can scatter," to food "that no eating can lessen," and to a "satiety" that "does not sunder us" from him (*C*, 10.6.8). Finally, he brings this figurative description of the relation between God and the soul to a conclusion by saying, "This is what I love when I love my God" (*C*, 10.6.8).

Having moved from what he knows to what he does not know, and from what God is not to what he is, Augustine passes the entire natural order in review, asking every part of it whether it is God and hearing in each case the reply, "I am not he!" (*C*, 10.6.9). Then he asks the things that he perceives to tell him something about God, and all of them cry out: "He made us" (*C*, 10.6.9). According to Augustine, creation is the fundamental relation between God and the world; and having come to know God through direct experience, he is able to understand what God is by observing the beauty of nature. The question that Augustine puts to nature and the beauty with which it responds allow him to hear the voice with which the natural order speaks about the ground of its existence (*C*, 10.6.9).

At this juncture, Augustine turns away from nature and turns inward toward the soul to continue his account of the journey toward God. He has traveled this pathway before by participating in mystical experiences that have given him access to God (*C*, 7.10.16, 7.17.23), but now he begins to generalize the pattern of these experiences by giving a systematic account of them. At this juncture, the one who asks nature where God is to be found begins to ask questions about himself (*C*, 10.6.9). In doing so, he attempts to find a place of access to the one who transcends him infinitely.

When Augustine asks himself, "Who are you?" the answer he gives is "A man!" (*C*, 10.6.9). However, at the level of philosophical analysis, he also claims that the body and the soul are in him and ready to serve him, one exterior and the other interior (*C*, 10.6.9). This means that he has both a soul (*anima*) and a body (*corpus*), that both principles make him what he is, and that these principles are to be distinguished from one another in terms of their distinctive functions. Augustine asks which of these principles ought to be his point of departure in seeking God (*C*, 10.6.9).

The author of the *Confessions* answers this question by saying that the soul (*anima*) is the principle through which the search for God should be conducted, claiming that the "inner man" is higher than the "outer man" because it rules and judges it (*C*, 10.6.9). Then in one of the most important but most misleading statements in the book, he says, "I, the inner man, know these things: I, I, the mind (*animus*), by means of my bodily senses" (*C*, 10.6.9). This is not to say that human beings have two kinds of soul (*anima* and *animus*), but that just as the soul and the body have distinctive functions, so the two kinds of soul play distinctive roles.

If we are to avoid misunderstanding at this juncture, it is important to notice that Augustine's identification of himself with his soul (*animus*) derives from his identification of himself as a man. His initial answer to the question, "Who am I?" is "A man!" where to be human is to be a composite of a soul (*anima*) and a body.[6] From an ontological point of view, this means that when he uses the word "I," he is talking first about himself and only derivatively about his soul or his body. The true man is not the soul, but the composite of the soul and the body, where the concepts of the inner and the outer man involve metaphorical extensions of the concept of a man to the soul and the body considered in themselves.[7]

When Augustine claims that the soul is better than the body, this does not mean that the soul is the true man, but simply that the inner man is *higher* than the outer man. The true man is the soul and the body taken together, where the soul is the higher part of man understood as a composite. On this basis, it is possible to distinguish three Augustinian concepts of what it means to be human against the background of his initial identification of himself as a man. First, to be a man is to be a composite of a soul and a body. Second, to be human is to be a soul, which Augustine calls the "inner man." Finally, to be human is to be a body, which Augustine calls the outer or the "exterior man." Augustine's strong identification of himself with his soul (*animus*) at this stage of his inquiry does not cancel the fact that he is a composite, but points to the distinctive function of the soul in his journey toward God (*C*, 10.6.9).

The power of the soul by which Augustine begins to ascend toward God is the power of sensation, but since God is not a body, he is not to be found in this way (*C*, 10.6.8). As a consequence, Augustine moves beyond sensation, and ascending step by step to his Creator, enters the "fields and spacious palaces of [his] memory" (*C*, 10.8.12). This way of formulating the nature of his journey is important because it points to the orderly progression of the stages involved in it. By moving toward God in stages that are arranged in a hierarchy, Augustine makes it clear that he is now attempting to give a systematic picture of the mystical experiences that have been recounted already in Book 7 (*C*, 7.10.16, 7.17.23).

The pivotal transition at this stage of the discussion allows Augustine to move beyond the dimension of the soul (*anima*) that he shares with the animals to the rational side of the soul (*animus*) that is distinctively human. It is the *animus* rather than the *anima* that will allow the language of God and the soul to develop as Augustine moves upward toward God (*C*, 10.8.12). When Augustine turns to the spacious halls of memory as a place where this language can unfold, he finds countless images of a great variety of things that have been brought there from objects perceived by the senses (*C*, 10.8.12). In addition to images generated by the activity of the senses, he also finds products of the activity of thinking that have been stored away in this context (*C*, 10.8.12).

Augustine's description of the way in which his memory functions is one of the classic passages in the *Confessions*, and it is of special significance because it undergirds the process that he undergoes in writing a book that requires him to remember so many things about his past experiences. Augustine says:

> When I am in that realm, I ask that whatsoever I want be brought forth. Certain things come forth immediately. Certain other things are looked for longer, and are rooted out as it were from some deeper receptacles. Certain others rush forth in mobs, and while some different thing is asked and searched for, they jump in between, as if to say, "Aren't we perhaps the ones?" By my heart's hand I brush them away from the face of my remembrance until what I want is unveiled and comes into sight from out of its hiding place. Others come out readily and in unbroken order, just as they are called for: those coming first give way to those that follow. On yielding, they are buried away again, to come forth when I want them. All this takes place when I recount anything from memory. (*C*, 10.8.12)

Having pointed to the ways in which acts of remembering occur, Augustine tells us that the images we remember are kept distinct and organized under categories. This is the finite, structural dimension of memory, which permits him not only to give a chronological account of events, but also to collect images from the storehouse of memory to reconstruct the story of his life.

Collecting the images that he needs for this purpose is made possible by the fact that they do not exist in his memory haphazardly, but according to kinds (*C*, 10.8.13).

In addition to the finite dimension of memory, Augustine suggests that it displays an infinite capacity by claiming that it has "hidden and inexpressible recesses within it" (*C*, 10.8.13). Memory as a context in which we can attempt to find God is finite and infinite at the same time; and in this respect, it reflects the structure of the soul as it journeys toward God. Once more, we find that the structure of memory is the condition that makes the journey toward God possible, and an image of that journey at the distinctively reflective level.

Augustine tells us that memory is "vast and unbounded" and that it is not possible to penetrate it "to its very bottom" (*C*, 10.8.15). In doing so, he reminds us again of the infinite dimension of memory that makes the journey toward God possible. On the other hand, he says that memory is a power of his soul (*animus*) and that it belongs to his nature. This suggests that he does not comprehend all that he is and that his soul (*animus*) is unable to possess itself. Yet if the infinite power of the soul (*animus*) is within Augustine rather than outside him, how is it possible that he is unable to comprehend it? The answer to this question is that Augustine is not only finite and infinite, but also present and absent at the same time.

"Great wonder" arises within Augustine, and "amazement seizes [him]" as he confronts the phenomenon of self-transcendence (*C*, 10.8.15). This phenomenon implies that self-consciousness is not self-contained, and that as a consequence, it points beyond itself toward a higher principle. The interplay between presence and absence and between finite and infinite dimensions of the soul calls our attention to the fact that we transcend ourselves by moving from one level of cognition to another. The journey toward God begins by turning away from objects toward the soul, but it can be brought to completion only when the soul's knowledge of itself leads to a self-transcendent knowledge of the ground of its existence.

Augustine continues to point toward the infinite side of himself by speaking about the immeasurable capacity of memory to store up knowledge. In doing so, he tells us that his memory contains all the things that he has learned from the liberal arts that he has not forgotten (*C*, 10.9.16). In this case, he does not carry the images of things in his memory, but the things themselves (*C*, 10.10.17). As a consequence, what Augustine knows about logic, literature, and rhetoric is in his memory in such a way that he has "not retained the image while leaving the reality outside" (*C*, 10.9.16).

Since the realities that he apprehends do not enter his soul through the senses, Augustine wonders whence and how they enter his memory; and in a much-disputed passage, he replies:

> How, I do not know, for when I first learned (*discere*) them I did not give credence to another's heart, but I recognized (*recognoscere*) them within my own, and I approved them as true, and I entrusted them to my heart. It was as if I stored them away there, whence I could bring them forth when I wanted them. Therefore they were there even before I learned (*discere*) them, but they were not in memory. Where, then, or why, when they were uttered, did I recognize (*agnoscere*) them, and say, "So it is; it is true," if not because they were already in memory, but pushed back as it were in more hidden caverns that, unless they were dug up by some reminder, I would perhaps have been unable to conceive them. (*C*, 10.10.17)

The obviously platonic dimension of this passage suggests that Augustine does not learn truths *from* the liberal arts, but that he learns them by recollection when he is placed within a context where the liberal arts are "taught" (*C*, 10.9.16). In addition, the Latin terms that are translated by the word "recognition" (*recognoscere, agnoscere*) point toward a doctrine of recollection: the meaning of the first word is "to know again," and the meaning of the second is "to know on the basis of previous acquaintance" (*C*, 10.10.17). Finally, Augustine seems to confirm this interpretation by moving back and forth between the dimensions of presence and absence as they pertain to the acquisition of knowledge. First, he claims that the truths of the liberal arts are present in his heart even before he learns them (*C*, 10.10.17). Then he says that these truths are not in his memory (*C*, 10.10.17). Yet when he asks where and why he recognizes them as true when they are uttered, he concludes that they are present in his memory after all (*C*, 10.10.17). This conclusion suggests the hypothesis that these truths have been pushed back into "hidden caverns" of the memory and that unless they are drawn forth by some reminder, he would have been unable to conceive of them (*C*, 10.10.17).

Despite the fact that these considerations point toward a doctrine of recollection, it is important to notice that Augustine does not know how the truths of the liberal arts enter his memory (*C*, 10.10.17). As a consequence, he turns away from telling a recollection myth as a way of undergirding the claim that learning is recollection of what we have "known" before.[8] In using words for "recognition" within the context of learning, Augustine also points beyond the platonic doctrine of recollection to the distinctively Augustinian doctrine of illumination, where a direct recognition of the truth can be identified with immediate insight that the light of Truth makes possible.[9]

Within the context of illumination, Augustine gives an account of how we learn the truths of the liberal arts apart from images. He tells us that by acts of thinking, we collect (*colligere*) things that memory contains here and there without any order and that we observe them and place them near at hand so they may occur easily to the mind (*animus*) that is familiar with them already (*C*, 10.11.18). However, the process of coming to know these things must occur repeatedly; for if I cease to recall them for only a short period of time, they are forgotten and must be called forth again as if they were new. As Augustine formulates the point:

> They must be brought together (*cogenda*) so they may be known. That is, they must be collected together (*colligenda*) as it were out of a sort of scattered state. (*C*, 10.11.18)

In giving an account of the process of learning, Augustine fails to mention a state of preexistence in which our knowledge is complete, but confines himself to the scattered condition of what we are trying to learn and to the process of collecting what is scattered that makes learning possible (*C*, 10.11.18). The scattered dimension of our epistemic condition is a theoretical reflection of the fall by which we are fragmented, and the process of collection that brings these scattered pieces together reflects the process of conversion in which the dispersed elements of our lives are bound together. Augustine says that the epistemic contents that we are attempting to learn are within our memories *before* we come to know them but that they are there in a scattered and neglected state. This use of "before" points to the scattered and neglected status of the contents of cognition in our memories rather than to a state of preexistence in which we have perfect knowledge of the contents in question.

At this juncture, Augustine moves beyond the problem of memory to the problem of forgetfulness, suggesting that when we say the word "forgetfulness" and understand what it signifies, we recognize the reality to which it points by remembering it. Indeed, if we had forgotten it completely, we would not be able to comprehend what the word in question means (*C*, 10.11.18). In addition, when we remember memory, memory is "present to itself through itself" (*C*, 10.11.18); and when we remember forgetfulness, "both memory and forgetfulness are present: memory by which I remember and forgetfulness which I remember" (*C*, 10.16.24).

Having claimed that when we remember forgetfulness, memory and forgetfulness are present together, Augustine holds memory and forgetfulness apart by suggesting that memory is the *act* by which we remember and that forgetfulness is the *content* toward which this act is directed. However, this distinction not only implies that memory is present and absent because it is self-transcendent, but also that presence and absence can be driven into the content of memory when what we remember is forgetfulness. This becomes especially clear when our memory of forgetfulness is brought into relation with our memory and forgetfulness of God. When we remember forgetfulness, a fissure opens up within the context of memory that makes our capacity to return to God problematic. Yet as we shall soon discover, Augustine does not believe that forgetfulness in general and forgetfulness of God are ever absolute. As a consequence, he suggests that forgetfulness of both kinds is present and absent in the structure of forgetfulness itself.

In his discussion of the happy life, Augustine claims that all of us remember God, at least in the minimal sense that we remember that we have forgotten him (*C*, 10.23.33). In this way, he uses the phenomenon of forgetfulness to advance his discussion of the nature of memory as a pathway to God. On the other hand, he believes that our forgetfulness of God and our consequent separation from him are so serious that more than a memory of God is required to overcome the chasm that separates us from him. As his analysis of the nature of memory moves in this direction, Augustine indicates how its structure not only permits us to transcend ourselves in our journey toward God, but also how the fissure of forgetfulness can become a "window" through which God manifests himself to the one who has forgotten him.

The most important point to notice about the relation between memory and forgetfulness is that the fissure of forgetfulness at the heart of memory makes it possible for God to manifest himself, where this self-manifestation is the ground for the philosophical conversion in which Augustine participates in Book 7 (*C*, 7.17.23). The relation between memory and forgetfulness is the condition that makes it possible for Augustine to undertake a journey toward God, and the structure of memory that includes forgetfulness is a reflective image of the relation between God and the soul that the mystical experiences of Book 7 presuppose (*C*, 7.17.23).

Before we pursue these issues in more detail, several other problems about the relation between memory and forgetfulness need to be considered. The first of these issues surfaces when Augustine asks the rhetorical question, "What is forgetfulness, unless it be privation of memory?" (*C*, 10.16.24). This question suggests that Augustine should have analyzed forgetfulness in the same way that he analyzes darkness and silence, where all three concepts are privations. Yet when we notice the rhetorical character of Augustine's question about forgetfulness, we should be prepared for a negative answer.

In discussing the status of forgetfulness, Augustine moves beyond the negative analysis of forgetfulness by suggesting that it has a positive role to play
in his discussion of the nature of memory.

When we move in this direction, we encounter a paradox: forgetfulness
is present so that we are not forgetful of it; but when it is present, we forget
(*C*, 10.16.24, 10.16.25). However, Augustine is no more confused in claiming that the forgetfulness we remember causes us to forget than he is in suggesting that when memory is present to itself, it is both present and absent
at the same time. In both cases, he is speaking about the *nature of memory*
within which the distinctions among memory, forgetfulness, and particular
acts of remembering and forgetting arise. Memory is self-transcendent when
it is present to itself in an act of remembering; and in a similar way, it negates
itself when it becomes aware of its forgetfulness (*C*, 10.16.25). In this second case, forgetfulness transforms acts of remembering into acts of forgetting; and it transforms memory into forgetfulness as a pervasive condition.
This moves Augustine to say:

> What man will search this out? Who can comprehend how it is? Lord, I
> truly labor at this task, and I labor on myself. I have become for myself a
> soil hard to work and demanding much sweat. (*C*, 10.16.24–25)

The anguish that these questions express and the confession to which they
lead remind us of Adam's exile from the Garden of Eden (Gen 3:17-19) and
it also reminds us of the existential wasteland into which Augustine wanders
as a result of stealing forbidden fruit from his neighbors' vineyard
(*C*, 2.10.18). When God casts Adam out of the Garden, he condemns him
to till the land and to labor with the sweat of his brow (Gen 3:23-24). After
identifying himself with Adam at the end of the pear-stealing episode, and
experiencing the existential anguish that sin always produces (*C*, 2.10.18),
Augustine extends the range of his anguish by identifying himself with the
land on which Adam labors, and by identifying the sweat of his brow with
philosophical reflection.

If we take this comparison between Augustine and Adam seriously, several aspects of our earlier discussion of the problem of forgetfulness begin to
fall into place. First, in suggesting that forgetfulness is more than a privation,
Augustine is pointing to the fact that our forgetfulness of God is a reflection
of the fall in which we have participated experientially. Second, forgetfulness
of this kind is the condition that makes the fall possible, where the analysis
of forgetfulness as a philosophical problem indicates that we continue to participate in it, even when we move to the reflective level. Finally, forgetfulness
is like the fall because it involves a *negative act of turning away from God*. The

ultimate reason that Augustine cannot analyze forgetfulness in the same way that he analyzes darkness and silence is that forgetfulness involves a *volitional* component that orients him away from the ground of our existence.

In this context, Augustine points once more to a comparison between the pear-stealing episode in which he falls away from God and the phenomenon of forgetfulness in which the fall is recapitulated in reflective terms. In both cases, he suggests that a dimension of the phenomena in question is incomprehensible and that it cannot be given a place within a rational account of the human situation. However, he also acknowledges the truth about our fallen condition and about the forgetfulness of God that makes it possible, even though he is unable to understand it. In doing so, he suggests that truth is prior to meaning, even though he is unable to comprehend the truth to which he is committed in both cases. Yet as we shall soon discover, Augustine will move from faith to understanding and from truth to meaning when forgetfulness becomes a window through which he passes beyond his memory to God.

Forgetfulness is a crucial element in Augustine's account of the nature of memory, and one of its most important roles is to suggest that we stand in contrast with what we need to remember because of the structure of memory. The mind is not a foundational principle that contains its own ground, and the forgetfulness that we often experience reflects this fact. In recognizing that the mind not only transcends itself, but also forgets, Augustine explodes the concept of the mind as a self-contained context. What first presents itself as a container that encircles its contents and that encircles itself opens out toward a content that lies beyond itself. In the process, forgetfulness points beyond memory to what transcends our powers of recollection.

At this stage of his argument, Augustine claims that he will pass beyond the power of his memory to reach God. The one he seeks is the Light he sees in the mystical experience of Book 7 (*C*, 7.17.23) and the Voice he hears in Book 8 (*C*, 8.12.29); in seeking them again, Augustine is attempting to trace out the pathway of the soul to God within the context of the soul itself. As he formulates the point:

> Behold, going up through my mind to you, who dwells above me, I will pass beyond even this power of mine which is called memory, desiring to reach you where you may be reached, and to cling to you there where you can be clung to. (*C*, 10.17.26)

Augustine says this because what is distinctive about us is the fact that we stand in a cognitive and volitional relation to God, where this relation will finally allow us to come to rest in God.

The problem that arises here is that Augustine must transcend memory to find God, but he cannot recognize what he finds without remembering God (*C*, 10.17.26). Memory must become self-transcendent if Augustine is to find what he seeks, but there are two sides of self-transcendence that it is important to distinguish. On the one hand, memory transcends itself as it moves toward the dimension of God that stands over against it. On the other hand, it must remember the one it seeks if it is to recognize God when it encounters him.

The two sides of the nature of God correspond to the two sides of self-transcendence that give us access to God. Our memory of God that has not been tarnished by the fall gives us access to his immanent side, while illumination gives us access to the transcendent side. It follows from these considerations that Augustine both remembers and does not remember God. He remembers God because he stands in a created relationship with him that is not obliterated by the fall, but he does not remember him because he has fallen away from God into an abyss. Our primary task in the following paragraphs will be to understand this complex ontological, epistemic, and volitional situation.

Augustine tells us that when we seek God, we seek the happy life that we have not forgotten completely. He never wavers from the conviction that this kind of life is the goal of philosophy (*C*, 10.20.29), and he remains oriented toward it from the time he reads the book of Cicero that exhorts him to embrace the love of wisdom (*C*, 3.4.7). However, he wonders how to seek the happy life; and he responds to his own question:

> Here I ought to tell how I seek it, whether through remembrance, as if I had forgotten it but still held to the fact that I had forgotten it, or out of desire to a thing unknown, whether one I never knew or one I had forgotten so completely that I did not remember that I had forgotten it. (*C*, 10.20.29)

Two possibilities that Augustine considers presuppose a radical discontinuity between himself and the happy life, while the other presupposes that an initial continuity between himself and what he seeks has not been obliterated by the fall. In the first two cases, we are cut off from the happy life so completely that it would be impossible for us to remember it. In the third case, we remember it sufficiently to reach for it by remembering the fact that we have forgotten it (*C*, 10.20.29).

Augustine is perplexed about whether our knowledge of happiness is in our memories:

> If it is there, then all of us have already been happy at some period, either
> each of us individually, or all of us together in that man who first sinned,
> in whom we all died, and from whom we are all born in misery. Of this
> last I do not now inquire, but I inquire whether the happy life is in the
> memory. (*C*, 10.20.29)

Augustine begins to bring this stage of his reflections to completion by
claiming that we could not love the happy life unless we know it. Then he
says that since we desire to possess it, we know it. Finally, he tells us that we
could not know the happy life unless it were in our memories (*C*, 10.20.29).

Augustine begins to elaborate what he means by happiness by comparing our memory of the happy life with our recollection of joy (*C*, 10.21.30).
The two are comparable because we can remember joy when we are sad, just
as we remember the happy life when we are unhappy. Both joy and happiness are not physical objects, but affections of the mind; and both of these
affections are positive or negative, depending on whether the objects toward
which they are oriented are good or evil. For example, when Augustine
remembers past joys that are evil, he remembers them with sadness; and
when he remembers past joys that are good, he remembers them with longing. In addition, when the good things that he desires are no longer present,
he remembers them with sadness (*C*, 10.14.21). In this case, his recollection
of the happy life points to a separation between himself and the object of his
deepest desire.

The fact that he can remember the happy life leads Augustine to ask,
"Where, then, and when did I have experience of my happy life, so that I
remember it, and love it, and long for it?" (*C*, 10.21.31). In order to place
this question within the broadest possible context, he says:

> It is not merely myself along with a few others, but all of us without
> exception desire to be happy. Unless we knew this with sure knowledge,
> we would not want it with so sure a will. (*C*, 10.21.31)

Once more Augustine suggests that we know what "happiness" means and
that we desire to be happy because all of us have experienced it. He also tells
us that this "earlier" experience takes place, either individually or in Adam
prior to the fall, where in this second case, we are present as participants
(*C*, 10.20.29).

Though Augustine believes that all of us remember the happy life, he
does not believe that all of us are happy. The recollection of the happy life is
the epistemic framework within which we can ask about the relation
between God and the soul; and without this framework, we would be unable

to undertake the journey toward the one whom we have forgotten. Yet Augustine insists that the joy we seek is not granted to the wicked, but only to those who worship God for his own sake and for whom God himself is joy (*C*, 10.22.32).Thus he tells us:

> This is the happy life, to rejoice over you, to you, and because of you: this it is, and there is no other. (*C*, 10.22.32)

Yet Augustine also calls our attention to a transcendent dimension of joy that manifests the grace of God. Though Augustine's recollection of joy generates the epistemic framework within which his thought develops, he experiences the transcendent side of joy only when *God addresses him directly* (*C*, 10.22.32–10.23.34). God has granted him joy of this kind in Milan and Ostia (*C*, 7.17.23, 9.10.24), and he describes his relation to joy in a fashion that reflects these earlier experiences.

By moving in this direction, Augustine does not forget about the epistemic framework within which he works. The immanent side of joy and happiness are accessible within this context, and he is able to climb toward it by using a Neoplatonic ladder (*C*, 9.10.24). However, the transcendent dimension of these same experiences requires a divine interjection (*C*, 8.12.28). As a consequence, Augustine distinguishes between true and false joy, not only by distinguishing joy from a certain image of it, but also by contrasting followers of God with those who turn away from him. The Neoplatonic orientation toward the happy life is a matter of the intellect (*C*, 10.23.33), while the Christian response to it depends on an orientation of the will (*C*, 10.23.34). Augustine participates in the Christian dimension of this dichotomy in the garden in Milan (*C*, 7.17.23), and he expresses it reflectively by distinguishing between those who embrace the happy life from those who merely seek an image of it (*C*, 10.23.34).

At this juncture, Augustine must face the problem of binding the immanent and the transcendent dimensions of his analysis together. In beginning to do so, he asks:

> Is it uncertain, then, that all men desire to be happy, seeing that they do not truly desire the happy life, who do not desire to have joy in you, which is the only happy life? Or do all men indeed desire this? But, since "the flesh lusts against the spirit, and the spirit against the flesh," so that they do not do what they wish, do they fall down to what they are able to take, and are satisfied with this? (*C*, 10.23.33)

Augustine responds to these questions by taking four steps that lead beyond his memory toward the transcendent side of God. The first broadens his definition of happiness and places this richer conception of it within the context of both the will and the intellect. The second deals with the problem of why he turns away from God in spite of his vague awareness of God's existence. The third focuses on how he comes to know the one from whom he has turned away. And the fourth considers the question of how God makes this knowledge possible by speaking to Augustine directly.

Augustine broadens his definition of happiness by connecting joy with Truth (*C*, 10.22.33). He asks whether we would rather rejoice in Truth than falsehood, and he replies that we would no more hesitate to say this than say that we desire to be happy (*C*, 10.23.33). On this basis, he defines the happy life as "joy in the truth." Thus he exclaims: "This happy life all men desire; this life which alone is happy all men desire; all men desire joy in the truth" (*C*, 10.23.33).

Yet why do we turn away from God who can be identified with the Truth that we can remember? Augustine says:

> It is because [we] are more strongly taken up with other things, which have more power to make [us] wretched, than has that which [we] remember so faintly to make [us] happy. Yet a little while there is light among men. Let [us] walk, let [us] walk, lest the darkness overtake [us].
> (*C*, 10.23.33)

In this passage, Augustine brings the cognitive and the volitional dimensions of his argument together by suggesting that our faint recollection of the happy life is not sufficient to overcome our infinite desire for finite things.

After the fall, this infinite desire displaces our longing for God; and it leads to a forgetfulness of God that manifests itself on two levels. From an epistemic point of view, the fallen soul retains only a faint memory of God (*C*, 10.23.33); from a volitional perspective, it turns away from God to embrace a world of its own (*C*, 10.23.33). In the first case, we have forgotten God intellectually; in the second, we have forgotten him volitionally. Though both kinds of forgetfulness presuppose that we remember God in the sense that we remember that we have forgotten him, Augustine insists that this memory is faint, on the one hand, and that it is misdirected on the other.

The first kind of forgetfulness is *privative*, which points to the truth of the claim that Augustine should have given an account of the nature of for-

getfulness as a privation of memory. However, the second kind of forgetfulness is *performative*, which suggests that the forgetfulness of God involves a
volitional orientation away from him, first toward finite things, and then
toward the *nihil* out of which these things are created (*C*, 10.23.34). Thus,
forgetfulness is not only a privation of memory, but also a chasm into which
we can fall toward nothingness. Yet when conversion occurs at both the
intellectual and the volitional levels, it becomes a window through which we
can return to God. In order to point to this window, Augustine reminds
those who have turned away from God that there will be light in the world
for a little while, and that they need to walk in it so darkness will not over-
take them (*C*, 10.23.34).

In the third stage of his argument, Augustine turns to the question of
how we come to know God experientially. In one of the classic passages of
the *Confessions*, he exclaims:

> Behold, how far within my memory have I traveled in search of you,
> Lord, and beyond it I have not found you! Nor have I found anything
> concerning you except what I have kept in memory since I first learned
> of you. For since I learned of you, I have not forgotten you. Wheresoever
> I found truth, there I found my God, truth itself, and since I first learned
> the truth I have not forgotten it. Therefore, ever since I learned about
> you, you abide in my memory, and I find you there when I recall you to
> mind and take delight in you. (*C*, 10.24.35)

First, Augustine says that what he knows about God has been kept in his
memory since he first learned of him. Second, he claims that since he learned
of God, he has not forgotten him. Third, he tells us that wherever he finds
Truth, he finds God, and that since he first learned the Truth he has not forgotten it. Finally, he says that ever since he learned about God, God abides
in his memory and that he finds him there when he calls him to mind.

There is a sense in which Augustine knows about God simply because
he is a human being in whom the image of God has not been effaced
(*C*, 10.24.35), and there is another sense in which he knows about God
since he first learns about him in childhood (*C*, 1.11.17). However,
Augustine's claims about his knowledge of God point beyond the doctrine
of recollection and beyond the early stages of his religious education to the
episodic moments in which he learns about God in the mystical experiences
that he recounts in Book 7 (*C*, 7.17.23). In these experiences, Augustine
does not learn about God by gathering and collecting what has been scattered and neglected, or by reflecting on what his mother and others within
the Christian community have taught him, but through his own experience.

In the final analysis, learning about God requires divine illumination, where illumination outstrips recollection, performs an important soteriological function, and allows God to abide within the soul to which he manifests himself (*C*, 10.25.36).

Memory gives Augustine access to the immanent side of God, and illumination gives him access to God's transcendent side. In the first case, he remembers a non-fallen relation to God that allows him to have a faint recollection of God; in the second, he encounters God as the standard of Truth that makes his intellectual conversion possible. There is also a voluntaristic dimension at this stage of the argument that reflects Augustine's Christian conversion. In the garden in Milan, Augustine finds God by responding to a voice that addresses him from beyond a garden wall (*C*, 8.12.29). Now speaking and hearing come to the center of our attention once more when Augustine says:

> Where then did I find you, so that I might learn to know you? You were not in my memory before I learned to know you. Where then have I found you, if not in yourself and above me? There is no place, both backward do we go and forward, and there is no place. Everywhere, O Truth, you give hearing to all who consult you, and at one and the same time you make answer to them all, even as they ask about varied things. You answer clearly, but all men do not hear you clearly. All men ask counsel about what they wish, but they do not all hear what they wish. Your best servant is he who looks not so much to hear what he wants to hear, but rather to want what he hears from you. (*C*, 10.26.37)

The voice of God rather than Neoplatonic recollection is the focus of Augustine's reflections at this juncture. Though he remembers the immanent side of God as a condition that makes it possible for him to look for the one he has forgotten, forgetfulness becomes a window through which the transcendent side of God manifests itself, not only as Truth, but also as the omnipresent voice that speaks to Augustine's heart. Yet the author of the *Confessions* is also careful to say that God transcends the distinction between the immanent and the transcendent sides of his nature and that there is no place within which he can be confined (*C*, 10.26.37). As a consequence, language about God must be stretched to the breaking point if we are to speak about him adequately.

Having moved from the nature of memory to a faint recollection of the happy life, from the memory of the happy life to a recollection of God's immanent side, and from a memory of the immanent side of God to an encounter with the God beyond the mind, Augustine admits that he has loved God belatedly (*C*, 10.27.38). Though God is "within," Augustine is outside himself; and as a consequence, he looks for God among the things that God has created. Augustine's preoccupation with finite things has caused him to "rush headlong" toward them, where he forgets God by falling away from him (*C*, 10.27.38). Augustine is not a character in a platonic recollection myth who forgets what he once knows, but a protagonist in a Christian drama that chooses to turn away from the ground of his existence. Yet there is a remedy for Augustine's fragmented condition, and he reminds us of it by remembering his intellectual conversion in Milan and his Christian conversion in the garden soon afterwards. In one of the most beautiful passages in the text, he writes about the immanent side of God in the following way:

> You have called to me, and have cried out, and have shattered my deafness. You have blazed forth with light, and have shone on me, and you have put my blindness to flight! You have sent forth fragrance, and I have drawn in my breath, and I pant after you. I have tasted you, and I hunger and thirst after you. You have touched me, and I burn for your peace. (*C*, 10.27.38)

Chapter 6

Hegel and the Problem of Difference

This chapter returns to some of the themes that I have considered already, including the problems of space and time, the question of the two directions in which religion and philosophy develop, the problem of difference as a central theme, and the topic of dialectic and analogy as alternative ways of bringing unity to the human situation. Before we turn to these topics it is important to notice that in the hands of his most persistent critics, philosophy in the aftermath of Hegel has focused on three pervasive themes: the problem of existence and individuality,[1] the problem of theory and practice,[2] and the problem of identity and difference.[3] From a systematic point of view, this final problem is the most important, for it epitomizes the fact that Hegel's religious and philosophical critics have always attempted to stand outside his philosophical system. The philosophies of existence, individuality, praxis, and difference that have been Hegel's most visible philosophical legacy are rooted in the primacy of difference and in the conviction that philosophy after Hegel is possible only if we can transcend the omnivorousness of his system from an external point of view.

Despite the force of these familiar responses to Hegel, there are two obvious difficulties with any external attack on the Hegelian enterprise. First, Hegel makes the phenomenon of negation the central element of his system so that any attempt to stand outside it becomes an indirect way of being imprisoned within it. As he expresses the point in both *Phenomenology of Spirit* and the *Science of Logic*, the kind of negation, opposition, and difference that appears to be external to the system is included in it as the moving principle that permits his thought to become a living unity (*PS*, 48–57; *SL*, 112, 118–25, 135–53, 158, 384). The critic who adopts an external point of view in relation to Hegel is placed from the outset at the center of his dynamically developing philosophical system. Second, Hegel claims that even if non-dialectical difference were possible, it would be unintelligible. He demands repeatedly that we say what we mean, but if we intend to speak on behalf of radical externality, we are unable to do so without embracing the dynamic structure that is under external attack (*PS*, 60, 62, 64, 66). Hegel insists that difference is always dialectical and that by itself, bare difference is just as unintelligible as simple identity.[4]

In order to avoid these difficulties, my own criticism of Hegel will be internal and will examine the problem of difference as a way of exploding his dialectical project from within. I will also focus my attention primarily on *Phenomenology of Spirit*, for it is the most perspicuous place where the presence of non-dialectical difference surfaces in Hegel's thought. The first example of the kind of difference I have in mind is to be found in sense-certainty, where Hegel begins with what is given, moves to an attempt to articulate it in terms of an abstract universal, and then suggests that the truth of sense-certainty is the process in which the particular articulated in this way both vanishes and is preserved as a constituent element of a concrete plurality (*PS*, 60). In describing the temporal dimension of experience, Hegel first suggests that it is present now, and that we might attempt to capture its conceptual content by claiming that the "now" is night. Yet if we make this claim, the temporal process negates it as it moves from night to day, and the process becomes the "now" as a concrete universal that is neither night nor day but both (*PS*, 60). The "now" preserves itself by negating abstract universality, and its self-identity is constituted by the fact that it remains unaffected by its own negativity. Thus, the momentary "now" with which we begin, and the abstract "now" with which we might attempt to bring time to a standstill, become the "now" as a self-identical process generated by its own self-negation (*PS*, 60).

We find an even more forceful formulation of this point in Hegel's brief characterization of the act of pointing to the temporal aspect of experience. In his formulation of this issue he says:

> I point out the "Now," and it is asserted to be the truth. I point it out, however, as something that has been, or as something that has been superseded; I set aside the first truth. I now assert as the second truth that it has been, that it is superseded. Yet what has been, is not; I set aside the second truth, its having been, its supersession, and thereby negate the negation of the "now" and thus return to the first assertion, that the

"Now" is. The "Now," and pointing out the "Now," are thus so constituted that neither the one nor the other is something immediate and simple, but a moment which contains various moments (*PS, 63–64*).

The movement in question is temporality understood as Absolute Process,
and the moments to which Hegel refers are a unified plurality of "nows,"
bound together by negating the negation of abstract universality.

In his phenomenological description of sense-certainty, Hegel provides us
with a profound account of the dialectical structure of time, where in Kantian
terms we find a dynamic reconstruction of the synopsis of sense (*CPR, 74*)
and of the temporal dimension of sensible intuition (*CPR, 77–78*). His characterization of the "now" is an attempt to articulate the nature of this synopsis, and his explication of the act of pointing is a dialectical reformulation
of the nature of pure intuition (*PS, 63; CPR, 77–79*). However, in this same
section Hegel implies that space is equally dynamic and dialectical, and it is
here that he begins to ignore a non-dialectical dimension of that difference
he should not have overlooked. Hegel claims that having referred to a particular spatial region, we find that when we turn around, another replaces it.
As a result, he says that the truth of space is universal, not simply because a
description of a particular spatial region must be universal, but because space
remains constant when a particular "here" vanishes as it is replaced by
another (*PS, 60–61*). Yet Hegel fails to acknowledge the fact that his own act
of turning around mediates this transition and that this act is non-dialectical. We can understand in a dialectical way the sequence of statements that
results when we express the determinate content of particular spatial regions
as we turn from place to place. Yet this is due to the fact that they form a
temporal series and does not imply that space is dialectical. In fact, we presuppose space as the non-dialectical context in which we turn around before
we can formulate these statements; and from a philosophical point of view,
it becomes the non-dialectical dimension of sensibility and pure intuition
(*PS, 63; CPR, 80–82*).

The difference between space and time as forms of intuition is that space
is non-dialectical while time is not. The temporal dimension of the phenomenological process unfolds of itself; and as Hegel reminds us, the
philosopher should simply observe this self-developing process without
interfering with it (*PS, 53–55*). However, the spatial dimension of this process, both religiously and philosophically, does not take care of itself in the
same way as temporality; for it unfolds dialectically only after the subject
makes a non-dialectical transition. And it does so even then only when this
same subject formulates a sequence of utterances that Hegel can take up into

a dialectical context. The most important conclusion to be drawn from this fact is that when we take the spatial and the temporal dimensions of experience together, we must not sublate the spatial element, since it is the non-dialectical presupposition that makes a series of "spatial" utterances possible. To move from one "here" to another is quite different from moving from one temporal moment to another in terms of a determinate negation; and we should acknowledge this structural difference by admitting that there is a radical externality in the relation between one "here" and another that we cannot capture in dialectical terms. We also cannot reduce difference to negation, and space displays a non-dialectical dimension of difference that is not reducible to the negative moment of a temporal process.

This non-dialectical element in Hegel's system is also reflected in his account of the role of the subject of consciousness in sense-certainty, though he refuses to acknowledge its presence in this admittedly more complex context. The transition to the subject first occurs in order to allow us to remain in contact with the particularity of the object with which we begin. We can prevent the transmutation of the "now" and the "here" into universals only if we hold them fast, where we see and hear that "now" is day rather than night and that "here" is a tree rather than a house. Yet as Hegel reminds us, another "I" can make a different assertion, and when it does, the dialectical development that we have traced reemerges. One bare assertion cancels the other, and all that survives is the "I" under which any individual can be subsumed (*PS*, 61–62). In Kantian terms, we can understand this "I" as the transcendental ego (*CPR*, 60, 61, 66) that we transmute into a dynamic center of activity, just as we have transformed sensibility and pure intuition in the earlier account.

In developing his account from an exclusively dialectical perspective, Hegel has overlooked once more the non-dialectical element at the heart of his position. He fails to acknowledge the fact that when a different "I" makes a different assertion than the first, there are two senses of difference involved, the first of which is the non-dialectical ground of the second. The two "I"s do not differ from one another in the same way that the contents of their utterances do; for both may speak independently, even though we may subject what they say to subsequent dialectical transformations. Indeed, this independence is necessary if there is to be another "I" who makes a different assertion that may take its place within a dialectical context. The transcendental ego proves to have two sides that parallel the earlier contrast between the two forms of pure intuition, one of which is dialectical, while the other is the non-dialectical ground of the first.

It remains to be seen whether we can state what we mean to do in drawing this distinction; for unless we can do this, we can only point out nondialectical difference rather than articulate it. We would then remain speechless; articulation would once again prove to be exclusively dialectical; and the empirical differences between the "now" and the "here" and between two centers of consciousness would have no philosophical significance. As a consequence, it is therefore of the utmost importance that we develop a mode of discourse in both religion and philosophy that enables us to express both the spatial and the temporal aspects of experience and both the dialectical and the non-dialectical dimensions of the experiencing subject.

Perhaps we can take our clue from Hegel's own procedure in this respect. In discussing the contrast between meaning and saying, Hegel confronts the problem of framing an adequate philosophical language by introducing an ambiguous sense of universality (*PS*, 60, 66). He claims that we can say what we mean straightforwardly by using abstract universals, and he demands articulation of this kind by the non-philosophical consciousness (*PS*, 60, 66). Yet he also acknowledges the fact that the concept of a concrete universal is difficult to articulate and that it is by no means clear that we can say what we mean about it without stretching philosophical language to the limit. As he formulates the point himself:

> The proposition in the form of a judgment is not suited to express speculative truths. [Moreover,] it is the form of simple judgment, when it is used to express speculative results, which is very often responsible for the paradoxical and bizarre light in which much of recent philosophy appears to those who are not familiar with speculative thought. (*SL*, 90–91)

Hegel responds to this problem by expanding the unit of meaning to include both the product and the process of reflection, generating a mode of discourse that is adequate to express speculative insights (*PS*, 39–42). Yet if he is able to remedy the defects of propositional language by developing a dialectical framework, perhaps we should stretch language a bit further to say what we mean by the concept of non-dialectical difference. In this way, we could satisfy Hegel's demands for articulation at the distinctively philosophical level at least as well as he satisfies them himself.

Before we turn to this problem, we can take the next step in framing an intelligible account of difference that is not exclusively dialectical by turning to the perception section of the *Phenomenology*, where once more the subject confronts an object that stands in contrast with it. Since the object we encounter in this context is in space and time, and since we have expressed the synopsis of sense and pure intuition dialectically, both the universal and the particular dimensions of the earlier discussion are present in the object at the outset (*PS*, 66–67). Indeed, Hegel suggests that if we have understood the dialectical consequences of the examination of sense-certainty, we can stand in between the subject and the object as abstractable aspects of a concrete process in which they both participate, where immediacy and abstract universality interplay with one another as a way of "taking things truly" (*PS*, 66). The ordinary consciousness fails to occupy this standpoint because it always makes the mistake of beginning with the primacy of the object (*PS*, 67), and we are willing to embrace it only if we understand this middle ground between the subject and the object as a process that overrides the non-dialectical dimension of sensibility, pure intuition, and the transcendental ego. From the religious and the philosophical perspective that I have been developing, this dimension should express itself as a non-dialectical difference between the subject and the object, where particularity and abstract universality fall on both sides of the contrast in question, and where to stand in between them is to occupy the standpoint of dialectical and non-dialectical difference simultaneously.

Yet what is the fate of non-dialectical difference in Hegel's discussion of the dialectic of perception? With respect to ordinary consciousness, he argues that we cannot sustain it and that under the pressure of dialectical reflection both the subject and the object of perception prove to be identical in content. More accurately, he claims that the same dialectical transitions occur on both sides of the subject-object distinction, and that as a result, each term is an expression of the same process (*PS*, 68–70). If we begin with the object of perception, it first presents itself as a unity; and the diversity of its properties falls within the subject as the conceptual elements that serve to make it accessible (*PS*, 68–70). Yet we might also regard the object as a plurality of properties and construe the subject as the seat of unity (*PS*, 70–74). In this case, unification is a function of the transcendental unity of apperception, where we can understand objective properties as the unified content of synthetic activity (*PS*, 69–70; *CPR*, 137).

When we take these two ways of proceeding together, Hegel claims that the subject and the object are identical, since we can understand them both in terms of unity and diversity (*PS*, 70–74). Yet if this proves to be the case, we cancel the non-dialectical difference between the subjects I question; and we return to the Absolute Process, not simply as a dynamic version of the synopsis of sense or of pure intuition, but also as a dialectical reformulation of the nature of pure synthetic activity. Indeed, we not only overcome non-dialectical difference once again, but the truth of the *Phenomenology* reveals itself as an experiential, a religious, and a philosophical version of the development of the Absolute toward its consummation (*PS*, 70–74). Like Cronus who devours his children,[5] the Absolute Process is at work within this context, repeatedly devouring non-dialectical difference so it can be at peace with itself as it unfolds its absolute content (*PS*, 70–74).

There is one problem that blocks the path of the dialectical development of consciousness; and this problem surfaces in the fact that before he identifies them with one another, Hegel ignores the order in which the dialectical transitions occur in the subject and the object. The order differs in each case non-dialectically, and it is this non-dialectical difference that holds the subject and the object apart for the reflective consciousness. In the dialectic of perception, the object moves from unity to diversity before it collapses into the unity of the Absolute Process (*PS*, 70–71), while the subject moves from its original diversity into a unity of properties before it collapses into the unity of this same process (*PS*, 71–74). This means that the subject and the object traverse different paths in their dialectical development, one beginning with diversity and moving toward unity and the other beginning with unity and moving toward difference. However much these two poles might be identical in conceptual content, they are not identical in directional orientation, and it is this vector difference that holds them apart as really distinct elements of the perceptual process.

At one point, Hegel seems to acknowledge this distinction; for having argued that the act of perceiving and the object of perception are the same, he says:

> In essence the object is the same as the movement: the movement is the unfolding and differentiation of the two moments, and the object is the apprehended togetherness of the moments. (*PS*, 67)

The concept of essence designates the dialectical development of the subject and the object respectively; and since a developmental dimension is present in each case, he assumes that the two poles of the subject-object relation are the same. Yet unless Hegel can show that vector directionality has nothing to do with the essence of a thing, he will not be able to demonstrate that the subject and the object dissolve into one another in the process of cognition. In fact, just the opposite is the case, since the vector difference that the development of the subject and the object displays hold them apart in a mirror-image relation that Hegel can never cancel by dialectical considerations alone. In characterizing the essence of both the subject and object, it is not sufficient to introduce a developmental dimension that allows Hegel to identify the terms in question. Since the subject and the object move in different directions, we must acknowledge their non-dialectical dimension; and when we do this, the essence of the perceptual consciousness reveals itself as an analogical separation between two terms that develop in different directions (*PS*, 67–71).

The analytic development of the object from unity to diversity and the synthetic development of the subject from diversity to unity are similarities that bind the knower and the known together, but they are also differences that allow these terms to remain separate as really distinct elements in the unfolding process of cognition. We can describe this moment of separation most adequately as a representational relation between the subject and the object in analogies that preserve both the differences and the identities of its terms. Formulated in a different way, analogy is the ontological foundation for the intelligibility of non-dialectical difference; and it makes it possible for us to say what we mean by this element of our earlier discussion.

There is a dialectical dimension present in perception, and it reveals itself in the fact that both the subject and the object undergo transitions involving identity, difference, and unity. However, these two dialectical poles stand apart because of a non-dialectical difference of directionality, and we can mediate this difference only by an imagistic relation of similarity. As Hegel suggests, we can articulate this mediation by claiming that the subject and the object are the same, but we must not understand the sameness in question in dialectical terms alone. Instead, we must formulate a judgment of analogy that preserves the identity and the difference of its terms non-dialectically. To say that the subject and the object are the same does not mean that these poles of consciousness develop dialectically, requiring us to expand the propositional unit of meaning to include both structural and developmental elements. Rather, we can express the sameness in question in a judgment that asserts that the object develops dialectically from unity to diversity, while the dialectical development of the subject moves from diversity to unity. This judgment of analogy is the foundation for an internal critique of Hegel, and it is the crucial element in preserving the intelligibility of both the dialectical and the non-dialectical dimensions of the experience of consciousness.

It is important to emphasize the fact that both dialectical and non-dialectical elements are present in the subject and the object of consciousness and that non-dialectical intelligibility is not to be confined to the representational relation between them. In my earlier discussion of the differences between space and time and between two centers of consciousness, I suggested that space involves non-dialectical difference, while time does not, and that we should draw a distinction between the dialectical difference present in a sequence of utterances and the non-dialectical difference that makes it possible. Since the subject and the object are both in space and time, and since two different "I's" can participate in a unified dialectical sequence, we can conclude that both kinds of difference are present in the subject and the object respectively. Yet what can we say about the intelligibility of non-dialectical difference in these two contexts? In framing his own response to this problem, Hegel attempts to demonstrate that it is impossible to articulate difference of this kind in its own terms and that it must be absorbed into the dialectical intelligibility of a relational nexus (*PS*, 73, 152).

As he formulates the problem of difference with respect to two or more objects of consciousness, Hegel claims that we can understand the first object as a One in contrast with a Many. But since this object is what it is only by contrast with others, it is not simply an independent entity, but depends for its integrity on the relations in which it stands with whatever else there is. These relations are essential to the thing, and what began as an independent entity ends as a term in a relational network of other terms that defines the being of the thing in question (*PS*, 74–76). In this way Hegel attempts to override non-dialectical difference, introducing a set of internal relations to undermine the apparent externality that holds a plurality of objects apart. However, an argument of this kind with respect to either subjects or objects overlooks once more the distinction between conceptual content and vector directionality, mistakenly suggesting that they collapse into one another as terms on the same logical level. A subject or an object is first oriented in space and time and then related to other things, and unless we can distinguish these two moments, there would be no term with respect to which Hegel could generate his own dialectical argument. Yet if this is so, order once more proves to be an essential ingredient in the discussion, not only for establishing the integrity of non-dialectical difference, but also for allowing us to show how difference of this kind is intelligible.

The importance of the concept of order becomes clear when we notice that if a second term is related to the first, what is first for each element is its own vector orientation, and what is second is the relational network in which it stands with other things. This means that what is first for term, is second for term, and term 2 is second for term 1. However much these terms develop dialectically, they also stand in a mirroring relation to one another, and it is the possibility of a cognitive judgment corresponding to this relation that serves to make their non-dialectical difference intelligible. We must therefore acknowledge the centrality of a judgment of this kind, not only with respect to the representational relation between subject and object, but also as it reflects the non-dialectical dimension of the subject and the object of consciousness.

It would be possible to continue these critical reflections at every stage of the phenomenological project, showing how a dimension of difference that is intelligible only in non-dialectical terms infects other dialectical transitions. Yet this is unnecessary, for what is at stake is the need for a revised conception of the entire Hegelian enterprise. In attempting to move the discussion beyond the level of an empirical protest into a philosophical context, and in attempting to show that we can make the subject, the object, and their relations intelligible in dialectical and non-dialectical terms, I have been suggesting that we must reconstrue the structure of the Absolute in terms of a broader conception of philosophical intelligibility. This reconstruction involves the supplementation of the kind of intelligibility appropriate to the concrete universal with the intelligibility of a non-dialectical concept of analogy. The concrete universal is an appropriate way of articulating the temporal dimension of experience, but we must stretch language even further to do justice to the irreducibility of space and to the truth expressed by the concept of spatial and temporal orientation. I have done this by claiming that an analogical relation can bind together two or more terms that are internally dialectical, where both the orientation and the abstract structure of the process are intelligible because of the mirroring relations in which they stand with other things and because of the judgment that relations of this kind obtain.

Just as Hegel extends the traditional concept of the abstract universal to capture the developmental dimension of both substance and subject (*PS*, 74–76), I have extended the traditional concept of similarity to capture the structure and the vector directionality that it often exhibits. This extension is applicable to the religious and philosophical dimensions of experience, and not simply relevant to the subject and the object of experience or to the representational relations that bind them together. Sense-certainty and perception are stages in the development of the experience; but if an adequate understanding of their "spatial" dimension requires a non-dialectical concept of analogy, we must place this concept alongside the concrete universal to make religion and philosophy intelligible throughout the entire range of human experience. Indeed, the concept of analogy is richer than Hegel's concept of dialectical intelligibility, for it includes the non-dialectical dimension of both the terms and the process that it makes accessible. This is not to say that this revised conception of analogy involves a sublation of the dialectical process, for it can be related to this process only because it allows us to image its structure, its orientation, and its development without subordinating the image to the process. As a result, we can preserve a dimension of radical externality, not only at the level of representation, and not simply as a constituent of the subject and the object of experience, but also in the kind of judgment that can make the non-dialectical aspect of religion and philosophy intelligible.[6]

I do not expect a Hegelian to be persuaded by my argument, not only because I have formulated it so generally, but also because Hegel himself would reject it. At a number of places in his writings, he says that space is an abstract reflection of the Absolute and that it is merely the skeletal form of time understood as developing dynamically (*PS*, 26–27; *PN*, 28–30). He also claims that directionality has no philosophical significance (*SL*, 105–6, 117, 147–48) and the kind of imagistic thinking that I have introduced into the Absolute Process in the transition to Absolute Knowing does not require it. Finally, in the *Science of Logic* Hegel describes the Absolute Process in such a way that dialectical difference is just as dominant as identity, insisting that the sameness of the process is as much the difference of dialectical identity and difference as it is their identity. In this respect, he is a modern Heraclitean; and in a context where he is free from the opposition of consciousness, he makes this clear by emphasizing the centrality of the category of becoming for his dialectical enterprise (*PS*, 473, 476–79; *SL*, 82–100). The unrelenting teleological dimension of Hegel's thought belies our insistence on the value of vector orientation; for from within the Absolute Process, he orients himself toward the ultimate expression of the Absolute in its richest and most comprehensive form (*PS*, 492). This comprehensive articulation of the Absolute Process forces us to insist on a non-dialectical sense of difference that we must make intelligible in its own terms.

If we are to take seriously Hegel's claim that sameness involves difference just as it involves identity, the sameness of the beginning and the end of philosophical reflection is as different as it is identical. Yet this fact demands a kind of articulation that is adequate to the way in which the beginning and the end of philosophy stand in contrast with one another. The concrete universal is not sufficient to describe this situation; for when Hegel introduces it, he attempts to comprehend an abstract beginning by dialectical sublation. If the beginning and the end of religion and philosophy are different, they stand apart in such a way that the kind of imagistic way of thinking I introduced becomes appropriate. To invert one of Hegel's most suggestive phrases (*PS*, 409, 493), the beginning and the end of things are God standing over against himself and over against those who recognize themselves as finite beings, charged with the task of making the Absolute Process intelligible. My own way of developing this point has been to mobilize the concepts of orientation and analogy, where we can describe the essence of the Absolute by the kind of sameness in which identity and difference are both preserved and held apart by imagistic thinking. Hegel is correct in claiming that sameness involves the difference of identity and difference just as much as it involves their identity, but an intelligible account of this fact requires the transformation of the Heraclitean flux into analogy as an irreducible ontological nexus.

Chapter 7

Heidegger and Jaspers:
Being and *Existenz*

In this chapter, I focus attention on space, time, and place; on the relation between Heidegger and Jaspers, on Being and creation *ex nihilo*, on the stories with which religion and philosophy begin; and on the metaphors and analogies that make these stories accessible. It is these themes that permit us to bring what we say about Heidegger and Jaspers into relation with the earlier chapters of this book. The best way to begin to elaborate these points is to notice that when we turn our attention to Heidegger's philosophical enterprise, the central theme is language and speaking rather than language as structure understood from a structural point of view (*BT*, 21–28, 55–58).[1] Heidegger makes this point explicit in the title of his first great book. Among other things, *Being and Time* repudiates representational discourse, where we can construe this way of speaking in terms of logic in a narrow sense of the term (*BT*, 127). Consider first a quotation from one of the earliest philosophical sources that influenced Heidegger's thinking.[2] This quotation takes us back to Aristotle's *Metaphysics*, where the philosopher tells us:

> We speak of being in many senses, but always with a view to one sense and to one nature, not simply in the way we use identical expressions, but in the way everything healthy is related to health in as much as it preserves or restores health or is a sign of health. In precisely this way we speak of being in many senses, but always with a view to one dominant sense. And just as there is one science of the healthy, so it is in all such cases.

Obviously, therefore, it is proper for one science to study being just in so
far as it is being.[3]

The passage before us is an example of what Aristotle calls "*pros hen* predication."[4] What he means by this expression is that when there are several
senses of a term, the meaning of these senses is derivative from the meaning
of a single sense to which they are referred. For example, Aristotle tells us that
healthy medicine and healthy urine are healthy with reference to health. If
instead of talking about various uses of the word "healthy" and their relation
to health, we talk about the many uses to which the concept of being can be
put in Aristotle's metaphysics, we can move from his concrete illustration
about *pros hen* predication to the metaphysical point that he wants to make
in terms of it. Just as we can relate health to other uses of "healthy," we can
relate being as *ousia* (substance) to other instances of being that would remain
systematically equivocal unless we could refer them to it.[5]

When Heidegger takes this quotation from Aristotle seriously, he has
already launched the project that comes to fruition in *Being and Time*.
Aristotle suggests that Being is reachable only as the *telos* to which he refers
the otherwise equivocal meanings of being; and in this respect, he launches
a tradition that comes to fruition in Hegel. Aristotle transcends the equivocity of Being by referring it to a single term, and the corresponding novelty
of the early Heidegger is that he construes the temporal development of
Dasein as a special manifestation of Being through which beings can be
brought into relation with Being understood as a *telos*.[6] Thus, when the eigh-
teen-year-old Heidegger reads this text, thinks it through, and takes it seriously, he has already launched the project that eventuates in *Being and Time*.[7]

My initial account of Heidegger has temporalized his project by introducing teleology into the picture in the guise of the many senses of Being
oriented toward a single meaning. I have done this to avoid the tendency to
reduce Being to a static content of consciousness and to unleash the dynamic
dimension that is present implicitly in the concept of *pros hen* predication.
Failure to do this will result in the kind of metaphysical sedimentation that
Heidegger wants to avoid (*BT*, 41).

When degeneration of this kind occurs, a thinker must appear who can
stir up the philosophical waters; and in Heidegger's case, this thinker is
Nietzsche. Consider the following sentences from the introduction of *Being
and Time* that make reference to Nietzsche. In *The Will to Power*, Heidegger
reads that being is a fiction (*WP*, 275–76). As Nietzsche formulates the
point: "[Being is] an invention of weary men who cannot endure a world of
ceaseless change and eternal becoming" (*WP*, 269).

The history of ontology, which in Nietzsche's view is the history of nihilism, seeks a world of definable beings in order to rescue man from time. Interest in Being, Nietzsche writes, "springs from revenge against time" (*WP*, 253). Nietzsche believes that the question of Being is not only anachronistic, but that its suspicious relation to time makes the pursuit of it a symptom of decadence (*WP*, 400–402). Indeed, the pursuit of Being becomes the quest for what is structured and is itself merely structural. The dynamic cosmos of Aristotle, where Being is the end of a sequence of processes of internal development, becomes in Nietzsche's hands a caricature of itself. Instead of being the eternal lure of a dynamic process, being is frozen and static and stands against time as a perpetual enemy (*WP*, 22, 76). Thus, the young Heidegger is influenced both by Aristotle, for whom Being and time come together,[8] and by Nietzsche, for whom they stand apart. In this second case, the quest for static structure becomes the expression of resentment in the face of our incapacity to conquer time.

In the introduction to *Being and Time*, Heidegger attempts to reawaken the question of Being by assuring us that it is not an empty category, which is the most universal concept (*BT*, 21). If it were, it would be impossible to recover the Aristotelian insight about the dynamic dimension of Being and to heed Nietzsche's warning that Being must not become an obstacle that prevents the philosopher from acknowledging the primacy of temporality. However, the more important point in Heidegger's introduction is his claim that the Being of beings is not itself a being. The Being that we understand tacitly in uttering the statements, "S is P" or "S exists," is not another being. As Heidegger might formulate the point, the first philosophical step in understanding the problem of Being is to avoid telling a story about it. That is to say, we must not frame a narrative that traces beginnings back to Being as the *arche* in virtue of which they are brought into being.

It is important to be clear about what is at stake here. Just as we have claimed that religion and philosophy begin with storytelling, Thomas Aquinas is telling a story when he gives an account of the relations among the being of predication, the *esse* of finite beings, and the divine *Esse* in virtue of which they come into existence. This is the *mythos* that Heidegger is prepared to repudiate; and he repudiates it by denying that your being and mine presuppose a ground, an *arche*, or an origin to bring them into existence (*BT*, 21). In this respect, Heidegger is siding with the Greeks against the medieval tradition. In the *Metaphysics* Aristotle says that the sentences, "S is a man" and "S is an existing man," are synonymous.[9] The reason for this is that for Aristotle, there is only one world; and it is gratuitous to add the qualification that something exists to make the transition from possibility to actuality.

When the Christian tradition emerges, the problem of existence becomes more complicated, for it involves a transition from what might be, to what is, to what is necessarily. It is this transition that Heidegger repudiates. In siding with the Greeks, he turns away from the Christian *arche* to return to another origin—namely, the original vision of Being that was accessible to the Presocratic thinkers (*BT*, 22, 76) tells us that the origin in question is not an origin to which a story gives us access, but a primordial encounter with Being itself.

How shall we make access to Being if not through storytelling? If we begin to do so, not by saying, "In the beginning" (Gen 1:1), but in some other way, only one option remains. In this second case, we can make access to Being only through the being who asks the question. The possibility of access to the meaning of Being, which we have understood tacitly and which we need to articulate, is grounded in our own being as the pathway that leads to being itself (*BT*, 24–26).

When Heidegger introduces the concept of Dasein, he does not mean to be pointing to human beings insofar as they exist (*BT*, 27). Rather, he is calling our attention to that dimension of human existence that sometimes expresses itself as a concern with, or an *ecstasis* toward the meaning of being, where the concept of *ecstasis* is the concept of standing outside oneself in relation to being (*BT*, 24–26, 32–33).[10] Just as the concept of Being has degenerated into a static and structural conception so that we can talk about language and logic in relation to it, so the notion of existence that meant originally "to stand outside oneself" has degenerated into a way of taking our place in the world alongside other things. The original concept of existence contains and hides the dynamism that allowed the young Heidegger to move from an original cluster of concepts of Being to one meaning of Being *pros hen* to which we can relate them. As a consequence, Heidegger presupposes the kind of dynamism that is built into Aristotle's account of this kind of predication in his use of the concept of *ecstasis*.

Heidegger argues that the ecstatic act whereby one stands outside oneself is the act by which the particular sciences are founded (*BT*, 29, 37). We can trace their founding to an ecstatic act in which Dasein stands outside itself in a constructive act of founding, where the clearest example of this is mathematical constructivism (*BT*, 29–30). But how does this founding act occur? It occurs through an ecstatic act of Dasein that lays the foundation for a scientific domain. This domain becomes what Husserl calls a "regional ontology," that is to say, a separate region where questions about being can be raised.[11]

At this juncture, Heidegger begins to undertake the task that any student ought to perform in relation to his teacher by generalizing the project in which the teacher is engaged (*BT*, 30). Heidegger reasons as follows. If the sciences are founded on an act of construction, there ought to be a corresponding fundamental ontology that is prior to regional ontologies, where what is founded is not simply a particular domain (mathematics, physics, chemistry, biology, and so on), but where the founding act is the founding and articulation of the meaning of Being for a particular epoch.

By analogy with the constructivism that gives us a sequence of regional ontologies, an act of construction can also be performed with respect to philosophy itself. As a consequence, Heidegger calls his enterprise fundamental rather than regional ontology. Notice that in this case, Heidegger does not intend to be telling a story or appealing to an *arche*, but tracing the founding act of philosophy to an ecstatic moment in which an existing being stands outside itself and acts constructively. This sounds like the Descartes of *The Rules for the Direction of the Mind*[12] or even like what I regard as the most accurate way of reading the *Meditations*.[13]

If Dasein not only provides the ontological pathway along which we can found mathematics, physics, chemistry, biology, and other domains, but also permits an ecstatic act to occur by which fundamental ontology comes into existence, we need to take seriously the fact that laying the foundation of ontology is temporal. It makes no sense to talk about an act of grounding, or an act of construction, without paying careful attention to its temporal dimension. If the act of construction must be temporal, we must say something about temporality; and when we do this, we begin to broach in a broader and richer way the problem of Being and time.

In what fashion does time manifest itself in the act of construction? The usual way of formulating the temporal modalities is to distinguish among the past, the present, and the future and to suggest that the present is more important than the other two. Heidegger is suspicious of this account of the nature of time because he wants to focus on the Aristotelian quotation with which we began, the quotation from Nietzsche to which we moved, and the ecstatic act on which fundamental ontology is founded. Thus, the dominant mode of temporality for Heidegger is not the present but the future (*CT*, 6; *WP*, 400) where some of his favorite passages from Nietzsche are the ones in which Nietzsche speaks about the philosophy of the future (*BT*, 42; *CT*, 6).

Heidegger has his own way of pointing to the primacy of the future. In doing so, he speaks about the present as "thrownness," and he suggests that thrownness is a function of both the past and the future (*CT*, 6). We bear the burden of the past because we have been thrown into the present; and we are oriented existentially, just insofar as we move beyond the present moment toward the future. As a consequence, the dominant temporal modality becomes the future rather than the present or the past, where we should understand the other temporal modes in terms of it (*CT*, 6).

By moving in this direction, Heidegger reveals once more his bias toward the Greeks. Since he regards finitude as a function of thrownness, Heidegger equates finitude with fallenness, embracing a position in which fate and finitude are bound together. By contrast, Christian anthropology distinguishes finitude from fallenness, understanding finitude to be a positive expression of creation *ex nihilo* and fallenness to be a negative expression of our attempt to turn away from God.

Let us continue to pursue the question of the meaning of Being in the light of Heidegger's reflections about fundamental ontology as involving a constructive act. According to this view, what can Dasein be but time itself? The problem of Being and time is not the problem of beings in time, but the problem of the identity of Dasein with time. This is due to the fact that Heidegger does not understand temporality from the standpoint of the present in which we point toward the past and toward the future, but as an act that emerges from the future and the past and constructs fundamental ontology (*BT*, 42, 46).

Heidegger continues to claim that Being appears in time; and when it does so, the meaning of Being is present. However, the more profound insight is that Being is not only present, but also "presencing," which means that it has its own "flow." The flow of Being is more fundamental than the flow of time (*BT*, 48), just as the act of construction that founds fundamental ontology is more fundamental than the act that founds mathematics, physics, chemistry, or biology.

As Heidegger develops his constructive philosophical enterprise, why does he try to destroy the history of ontology? He claims that he does this because earlier philosophical positions tend to freeze gerunds into nouns, and by implication, to transform the act of presencing into being present (*BT*, 42).[14] What has to be destroyed is the tendency to turn the act whereby Being becomes present into a standard by which subsequent manifestations of Being are measured (*BT*, 48). The gerund is never measured by the noun. Or to put the point in the language of *An Introduction to Metaphysics*, the noun never measures the infinitive. Rather, the situation is always the other way around (*IM*, 60).

According to Husserl, a phenomenon is something that shows itself.[15] Yet when this Husserlian insight is extended to the level of fundamental ontology, Heidegger claims that Being presents itself and that what is called for in response to it is an act of speaking that expresses its richness (*IM*, 77, 83, 87, 190–91, and 193). As a consequence, phenomenology follows Augustine in bringing together the phenomenon that shows itself with the *logos* that expresses it. What needs to occur in the phenomenological act is that Being manifests itself (*BT*, 69).

Heideggerian phenomenology is not merely structural; but as Augustine argued many centuries before (*C*, 10.17.26), it involves the development of a language than can be responsive to the presence and the absence of Being at the same time. The purpose of phenomenology in speaking about what shows itself is to allow it to be unveiled, uncovered, and rescued from forgetfulness. All of us have drunk from the stream that passes over into the other world, and when we wake up, we forget the meaning of Being. However, as the alpha privative suggests, truth is the negation of forgetting, where the phenomenon, *logos*, and truth are always connected, and where truth is the unveiling of what shows itself, even though the phenomenon that reveals itself also remains hidden.

In *An Introduction to Metaphysics,* Heidegger continues to explore the question of Being by calling our attention to the most fundamental question that he ever raises with respect to it. The best way of formulating this question is to ask: Why is there something rather than nothing? Heidegger claims that this is the widest question we can ask because it has to do with everything, and it is the deepest question we can raise because we are unable to get underneath it (*IM*, 1–2, 6). As a consequence, the question of the meaning of Being is the most fundamental question we can consider. Heidegger also claims that the question of Being is more radical than other questions because it is the only question that is self-questioning. This is so because the question that he raises is an expression of Being (*IM*, 4–6). If one asks, "Why is there something rather than nothing?," what is in the question, among other things, is the Being of the question that is formulated by it (*IM*, 9, 12).

If the question, "Why is there something rather than nothing?" is fundamental because it is a self-questioning question, it follows from this fact that there is no prior ground that can give an answer to it. It is not possible to ask, "Why is there something rather than nothing?" and then suppose that there is something prior after all that will serve as a metaphysical foundation for it. This pattern of reflection leads Heidegger back to his original affinity with the Greeks as opposed to the thinkers of the medieval tradition.

Having asked, "Why is there something rather than nothing?," Heidegger turns immediately to a discussion of the Greek conception of *physis*, or to what we can translate into Latin as *natura* (*IM*, 13). Heidegger tells us that *physis* is a process in which things emerge, come to stand, and endure for a while (*IM*, 14–15). As a consequence, *physis* points in two directions simultaneously: on the one hand, it points toward a process of generation and becoming in which things come to be and pass away; and on the other hand, it points toward the stability of what stands forth and presents itself as enduring.

Despite the interplay between generation and stability, Heidegger claims that *physis* is often reduced to stability, causing us to forget about the dimension of becoming. As a result, a series of ontologies emerges that presents itself as a sequence of stable systems (*IM*, 39, 117). However, to the extent that the meaning of being is connected intimately with the meaning of time, these stabilities must be put into question (*IM*, 84, 118). Therefore, if we ask the question, "Why is there something rather than nothing?," and if in doing so we embrace the Greek conception of *physis*, the primacy of this concept will not allow us to commit ourselves to an absolute and unchanging foundation.

According to Heidegger, philosophy and poetry are twins. Heidegger claims that the task of philosophy, on the one hand, and of poetry, on the other, is to celebrate *physis*. Whatever principles of criticism one brings to bear on it, a poem is always richer than what can be said about it. Yet if this is so, poetry reveals itself as the counterpart of philosophy, provided that the philosopher knows that there is a dimension of open-endedness in philosophy as well. These two trees, as Heidegger puts it in one of his later writings, are planted side by side, do not overlap, and have their roots in common ground. They are two ways of celebrating the interplay between the determinate and the indeterminate dimensions of becoming that will never yield their truth to the monomaniacal quest for stability (*IM*, 80).

Heidegger takes the question of the meaning of being to a deeper level by suggesting that if we ask the question, "Why is there something rather than nothing?," we not only catch a glimpse of becoming as fundamental, but also look down into the abyss of nothingness. As a consequence, the question "What is Being?" becomes "What is the Nothing?" Yet that, of course, appears to be an incongruous concatenation of words. At this juncture, Heidegger implies that Being is a "part of" Nothing, or at the very least, that it is determined dialectically by it (*IM*, 25–26). In this respect, he is placing himself alongside nearly every other thinker in the Western tradition. If one asks, "What is Nothing?," one is already presupposing a tacit understanding of Being in virtue of which the question can be formulated. This might lead us to ask, "Which is more objectionable, to ask 'What is Nothing?' or to ask 'What does it mean to have been created out of nothing?' "

There is an Hegelian dimension to be found in *An Introduction to Metaphysics* that will require some discussion for elaboration. Consider the following passage:

> If we put the question in the form of our original interrogative sentence, "Why are there beings rather than nothing?" this addition [the reference to nothingness] prevents us in our questioning from beginning directly with an unquestionably given being, and having scarcely begun from continuing on to another expected being as a ground. Instead, this being, through questioning, is held out into the possibility of non-being. Whereby the "Why?" takes on a very different power and penetration. Why is the being torn away from the possibility of non-being? Why does it not simply keep falling back into non-being? Now the being is no longer that which just happens to be present, it begins to waver and oscillate. (*IM*, 28)

If Heidegger is to be a fundamental thinker, he knows that he must outflank Hegel's dialectical ontology. However, it is not evident that he does this in the previous passage. It is also not so clear that he does so in this additional passage:

> For the present our question is only to open up the being in its wavering and oscillating between non-being and being. Insofar as the being resists the extreme possibility of non-being, it stands in being, but it has never caught up with or overcome the possibility of non-being, which is precisely what becoming has as its photograph. (*IM*, 30)

This picture of becoming never catches up with either pole that constitutes its nature. However, what separates Heidegger at this point from a simplistic version of Hegelianism?

There is a quite lengthy dispute in *An Introduction to Metaphysics* with the linguists, or what might be regarded as the scientific students of language. It is a dispute that is analogous to the conflict with the philologists that characterizes some of Nietzsche's early writings (*IM*, 36–40). Heidegger and Nietzsche are both philologists in their own right; but at this juncture, they repudiate their genealogy. The question at stake for Heidegger is whether the infinitive, *sein*, is prior to the substantive, *Sein* (*IM*, 37, 39, and 69). In English, the question is whether "to be" is prior to "Being" or whether "Being" is prior to "to be."

From an etymological and philological point of view, the question at stake is which comes first in the development of a language, the richly inflected domain of which nouns are constituents, or infinitives that might seem to be derivative from them. It is easy to make the philological argument that the infinitive is merely an abstraction. The infinitive comes very late historically, and inflected language with its nouns, finite verbs, and modifiers appears much earlier. From this point of view, the infinitive is nothing more than an abstract and desiccated sediment left over after inflected language has done its work.

It should come as no surprise that Heidegger embraces the other alternative. He argues that far from being an abstraction, the infinitive is fundamental and that the inflectional use of verbs, on the one hand, and of nouns on the other, arise out of infinitives. According to Heidegger, the notion that *sein* is a philosophical abstraction is an example of what it means for fundamental philosophical notions to degenerate. What was originally a rich conceptio—*physis*—with its upheaval, struggle, and becoming, becomes *natura*; and as we have noticed already, this concept leads to the modern conception of atoms in the void. The claim that the infinitive is prior to the noun and to inflections of the verb that flow out of it is an attempt on Heidegger's part to recover an ontological context that is more fundamental than any ontic domain. In fact, it is the attempt to recover this ontological domain that thrusts us back into Being and time.

If the infinitive is an abstraction, Being does not have anything to do with time. On the other hand, the kind of Being to which fundamental ontology calls our attention has everything to do with it if the infinitive implicates the same kind of dynamism to which the concept of *physis* points. Heidegger believes that if we move back far enough behind the classical Greek thinkers, we will be able to lay hold of this more primordial conception. Consider one last quotation in this connection from *An Introduction to Metaphysics:*

> Over against the fact that the meaning of the word "Being" remains an indeterminate vapor for us, and it does if it's an abstraction, the fact that we understand Being and differentiate it with certainty from non-being is not just another second fact. Rather, the two belong together. They are one. (*IM*, 62)

Let us read these sentences with Hegelian spectacles. "Over against the fact that the meaning of the word 'Being' remains indeterminate," [Being is the most indeterminate of all categories], "the fact that we understand Being and differentiate it with certainty from non-being" is not just a second fact— [Being and nothing are not distinct]. "Rather, the two belong together. They are one, [that is to say, they are the same, they are becoming]."[16]

Let us see how Heidegger moves beyond the question of the relation between Being and Nothingness in one of his later writings. In the traditional understanding of metaphysics, philosophers tried to find a ground—an origin, an *arche*, an original principle, a prime mover, or a Creator. By contrast, what Heidegger proposes to do in *Identity and Difference* is to turn away from the concept of a ground to think about identity as a relation—a relation between Being on the one hand and Dasein on the other (*ID*, 39).

Like most contemporary thinkers, Heidegger wants to stand in the middle ground between the subject and the object and between Being and beings. Indeed, he wants to be a philosopher of what Gillian Rose has called the "broken middle."[17] What I have suggested is that he has succeeded in being a philosopher of the middle insofar as he has been a replica of Hegel. The question before us at this stage of the argument is whether Heidegger can occupy the middle ground he seeks to embrace without becoming a Hegelian.

The theme of *Identity and Difference* is that to think about identity in terms of the relation between Being and beings is to think about their belonging together, where belonging together is to be both together and apart. When this occurs, things "vibrate," or to use Heidegger's metaphors, they "waver and oscillate" (*IM*, 28). At this point, it is important to notice that a concept of space begins to appear for the first time. It is this concept in terms of which the thinking of the later Heidegger is formulated. He says that the most important of his works other than *Being and Time* is *Identity and Difference* (*ID*, 31–33). Why? Because in this book he finally locates a way of speaking about the middle that is not simply a reflection of the Hegelian drive toward the primacy of becoming as the unity of Being and Nothing. In *Identity and Difference* to belong together in such a way that these categories are both together and apart is not to be a function of an Absolute Process, whatever else it is.

However, our fundamental question for Heidegger only pertains to the extent to which he gives us access to a mode of discourse that transcends dialectical language. One might say that the moments of a process are both together and apart and that they merge with one another in the moment they separate. Self presupposes togetherness so that belonging together might seem to be nothing more than a process of self-development.

Heidegger must think beyond this level if he is to think beyond Hegel. What language does he choose to use in trying to do so? The best he can do is to effect what might be called a "Kierkegaardian retrieval." In this connection, he speaks about a "leaping out," or a "stepping back" (*ID*, 37–38). This is admittedly a refreshing change from a philosophy of the future. By stepping back, one stands in the middle ground where what is to be thought is the identity of the relation between Being and being there, and where this amounts to belonging together in the sense of being both together and apart.

Yet notice that we cannot step back in any fundamental way if the truth of the context in which the stepping back occurs is Absolute Process. There is no stepping back once the Heraclitian river rushes over us. One must simply hope to be spun out to the edge of the water if deliverance is to occur. What we must ask Heidegger is how to articulate what standing together and standing apart has to do with a "leap" and a "stepping back," and what the structure of the leap and the stepping back amount to. Let us turn to the task of understanding these structures with respect to belonging together in its twofold guise.

My suggestion is that what we are looking for is like the analogy of Being, provided that the terms of the analogy are dynamically self-developing. One way to articulate belonging together in such a way that things are both together and apart is to speak about an analogical nexus. What is crucial to notice is that the terms of this nexus must not be geometrical structures, but partially indeterminate and selfdeveloping centers of power.

Heidegger sees this point, and this is the permanent truth of *Identity and Difference*. Being together and being apart does not simply raise the question of Being and time, but also opens us up to the question of Being and space. In addition, the question that Heidegger faces is not only the relation between Being and time and Being and space, but also the question of the Place of places with respect to which the other ontological categories can be understood. This Place is the most comprehensive philosophical context where Being and time and Being and space come together.

How does one name the Place where belonging together involves both being together and being apart? We must not let the word trip off our tongues so lightly that we are freed from the need to struggle with the issue to which the problem of identity and difference calls our attention. As we try to do this, perhaps we can begin to understand how Moses felt when after tending sheep for forty years in the desert, he stood at a burning bush that was not consumed (Exod 3:1-17). Moses asked God for his name, and the context became an occasion for self-naming. Could this be what is required with respect to the issue before us?

It is not my intention to transform the history of the Western tradition into Mosaic commentary. However, I am convinced that every great philosopher can be understood as attempting to find a name for the Place where Being and beings, Being and time, Being and space, and identity and difference come together. This claim does not suggest that these expressions are coextensive or that every term is just as good as any other. However, it is to point to a common direction in which what might often seem to degenerate into a babble of voices is oriented. As I have tried to indicate, Heidegger moves from time, to space, to identity and difference as a way of raising the question before us; and in this way, he struggles valiantly with what I have begun to describe as the problem of the Place of places.

At this stage of the chapter, I turn to the thought of Karl Jaspers, returning to the Augustinian themes of the finite and the infinite dimensions of the soul, to the self-transcendence that allows us to move beyond ourselves toward what is ultimate, to the theme of creation *ex nihilo*, to the role of metaphor and analogy in philosophical and theological reflection, and to the middle ground between the finite and the infinite dimensions of human existence.[18] I will also continue to focus on the fact that in contemporary philosophy, the pivotal question that has perplexed philosophers more than any other is the question of the meaning of Being. Like his more celebrated colleague and political antagonist, Jaspers asks this question; and like his more famous contemporary, he approaches and attempts to respond to it with delicate indirectness (*RE*, 77).

Together with Heidegger, Jaspers knows that the question of the meaning of Being is unanswerable if we ask "What is it?," not only confusing the "what" with the "that," but also failing to notice that Being transcends the distinction between essence and existence altogether (*RE*, 80). In order to permit the question of Being to arise without overdetermining the answer, both Jaspers and Heidegger follow the Kantian pathway in asking how Being manifests itself to us rather than what Being is in itself (*RE*, 80; *BT*, 24–26). Accordingly, both thinkers begin within a transcendental framework, where the central question becomes, "How does Being disclose itself?; and at the same time, how does it protect itself from epistemic and onto-theological encroachments?" (*RE*, 81) Throughout his philosophical career, Jaspers answers this question in a rich variety of ways; but from the outset, his answer focuses on a single conception. He tells us that Being manifests itself as encompassing the subject-object distinction, where modes of the Encompassing fall on both sides of the subject-object opposition (*RE*, 81). Moving from subject to object, the modes of the Encompassing are *Existenz*, Existence, Consciousness, Spirit, Reason, World, and Transcendence; where for the purposes of this chapter, *Existenz*, Reason, and Transcendence are the most important (*RE*, 80–84, 91–94).

Jaspers's enduring contribution to philosophy was to recognize the bottomless depths of *Existenz*, the infinite richness of Transcendence, and the self-transcendence of Reason that binds them together. We can never objectify *Existenz*, Transcendence, and Reason, for they are the ultimate horizons in which objectification occurs (*RE*, 92). Yet these concepts are important, not only because they are conditions that make experience possible, but also because they point beyond the confines of the spatio-temporal dimension of human existence to regions where the ultimate dimension of experience manifests itself (*RE*, 92).

The horizons within which we move are not placid media in which existence and reflection unfold, but are the overarching contexts in which we come face to face with our limitations. Struggle, suffering, guilt, and death are ultimate situations that we can never outstrip; and when they take us to the limits of human experience, we not only flounder, but also suffer shipwreck (*RE*, 96). Jaspers responds to the problem of shipwreck, first by being open to the Encompassing; then by pointing to communication as the act that binds us together; and finally, by inviting us to participate in a philosophical community, sustained by the thinkers who have forged the philosophical tradition (*RE*, 105).

I want to respond to the invitation that Jaspers extends by distinguishing four modes of self-transcendence that make philosophy possible in the contemporary situation. These expressions of self-transcendence are epistemic and ontological at the same time; and they presuppose an interplay between the finite and the infinite dimensions of the soul that point to the depths of *Existenz*, the heights of Transcendence, and the ecstatic character of Reason that binds them together.

As Augustine was perhaps the first to notice (*C*, 2.8.16), the first mode of self-transcendence created finitude, and it points to the (finite–infinite) structure of human existence in which the two poles exist in perfect harmony (*RE*, 78–79). In this case, we are finite and infinite at the same time; where self-transcendence allows us to move beyond ourselves without losing contact with the finitude that individuates us. Our finitude ties us to the earth; our infinitude allows us to reach beyond ourselves; and the tension between them is the vibrating center of created goodness that permits us to stand in the middle ground between beasts on the one hand and gods on the other (*RE*, 78–79).

The second mode of self-transcendence is fallen finitude, and it points to the (finite–infinite) structure of human existence in which the infinite pole attempts to break the hyphen that binds it to the finitude that individuates it. In this case, self-transcendence turns away from the finitude that it can never escape; and in doing so, it attempts to become infinite (*C*, 2.8.16). As a consequence, we negate the finitude that binds us to the earth; our infinitude tempts us to identify ourselves with the heights and the depths to which it points; and we break the tension between them as we vainly attempt to become a creature other than ourselves.

The third mode of self-transcendence is transformed finitude, and it points to the moment when the infinite side of ourselves returns to its finitude (finite–infinite), not only to accept it as inescapable, but also to embrace it as good in its own right. In this case, self-transcendence returns to the finitude it must never reject; and in doing so, it remains infinite without denying the finite dimension that individuates it and that gives it a place to stand within a larger community (*C*, 8.12.30, 9.10.23). As a consequence, we affirm the finitude that binds us to the earth and to one another; our infinitude brings the heights and the depths of experience into a determinate relation with us; and the tension between them is reestablished as the middle ground in which we can finally come to ourselves.

The fourth mode of self-transcendence is fulfilled finitude, and it points to the occasions in which the infinite side of ourselves begins to express itself fully (finite–infinite) in and through our finite limitations. In this case, self-transcendence moves beyond finitude toward the heights of Transcendence and toward the depths of *Existenz*; but it does so without negating the finitude that permits it to exist within the spatio-temporal matrix in which its life unfolds. Thus, we move beyond the earth to which we are bound and the community in which we are embedded, and our infinitude uses the finite materials available to us as expressions of Freedom and as ciphers of Transcendence.[19] As a consequence, the tension between the finite and the infinite dimensions of our nature becomes the medium through which we can express the richness of our middle ground existence.

The four modes of self-transcendence are accessible to philosophical analysis because they present themselves as phenomena encountered when we reflect on our nature and existence. However, the acknowledgment of self-transcendence in all its modes rests on controversial philosophical presuppositions that we must consider if we are to come to grips with ourselves within the boundless horizons of *Existenz*, Reason, and Transcendence. Only in this way can we move to a philosophical context that establishes our self-transcendent place in the world as creatures that are finite and infinite simultaneously.

Individuals who display both finite and infinite dimensions move from created to fallen finitude by encountering shipwreck; but in this case, it is necessary to distinguish two concepts of shipwreck, only one of which Jaspers recognizes. In claiming that we experience shipwreck when we encounter struggle, suffering, guilt, and death, Jaspers conflates two problems that are natural consequences of created finitude with two others that reflect the fact that we participate in fallen finitude as well. Finite beings struggle and suffer because they are limited by negation, which expresses itself in the fact that their past is no longer and their future is not yet, that they are here and not there, and that they are this rather than that. Negation of this kind is relative rather than absolute; and the struggle and suffering that finite beings must endure is a natural expression of the fact that they have a delimited place in the cosmos (*RE*, 93–94). To be a finite being is good, where created finitude points to what is positive about a creature rather than to a privation that makes it less than it should be. In this case, the shipwreck we face as created individuals is a natural fact, demanding that we mobilize our (finite–infinite) resources to respond to the limit situations posed by the relative non-being of our finite situation.

By contrast, when we make the fatal transition from created finitude to fallen finitude, we face shipwreck at a deeper level than the struggle and the suffering implied by our finitude suggests. When we suffer guilt and face death we are not simply limited by negation, but come face-to-face with the fact that the infinite side of ourselves often seeks to be self-sustaining, turning away from the spatio-temporal framework in which we are both limited and self-transcendent (finite–infinite) (*C*, 2.7.15) to a context in which we fall away from our created goodness by acts of our own (finite–infinite) (*C*, 2.8.16). When we do this, we orient ourselves toward absolute rather than relative non-being, where our fall toward the absolute *nihil* expresses itself in the shipwreck of guilt, on the one hand, and the shipwreck of death on the other (*C*, 8.8.19). In this case, guilt and death are not simply natural results of created finitude, but willful results of fallen finitude (*C*, 2.6.12); and the shipwreck to which they call our attention points beyond our natural limitations to the price we must pay for refusing to accept the tension of the (finite–infinite) situation that defines our original condition (*C*, 7.3.5). On occasions of this kind, the shipwreck we face is the unnatural result of our choice to infinitize ourselves, pointing toward absolute non-being, and demanding more than the (finite–infinite) resources we mobilize to respond to the limit situations posed by the relative non-being of our finite situation (*C*, 7.11.17).

There are two ways of coming to terms with limit situations, one which focuses on the restrictions imposed by our created finitude, and the other which focuses on the more serious limitations generated by our fallenness. In the case of struggle and suffering, the appropriate response is openness to the infinite horizon of Transcendence, where our willingness to take responsibility for our finite situation correlates with the richness of the Encompassing within which we stand (*RE*, 93–94, 103). To accept responsibility for ourselves is to participate in the encompassing dimension of *Existenz*, and to stand within this horizon brings us into an appropriate existential correlation with the horizon of Transcendence (*RE*, 92). By contrast, in the case of guilt and death, accepting responsibility for ourselves is not sufficient to bring our fallen finitude (finite–infinite) (*C*, 7.11.17) into correlation with the horizon of horizons that encompasses us (*RE*, 103).

When we fall away from the (finite–infinite) structure of our created finitude through self-accentuation and plunge toward the absolute *nihil*, we are responsible for the guilt and death that result (*C*, 8.8.19). Yet in this case, accepting responsibility for our existential situation is not an adequate response to it. Openness to Transcendence enables us to respond to struggle and suffering by embracing an infinite horizon in which we must work out our own salvation in fear and trembling, and it is to this task that the concept of philosophical faith to which Jaspers commits himself is relevant (*RE*, 94). However, guilt and death cannot be worked out within this same horizon because they cannot be worked out at all by anything we can do to atone for the predicament that generates them. In this case, we must supplement philosophical faith with faith of a radically different kind, not only opening ourselves to the infinite richness of Transcendence, but also to the possibility that what is transcendent might participate in a process of redemption (*C*, 9.1.1). It is to this possibility that both Paul and Augustine point when they exclaim, "Who will rescue me from this body of death?" (Rom 7:24; *C*, 8.5.12).

Religious faith differs from philosophical faith because it moves beyond openness to Transcendence, and further to the active work of Transcendence in correlation with the boundless depths of *Existenz*. In the face of struggle and suffering, philosophical openness to the horizon of horizons is sufficient (*RE*, 98–100); but when we confront guilt and death, something more is required. Having accepted responsibility for the fallen finitude that generates them both, this does not resolve the issue. Rather, it leads us to the Place where openness to Transcendence can become the occasion for existential transformation. If this occurs, Transcendence must reveal itself, allowing us to move from the fallen finitude that defines our deepest existential predicament to the transformed finitude that we are unable to work out for ourselves in the face of guilt and death (*C*, 8.7.18).

The self-transcendence of transformed finitude, where the (finite–infinite) being that falls away from its finitude comes back to itself and accepts its limitations, is possible only if the infinite horizon of Transcendence expresses itself in human form (*C*, 8.8.19). This is so, not only because we need an example of a (finite–infinite) being that accepts itself, but also because we need the power to accept ourselves that can never come from our own resources, either finite or infinite (*C*, 8.8.20). Having fallen away from ourselves toward the absolute *nihil*, we have exhausted our resources in making the transition from created to fallen finitude, where we break the hyphen of the (finite–infinite) structure of the human situation in the direction of self-accentuation (*C*, 8.11.27). When this occurs, we can only reach toward the power of Transcendence that not only encompasses us, but also transforms the brokenness into which we have fallen and from which we are unable to extricate ourselves (*C*, 11.29.39).

If we reach the place where we not only move from created to fallen finitude, but also make the transition from fallen finitude to transformed finitude (finite–infinite), it then becomes possible for us to begin to contemplate the possibility of existential fulfillment. In the mode of self-transcendence that leads from transformation to fulfillment, the (finite–infinite) being not only affirms itself by accepting the power of Transcendence, but also moves beyond itself, using both the finite and the infinite sides of itself to express itself infinitely (finite–infinite) (*C*, 2.4.9). When we do this, we not only read the ciphers of Transcendence,[20] but also become ciphers of Transcendence in our own right, where the fulfillment we seek manifests itself in a "satiety without satiation" (*C*, 9.10.23, 11.29.39) in relation to the transforming power of Transcendence that stands over against us.

When Transcendence ceases to be simply the ultimate horizon that encompasses us, and becomes the Radical Otherness that stands over against us, we can reach beyond ourselves toward a positive term that corresponds to the negative conception of the absolute *nihil*. Just as the boundlessness of *Existenz* stands in a positive correlation with the horizon of Transcendence (*RE*, 103), so the *nihil* out of which we are created can be brought into a positive relation with Radical Otherness by an act of creation *ex nihilo* (*C*, 12.3.3, 12.9.9). In addition, when we make the non-dialectical transition from created to fallen finitude, we turn away from Radical Otherness, not only through a lack of resoluteness (*RE*, 102–3), but also through an act in which we attempt to deify ourselves (finite–infinite) (*C*, 12.11.11). This attempt to become infinite without qualification not only leads us toward the *nihil*, but can be brought into a positive relation with Radical Otherness only by an act of self-manifestation on the part of Otherness itself (*C*, 10.27.38). In this case, our pathway toward redemption leads, not only through existential resoluteness, but also through a willingness to embrace the grace that Radical Otherness sometimes manifests (*C*, 10.29.40). This leads, in turn, to two ways of living within the horizon of horizons that encompasses us: on the one hand, we can respond to Transcendence with an existential act of metaphorical openness; on the other hand, we can respond to Radical Otherness by accepting the gift of analogical otherness in our own existential situation.[21]

By introducing the absolute *nihil* and Radical Otherness into the discussion of the themes into which Jasper's philosophy leads us, I am introducing two terms to supplement the canonical list of expressions he uses to characterize the Encompassing. In addition to *Existenz*, Existence, Self-consciousness, Spirit, Reason, World, and Transcendence, we should place the absolute *nihil* underneath these other domains and Radical Otherness beyond them as the limits to which ontology points. In linguistic terms, this leads to a complex semantics of self-transcendence and Radical Otherness in which Reason binds *Existenz* and Transcendence together by using metaphors that permit the first to open out toward the second and by using analogies that bring *Existenz* into relation with the Radical Otherness that stands over against it. In the first case, the metaphor of the Encompassing allows the boundlessness of *Existenz* to stretch forth toward the boundlessness of Transcendence (*RE*, 95). In the second case, the analogy of faith and the incursion of grace to which it responds allow the transformed finitude of *Existenz* to stand in a positive correlation with Radical Otherness (*C,* 12.16.23).

In this correlation, the Otherness that creates us, from which we fall away, toward which we can be reoriented, and in which we can be fulfilled become four modes of self-transcendence that not only bind *Existenz* and Transcendence together, but also hold them apart. The semantics of self-transcendence becomes, in turn, the positive interplay between metaphorical openness and analogical otherness, where Reason not only stretches toward the horizon of horizons, but where Faith allows us to dwell over against Radical Otherness as transformed individuals in search of ultimate fulfillment. Indeed, when we add the absolute *nihil*, Radical Otherness, and Faith responding to Grace to the list of expressions with which Jaspers begins, seven terms become first nine and then ten, leading us to the place where Reason and Faith stand together in binding us to Transcendence, on the one hand, and to Radical Otherness on the other. When this occurs, philosophy begins to play across the middle ground of our existence, where metaphorical openness gives us access to Transcendence and analogical otherness brings us into a positive relationship with God.

PART THREE

Mystery, Power, and Structure

Chapter 8

The Quest for Wholeness

This chapter introduces the concept of the quest for wholeness[1] for the first time. However, there are analogues to this conception in some of the other chapters; and the concepts of metaphor and analogy and of the Place of places that I use to explain it are central elements in my earlier reflections. The quest for wholeness stands in contrast with the fragmentation into which our lives often degenerate, and it is important to try to understand how we can move beyond fragmentation toward fulfillment. Only by doing this can we find a place to stand that will bind the fragments of our lives together.

One way to elaborate the concept of fragmentation is to notice that the two opposing cultures into which our intellectual lives often divide are merely one illustration of a fundamental bifurcation that pervades our contemporary consciousness. The arts and the sciences, the human realm and the non-human products of a technological age, the quest for political order along typically Western lines, and the emergence of a Third World with its own legitimate demands call our attention to the fact that the world is not a seamless fabric, but is a context in which opposing forces are engaged in a conflict for which there seems to be no resolution. In fact, the contemporary situation sometimes seems to manifest itself more as a cluster of fragments than as a series of competing forces, for the surface rationality of direct and clear-cut opposition expresses itself less frequently than the confusion generated by the virtually unmanageable complexity of the contemporary cultural and intellectual world. It is not so much the oppositions between art and science, humanity and technology, Western culture and non-Western aspirations that define our predicament, but the impossibility of characterizing their interrelations in intelligible terms. The essence of technology is often dissociated from the essence of humanity, and as a consequence, art and science, East and West, humanity and what lies beyond the human realm collapse into a collection of fragments without a coherent focus that can bring unity to human experience.

It is important to notice that there is a more fundamental source of fragmentation that lies at the foundation of human experience and that reveals itself as a structural feature of the human psyche. One of the defining characteristics of the human realm is the intentionality of consciousness,[2] and because of this intentional structure, we are oriented toward objects of consciousness, not only in the act of knowing, but in the activities of doing and making as well. Yet it is also tempting to assume that these intentional activities display a futuristic orientation and that intentionality is an intellectual reflection of the erotic structure of the soul, which always orients itself to what lies beyond its reach (QW, 125–26). This erotic structure often leads us beyond the confines of the family and the city toward the larger world; and in reflective contexts, it even leads us to the rim of the world to find fulfillment (QW, 104, 150). The Faustian journey that the philosophical consciousness sometimes undertakes is not merely the expression of divine madness,[3] but the prototype of the development of the erotic dimension of consciousness, oriented as it always is toward the heights that lie beyond the human realm.[4] Yet there is not only a tendency in human experience to move outward toward a larger world, but also a wish to return to our origins and to recapture the integrity and the richness of the place where we began (QW, 4, 7, 48). A counterthrust that drives us in a different direction often interrupts our outward journey; when this occurs, the psyche becomes the battleground of these two competing tendencies. In the final analysis, human fragmentation is not merely a cultural phenomenon, but a function of the more fundamental conflict that can arise between two directional orientations of the human soul. We long for what lies beyond, but also for a sustaining ground. We orient ourselves toward a larger world, but we cannot escape the wish to return to our origins. With Socrates, we seek to become citizens of the cosmos[5] but when we consult our inner compass, we also wish to go back home. It is the conflict between these tendencies that lies at the foundation of our fragmented condition (QW, 48–58, 75–79).

At the philosophical level, there is a temptation to deal with the problem of fragmentation in two equally defective ways. On the one hand, we can abandon philosophical reflection for experiential immediacy, seeking to solve the problem of fragmentation by immersing ourselves in a mode of experience that is free from every form of opposition. In this way, we can seek to replace reflection with experience by returning to the experiential origins with which reflection begins. These origins then become the source to which we might turn to seek a foundation for human existence. On the other hand, we can attempt to remedy the defects of existential fragmentation by undertaking a quest for comprehension, seeking to reweave the fragments of both experience and reflection into a systematic unity (*PS*, 430). In this way, experience is subordinate to reflection and we find the unity we seek in reflective terms alone. However, the first attempt to deal with the problem of fragmentation overlooks the fact that the opposition between experience and reflection fragments the person in whom both dimensions are present. Even if existential opposition never arose within the context of experience, the contrast between immediacy and mediation that the preference for immediacy presupposes fragments us when we hold apart these poles in absolute opposition. In the history of Western culture, immediacy has been so attractive because it leads us away from the problems of reflection; but it is equally clear that any term that is defined by the negation of another carries this negation with it as an irreducible element. As a result, immediacy can never escape the mediation involved in the interplay with its opposite and can never give us access to the ultimate dimension of experience and reflection that can bring the human soul to rest.

The attempt to move beyond fragmentation by undertaking a quest for complete comprehension is equally defective, primarily because it assumes that we can give every problem, existential or otherwise, a reflective resolution (*PS*, 431). Yet just as reflection inserts itself within immediate experience in the guise of negation, fragmentation resists theoretical resolution in the guise of a moment of difference that we cannot articulate in theoretical terms. The experiential fragmentation that is rooted in the two directionalities of the human psyche and the cultural dimensions of the problem that arise from this existential foundation bring us face-to-face with a dimension of Radical Otherness in human experience that systematic reflection can never encompass (*QW*, 178). If a failure to do justice to the legitimate demands of reflection has been the defect of experiential immediacy, the failure to acknowledge the otherness and the integrity of existential opposition has been the equally obvious defect of the quest for absolute comprehension. We must avoid both defects if we are to deal with the problem of fragmentation in a fashion that is both adequate and intelligible.

In the following paragraphs, I will approach this problem of fragmentation neither from the standpoint of experiential immediacy nor from a perspective that demands absolute comprehension, but from a point of view
that stands in between these two extremes. We should approach the cultural
dimension of the problem before us, the two directionalities of the human
psyche, and the opposition between experience and reflection that we have
just considered from the middle of life rather than from either the beginning
or the end. Human wholeness stands between fragmentation and completion, and it is the midpoint in terms of which we can deal with the fragmentation we experience in both experiential and reflective terms. In the
process, we can make access to ultimate reality without committing ourselves
to a doctrine of immediate experience or to the impossible demands that the
quest for absolute comprehension imposes.

One of the clearest indications that wholeness is a middle-ground phenomenon is that we can never define it. The question, "What is X?," presupposes that the term under discussion is identical with a set of structures
to which we can make access and articulate in clear and intelligible terms. In
fact, the quest for an explicit definition assumes that the term we seek to
define is conceptually complete and that we can formulate the definition by
enumerating its features in structural terms. Perhaps we can define abstract
terms like "triangularity" and "circularity" in this way; but as the Platonic
dialogues suggest, we cannot give a satisfactory definition of this kind for the
terms we use to characterize the human situation. We can never define "tem-
perance," "courage," "wisdom," and "justice" explicitly because they are not
identical with a cluster of abstract characteristics that we can enumerate
explicitly. Yet if this is true with respect to these concepts, it is even more
clearly the case with the concept of wholeness, which is the single concept to
which we must relate these other conceptions. On the other hand, even
though wholeness is not identical with a set of abstract structures that we can
enumerate clearly, it does not follow from this fact that we can neither
describe nor understand the concept of wholeness and the ultimate dimension of experience to which it gives us access. As a middle-ground phenomenon, wholeness is neither a fragmented plurality nor a completed
totality; as a result, we can characterize it without the description degenerating either into conceptual incoherence or into a cluster of abstract properties. In fact, what we need with respect to the concept of wholeness is an
account of its nature that preserves the demand for intelligibility without
sacrificing the philosophical demands for clarity and precision.

In *The Quest for Wholeness*, I have attempted to characterize the concept
of wholeness by engaging in a series of concrete reflections about its nature

and significance (*QW,* 12, 193). Reflection of this kind attempts to weave the experiential and the theoretical dimensions of the problem of fragmentation into a series of stories that lead us toward the concept of wholeness in existential and reflective terms. In this context, however, let me tell a different, more abstract story by discussing the concept of wholeness as it pertains to the problem of knowledge. This is an appropriate place to focus our reflections, for we can understand the fragmentation of the contemporary situation as a crisis of knowing and as a crisis generated by the inevitable limitations on the knowing process that the recalcitrance and complexity of the pressing problems that confront us impose. In these terms the question before us expresses itself in a twofold form: first, how can wholeness be possible within the context of knowledge when the complexity of human experience confronts us; and second, how can we understand wholeness when we come face-to-face with the resistant otherness that characterizes the fragmented cultural context in which we are immersed? In attempting to answer these questions, I will bring together the cultural, the existential, and the theoretical dimensions of our previous discussion and will frame a philosophical story about what human wholeness means.

As we move through the complexities of human experience, the process in which we engage exemplifies three distinguishable dimensions:

1. the power to be and the power to develop, both in ourselves and in what we encounter;

2. the capacity to recognize or produce a minimal structure in what stands over against us, and by implication, to reproduce this structure in ourselves as the process of inquiry transforms us;

3. the partial indeterminacy both of ourselves and of what we encounter that enables the forming process to occur, binding together the moments of reproduction and recognition into a stable unity.

Let us call the first of these factors the dimension of power; the second, the dimension of structure; and the third, the element of mystery or of partial indeterminacy. When we take these factors together, the power, the structure, and the indeterminacy of the process of inquiry intertwine to generate a series of products that exhibit unity but that are also subject to further development. Formulated in somewhat different terms, the knowing process issues in a series of open-ended wholes that transcend fragmentation but that also fall short of the completeness to which we have referred already. In these terms, human wholeness consists in embracing the process of inquiry and in affirming the open-ended unities that emerge in the course of our cognitive interactions with the world. The complexity of experience will yield its rich-ness to the epistemic quest for unity only if we understand this quest in terms of the concept of wholeness rather than the concept of completeness. In addition, the philosophical story appropriate to the quest for wholeness transcends the fragmentation that a capitulation to the complexity of expe-rience would entail; and it does this without transforming the quest for wholeness into a quest for complete comprehension.

Yet what can we say from this perspective about the otherness and the recalcitrance of experience that sometimes seem to constitute a barrier to the epistemic quest for unity? Granted that a sequence of open-ended wholes stands between fragmentation and completeness and makes the complexity of experience partially accessible, how can we connect the con-cept of wholeness with the resistance that we sometimes encounter? Somewhat surprisingly, the dimension of indeterminacy involved in the process of inquiry allows us to deal with the problem of radical opposition in philosophical terms. Both the knower and the known are partially inde-terminate when they come together in an epistemic nexus, but this means that indeterminacy can serve as a medium in which these two partially structured centers of power can confront one another in the process of knowing. As the process of inquiry continues to develop, what allows these terms to become epistemic elements in a partially bounded yet open-ended whole are structural similarities between them that can serve both to bind them together and hold them apart. However, this means that analogy can mediate the otherness and the recalcitrance of the objects of experience by serving to make knowledge possible without obliterating the dimension of difference between the knower and the known. Both negation and differ-ence are always involved in the knowing process as it unfolds into a sequence of partially open-ended unities. The moment of negation allows the process to move and to develop by transcending previous stages, while the moment of difference acknowledges the autonomy of both the subject and the object of the knowing process as elements that will display their irreducible integrity.

This account of the knowing process and the concept of wholeness that it presupposes avoids the defects of the quest for absolute comprehension and the equally serious problem posed by the wish to embrace experiential immediacy. These alternatives produce a fragmentation of their own, pre-venting them from giving us access to the ultimate reality we seek. The quest for immediacy carries with it the negation of reflective mediation, while the quest for completeness fails to come to terms with the moment of difference that the process of knowing encounters. It is in attempting to stand in between these two attractive, but fatally flawed positions, that the wholeness of the account I am proposing here consists. In addition, in telling this epistemic story, I am attempting to do justice to the two directionalities of the human psyche and to relate them to the existential dimension of the problem of fragmentation with which we began. The conception of knowledge as an unfolding process that involves an unending sequence of open-ended unities reflects a thrust toward the larger world, while the acknowledgment of the otherness of the objects of knowledge calls our attention to an epistemic counterthrust that presupposes a real ground that resists holistic encroachments. The interaction between these two directionalities defines our epistemic condition and makes this account of the knowing process relevant to our existential situation.

If wholeness is a middle-ground phenomenon, and if we refuse to transform the quest for wholeness into a quest for complete comprehension, how can we elaborate the concepts required to make the concepts of wholeness and of ultimate reality intelligible; and how can we develop the language we should use in order to express its significance? I have suggested already that mystery, power, and structure are crucial elements in describing what human wholeness means and have implied that a living language is necessary if we are to move beyond the abstract opposition between immediate experience and the philosophical quest for absolute comprehension. In what follows, I will develop both suggestions briefly, first by focusing on the concepts of space, time, and eternity as ways of articulating the mystery, the power, and the structure of wholeness, and then by pointing to metaphor and analogy as the modes of language that are most appropriate for articulating the meaning of ultimate reality in human terms. As I shall attempt to indicate, it is the interplay between space, time, and eternity, on the one hand, and figurative uses of language on the other that gives us access to the meaning of wholeness and establishes the conceptual ground between fragmentation and completeness where this concept can be understood.

When I developed these points in the chapter about Hegel, I suggested that the quest for wholeness unfolds in existential and cognitive terms that it displays as a temporal dimension, and that this dimension underlies the open-endedness of the human journey at both the experiential and the theoretical levels. The quest for wholeness as an open-ended process requires us to tell a philosophical story because time unfolds as a plurality of moments, generating a sequence of "nows" that constitutes a potentially unending series of temporal determinations. However, as Hegel was the first to recognize, these "nows" are intelligible because they participate in "nowness" as an abstract universal so that the temporal sequence relevant to philosophical reflection is not merely the original series of temporal moments, but the intelligible transition from an original "now" to a series of "nows" through the mediation of "nowness" as an intelligible unity (*PS*, 60, 62).

The open-endedness of the temporal series is able to provide an intelligible foundation for the process of inquiry, not only because its openness makes inquiry possible, but also because its intelligibility allows this process to issue in intelligible results by analogy with the intelligible unity of the process. Just as a sequence of "nows" unfolds in a temporal series, the reflective movement from a single "now" to other "nows" in terms of "nowness" as their common content is a sequential process itself. This reflective process is more primordial than the generation of the ordinary temporal sequence; for it brings together in a single context the "now," a set of "nows," the abstract category in terms of which we can understand them, and the process of reflection in terms of which we move from one of these elements to another. Thus, the form of time, the moments of time, and the process of reflection stand together in a unity, generating a dynamic and intelligible temporal matrix in which the process of inquiry unfolds as an intelligible activity (*PS*, 63–64).

However, cognitive inquiry also presupposes a spatial dimension; and we encounter this dimension most clearly when the subject and the object of inquiry stand apart in experiential and cognitive contrast. As we discovered in our discussion of Hegel, just as time unfolds as a sequence of "nows," so the spatial continuum displays a plurality of "heres" that constitutes a network in which the subject and the object stand apart and stand together. Moreover, just as the sequence of temporal moments is intelligible because of the concept of "nowness" and because of a process of reflection that connects these moments with this abstract universal, so the network of "heres" is intelligible because of the concept of "hereness" and because of the reflective process that connects these spatial determinations with this intelligible dimension. However, as we saw with reference to Hegel, there is a crucial difference between space and time that has a bearing on our attempt to provide intelligible foundations for the quest for wholeness as a cognitive activity.

Though time unfolds of itself to generate a series of temporal moments, space is a framework that requires the active participation of the inquirer as he turns from here to there in the attempt to bring the process of cognition to focus. Among other things, this means that we must make choices in the course of reflection and that as a result, we must supplement the openendedness and the partial indeterminacy of the temporal dimension of inquiry with the power to choose the direction in which to turn and with the power to move freely from one content to another as the process unfolds. In addition, the need to make choices and the power to move from one content to another presupposes that the subject and the object of cognition remain radically distinct from one another and are not simply aspects in the unfolding rush of temporality. A mirror-image relation between subject and object serves to secure the intelligible relation between them without canceling the irreducible moment of difference that holds them apart (*QW*, 190, 193). If time makes the open-endedness of inquiry possible, space makes the equally important dimension of difference possible; and taken together, they provide an intelligible framework within which philosophical reflection can attempt to attain the satisfaction it seeks.

The concept of Place unifies the spatial and the temporal elements that the quest for wholeness as a cognitive activity presupposes. When inquiry reaches a preliminary termination, the temporal and the spatial dimensions of the process of inquiry and the openness, the otherness, and the intelligibility that characterize an adequate description of what wholeness means emerges. Place brings the open-endedness of time, the otherness of space, and the intelligibility of both conceptions together, where this Place is a provisional termination of the cognitive process and an instance of wholeness formulated in the language of cognition. The Place to which a process of inquiry moves is not an instance of fragmentation, since the interplay between the subject and the object involved in such a Place is too coherent for us to understand it merely as a fragmented plurality. On the other hand, this Place is also not complete; for any termination of inquiry is always provisional, not only because of the partial indeterminacy of its results, but also because of the moment of difference that holds the subject and the object apart even as they come to rest in a provisional conclusion. Thus, we find once more that the concept of wholeness is a middle-ground phenomenon, standing in between the fragmentation with which inquiry begins and the completeness to which it might sometimes seem to lead. The concept of Place is the most crucial element in our attempt to explicate what wholeness means in cognitive terms, for it is at the Place where space and time intersect that we can find wholeness as a provisional termination of cognitive inquiry (*QW*, 193–95).

In conclusion, let me ask about the status of the language that we need to describe the concept of wholeness, and by implication, characterize the concept of Place as a unity of spatial and temporal dimensions. As I have suggested already, the language required to do this is metaphorical and analogical and is a language that is appropriate to the middle-ground status of the human situation. In discussing the concept of time as the foundation of the open-endedness of inquiry, it is important to notice that the temporality in question is not time in the ordinary sense, but time as a process that the concept of "nowness" and the reflective activity that connects this concept with a dynamic sequence of moments mediates. However, this means that the concept of time that underlies the process of inquiry is a metaphorical extension of the more familiar conception and is the metaphorical ground that allows the process of inquiry to unfold as an open-ended activity (QW, 188–89. In addition, the concept of space incorporates the intelligible dimension of Hereness and is a reflective transformation of space in the ordinary sense of the term into a region in which a series of mirror-image relations binds the subject and the object together and also holds them apart. This means that the concept of space that is relevant to a discussion of the quest for wholeness as a cognitive activity is an analogical extension of the more familiar concept and is the analogical ground that allows both the subject and object of the process of inquiry to maintain their integrity (QW, 191–93). As a result, the metaphorical openness of inquiry and the temporal relations that underlie it merge with the analogical otherness of the subject and the object to constitute a Place where inquiry comes to a provisional termination, and where we can find wholeness in cognitive terms.

Yet what is the crucial metaphor and analogy that lies behind the foregoing account, and how can language of this kind serve to give us access to ultimate reality? The term with which I wish to conclude this chapter and that epitomizes our earlier reflections is the notion of a Place of places. This concept stands at the center of our inquiry, for it points both to the metaphorical openness that makes the process of inquiry possible and to the analogical otherness that prevents the transformation of the quest for wholeness into a quest for complete comprehension. In this respect, the concept of Place stands in between fragmentation and comprehension and makes the concept of wholeness accessible in metaphorical and analogical terms. The Place to which this concept refers is not a place in any ordinary sense, but is the ultimate Place where we can acknowledge the openness of cognition and the integrity of the subjects and objects within it.

Insofar as I have attempted to do this, this chapter is a Place where the metaphorical and the analogical dimensions that are necessary for explicating the quest for wholeness in cognitive terms come together. And if it has been necessary in the course of our argument to strain language beyond its ordinary uses, this should not be surprising if there is any truth in the suggestion that metaphor and analogy are appropriate ways of expressing the wholeness to which I have attempted to call your attention. Metaphor and analogy are ways of speaking that drive philosophical reflection beyond the confines of familiar modes of discourse and that allow us to seek wholeness in philosophical terms. It is in this sense that the Place of places is a metaphorical and analogical way of characterizing the meaning of ultimate reality and a way of bringing together the stretched uses of language that are necessary to make this cognitive framework accessible.

Chapter 9

Being and God

In this chapter I return to the concepts of space, time, and eternity as the framework for our inquiry; to the categories of mystery, power, and structure that make them intelligible; and to the figurative, performative, and intelligible uses of language that give us access to them. I will also develop the suggestion that I made in chapter 5 that I can unify the concepts of perfection, mystery, concreteness, and holiness by developing an unorthodox concept of Being. The first step in doing this is to notice that wherever he begins, the philosopher and the theologian must at some point attempt to understand what is ultimate and unconditioned. They begin with belief and opinion, but will remain unsatisfied until they transform them both into wisdom. We might interpret the quest for wisdom as the philosophical attempt to understand the meaning of Being Itself; by contrast, we might adopt the equally ancient religious approach to wisdom that identifies what is final and unconditioned with God. The concepts of Being and God thus emerge as alternative conceptions in terms of which we can understand the quest for wisdom.

The emergence of these alternative conceptions confronts us with a choice about the relation between them: Which term should we regard as genuinely ultimate? Alternatively, we can ask whether a choice between them is necessary: Is it possible to construe both concepts as equally fundamental? If we take these questions together, two kinds of relation emerge between the concepts in question. The first involves the relation of subordination and presupposes that one of the terms is more nearly ultimate than the other.

Thus, God is subordinated to Being, or Being is subordinated to God. The second presupposes that both concepts have equal status and that a choice between them is unnecessary. Accordingly, God and Being are regarded as identical, or they are thought to be strictly coordinate. We will now consider the nature of the four alternatives that these distinctions make possible.

According to the first, we should subordinate God to Being so that God appears to lose his status as ultimate. As a consequence, the question of his reality emerges as a meaningful, though problematic issue. Within this context, we characterize God as a being; and a dispute arises about whether we are to assign him a place within the whole of Being. Because Being Itself is the fundamental concept, we characterize God as a being who may or may not be, depending on a proper evaluation of the arguments for his existence.

By contrast, an alternative relation is possible in which God rather than Being is the basic concept. The meaningfulness of disputes about the reality of God is thereby called into question. If we subordinate Being to God, it is inappropriate to attempt to assign him a place within the whole of Being; and it is equally inappropriate to claim that he does not exist. From this perspective, it is also mistaken to claim that we can interpret the concept of God by means of ontological categories. God not only transcends the distinction between something and nothing, but also the ontological framework in terms of which finite things can be understood. He thus transcends the concept of Being Itself—the fundamental concept of traditional ontology.

There remain, however, two further ways in which we can bring the concepts in question together. According to the first of these alternatives, Being and God are identical. As identical with Being Itself, God is not a being who can or cannot be. As a consequence, a question about the place to which he is to be assigned within the whole of being fails to arise. On the other hand, though God transcends the distinction between something and nothing, he does not transcend the ontological framework altogether. Rather, as identical with Being Itself, he is identical with the most fundamental concept of the traditional philosophical enterprise.

Finally, we can draw the concepts of Being and God together in such a way that each coordinates with the other and is the fundamental concept within its own domain of discourse. This position commits us to the view that we must distinguish ontology from theology in a radical way and that we must acknowledge two ultimate concepts as mutually exclusive. Accordingly, philosophical criticism is irrelevant to religion; and we can undertake traditional ontology without making reference to the standpoint of religion.

In this chapter, I will examine the problem of the relation between Being and God from the standpoint of the first and third of these options—namely, the view that claims that God is subordinated to Being and the position that holds that Being and God are identical. I will not consider the other positions in detail, for each is committed to the thesis that philosophical analysis is inappropriate for the proper understanding of the nature and existence of God. For the position that claims that we should subordinate Being to God, God transcends the categories that we employ in ontological inquiry; and according to the view that God and Being are coordinate, God stands outside the framework of categories that we use within philosophy. Since an adequate treatment of these positions presupposes a discussion of the proper relations between philosophy and religion, I will lay aside this second-order inquiry and focus instead on the views that are more readily accessible to philosophical examination.

At the outset, I will assume that these positions are mutually exclusive. On this basis, I will set forth a brief account of the view that God is subordinated to Being and will examine it from the standpoint of the view that Being and God are the same. I will then explore the identification of Being and God dialectically in the attempt to give its terms a richer, concrete content. I will argue that Being and God involve a unity of structure, mystery, and power and that their unity can be understood by analogy with the unity appropriate to concrete things. This makes it possible for us to deny the ontological difference between Being and beings (*BT*, 28–31). I will maintain that Being is a special kind of being and that the opposition between the initial alternatives is not so fundamental as it appears. In conclusion, I will raise a question about the proper relation between the view of Being that I will develop and the traditional concept of Spirit. In doing so, I will maintain that Being remains the fundamental name for God, in spite of the Hegelian suggestion that we should understand the Absolute in terms of the concept of Spirit.[1]

As we noticed in chapter 5, when we subordinate God to Being, he is often accorded a special existential status as a perfect being.[2] In his perfection, God is supreme among the concrete things that have a place within the cosmos; and as supreme, he also embodies a mode of being that is infinite. God is thus the ultimate, concrete being and is different in kind from every other entity. As ultimate and concrete, God is sacred; and as a consequence he becomes the supreme object of worship. Finite entities stand in contrast with God as a perfect being, and the contrast between these two such different modes of being is mediated by man's unreserved respect and devotion.

We must not forget that the foregoing account of the nature of God has received the sanction of a number of strands within the classical tradition. On the other hand, we must notice that the critic can urge decisive objections against it from the standpoint of the view that God is identical with Being Itself.[3] As noted in chapter 5, when we define "God" as a "perfect being," it might seem that the concept of a being is incompatible with the concepts of ultimacy, absoluteness, and perfection. We also should distinguish items that have being from the Being that they have; and as a consequence God would be distinguishable from the Being he possesses. Accordingly, we should not define "God" in terms of the concept of a being, for this concept reveals its own imperfection in that it presupposes the concept of Being as more nearly basic than itself.

Though every kind of being presupposes the concept of Being, God as identical with Being presupposes nothing other than itself. In the language of the tradition, God is self-caused.[4] For this reason, and in contrast with the alternative interpretation, the identification of God with Being preserves the concept of God as ultimate reality.[5] It is important to notice that we can elaborate the foregoing conclusion in a different way by means of an analysis of the concept of a being. Beings are individualized entities, they comprise a framework of actual and possible beings. If we were to define "God" as a perfect being, he would be a term within this framework; and the restriction of God to a place within this more inclusive scheme is incompatible with the ultimacy of God as the appropriate "object" of religious concern. Worship requires that its "object" be infinite; but if we give God a place within a framework of beings, he is limited by contrast with them and becomes a finite being in a larger whole.

In addition, an individual entity, as individualized, is deficient in the manner in which it participates in beings other than itself. Beings are entities in which the polarity of individualization and participation is not balanced perfectly. As a consequence, they are entities in which the primacy of individualization prevents perfect participation. Since what is ultimate cannot be deficient, the concept of a perfect being is doubly inadequate as a concept of God. That concept mistakenly presupposes that an individual entity, really distinct from other beings, can participate perfectly in the reality of beings other than itself (*ST*, 1:204–8).

If we were to reject the concept of God as a perfect being and to identify God with Being, we might overcome the foregoing difficulties. As Being Itself, God is not a term within the framework of actual and possible entities, but is the most fundamental presupposition of the framework itself. We must thus restrict him to the domain of finite beings. Yet as identical with

Being Itself, he participates fully in the reality of every being. Wherever beings are to be found, Being appears as immanent in them. As presupposed by them, God must be distinguished from the domain of actual and possible entities: but this fact does not entail that he is deficient in the mode of his participation in them.

In response to this account, a proponent of the opposing view could claim that the foregoing considerations fail to acknowledge a crucial distinction that was implicit in the earlier contrast between perfect and imperfect modes of being. The critic might claim that this distinction not only involves a difference between two radically different kinds of being but also a difference between two modes of existential status. He might contend that the perfect being exists necessarily (*M*, 1–5; *P*, 2–3), and that it is mistaken to attempt to assign God a place within the realm of finite things. To make this mistake fails to take seriously the earlier distinction between the modes of being mentioned.

This is not the proper context for a detailed examination of the ontological argument. However, it is necessary to indicate that the conclusion of that argument makes no reference to a being that one must subordinate to the more basic concept of Being Itself. The proof rests on the conviction that the essence and the existence of God are identical. Within the context of the proof, God is scarcely to be regarded as a perfect being, but as the one whose essence is strictly identical with his being. For this reason, the argument fails to support the thesis that a necessary being exists as a special kind of entity within the cosmos as a whole. To the contrary, the ontological argument points to the conclusion that God and Being are identical (*ST*, 1:204–8).

Before I turn to a dialectical examination of this conclusion, I should mention three further considerations that seem to support the view that we should embrace the identification of Being and God. These considerations evoke the distinctively religious dimension of the issues before us and pertain to the relation between the one who worships God and God as the proper "object" of worship. This relation can be either idolatrous or genuine, but if it is the latter, one must direct it toward an "object" that is ultimate. Since Being is the ultimate concept, we might regard it as the proper "object" of religious devotion. As we have noticed already, Being is the appropriate "object" of worship, since it constitutes the primal mystery, while the essence of a being is transparent to reflection, at least in principle.

Finally, the religious attitude of worship is incompatible with a stance of detached reflection or speculation, for religious concern demands unreserved existential commitment. Since man as a being participates in Being Itself, he must not detach himself from Being that appears as immanent in him, where for this additional reason, Being is the proper "object" of religious concern. Being is inescapable; it is ultimate; and it produces awe and wonder. Accordingly, the identification of Being and God preserves the meaning of worship as the proper relation between man and the ultimate "object" of religion. Let us now return to a dialectical examination of this view.

In considering the position before us, we must ask an initial question about the meaning of Being and God. The question can be formulated as follows: If God and Being are identical, what further characterization of these concepts can we give as they stand in contrast with the concept of a being? The first alternative that might be considered is the one that identifies Being and God with the totality of beings, either actual or possible. This totality is presumably infinite and is not an individual, at least in any ordinary sense. As a consequence, we should distinguish it from any given being. It also contains all beings as parts of itself and appears as immanent in them. In fact, this view of God and Being might seem to represent a form of religious pantheism that we can find within the history of religion (ST, 1:233–34). How are we to appraise this position as an attempt to provide an initial explication of the concepts in question?

I believe that we must conclude that the position before us fails to disclose the meaning of Being that it claims to articulate. To see this, we must distinguish the concept of the whole of being from the concept of Being taken as a whole. The primary subject matter of the philosopher is not the totality of beings, but the pervasive structures that transform this totality into a cosmos. For the position that identifies Being and God with the totality of beings, the categories of individualization and participation are the most important of these pervasive structures. To be is to participate as an individualized part within an infinite collection. The meaning of Being that this position presupposes is not Being as an infinite totality, but Being as the categories of individualization and participation that transform this totality into a cosmic whole. To mention merely the infinite collection of beings is to leave unmentioned the meaning of Being that the totality of beings presupposes.[6]

The distinction between the whole of Being and Being taken as a whole presupposes a contrast between Being and the structure of beings. This structure may comprise a plurality of levels, and we can describe it in a variety of ways. We shall not attempt a detailed description of it here, since it is sufficient for our purposes to indicate that a distinction obtains between the structure of beings and the totality of beings. If we identify God and Being, and if the structures of beings are more nearly basic than the beings structured by them, a problem arises about the proper relation of Being and God to those structures taken in themselves. Indeed, Being transcends the realm of beings, but what are we to say about the relation of beings to the structures presupposed by them?

On the one hand, the structures of beings, like Being Itself, are not merely beings among others. On the other hand, it follows from this fact that the original distinction between Being and beings is too simple and undialectical. Since the structures of beings are to be distinguished from the beings structured by them, the original contrast is not simply between Being and beings, but between Being, God, and the structures of being, and all the beings, subject to structure, to determination, and to the categories of existence. Since from this perspective, both Being and the structures of beings are to be distinguished from the realm of beings, the problem of the relation between Being and structures requires a different solution from the one provided by the Being—beings contrast.

We can give two solutions to this problem. On the one hand, we can claim that Being and the structures of being are related intimately. For this reason, we might not only conclude that Being and structures stand in contrast with beings, but that they also stand in contrast with them as a structured unity. Being and God would then be structured; and they would stand in contrast with beings, which are subject to a structure of their own. On the other hand, we might claim that beings and the structures of beings are not distinct. We might regard these structures as abstractable aspects of things, but we might still maintain that Being and the structures of being comprise an indissoluble unity. Accordingly, we could regard both Being and the structures of being as abstractable aspects of the realm of concrete things. Both of these solutions require that we draw a distinction between the ways in which Being and beings are subject to structure. The structures of beings are structures of finitude, and beings that are structured by them are limited and finite. We thus must ask, regardless of whether Being is really distinct from beings, how are we to distinguish it from beings that are finite?

Perhaps we can express the answer to this question by claiming that though the structures of Being imply finitude, this means only that the beings structured by them are finite and limited. We could add that though Being and God are related to that structure, the relation is one of identity rather than subsumption. Since the structures of Being need not be finite, we could conclude that Being and God are identical with the structure of Being, without implying the finitude of either God or Being.

The plausibility of this position rests on the distinction between ontic concepts and ontological categories. Ontology is possible only because there are concepts that are less universal than Being, but more universal than any ontic concept that designates a special realm of beings. These ontological concepts, as contrasted with ontic concepts of a limited range of designation, comprise the structure of Being and the structure of everything that is. As universal in their scope and application, it might seem that they are identical with *ipsum esse*.

The religious equivalent of the view that Being is to be identified with the structure of Being is to be found in the traditional suggestion that God is to be equated with structure. When this structure is said to be distinct from the world, it is usually regarded as the God of justice. God stands over the world as a judge and is to be identified with the demands of a normative nature that he makes on the beings that comprise the cosmos. By contrast, when the structure of Being is regarded as an abstractable aspect of the world, God is identified with what Spinoza called the "soul or essence of the world."[7] According to this position, God is not to be equated with the totality of beings, but with the intelligible structure of the cosmos taken as a whole. This position represents a sophisticated version of pantheism and is one of the forms in which the view that Being is to be identified with structure receives a concrete religious expression.

Despite the initial plausibility of the suggestion that Being is to be identified with the structure of being, further examination reveals that this position must be rejected. Persuasive and cogent considerations to this effect emerge from careful reflection on the phrase, the "structure of being." If the question of the meaning of Being is a question about what it means for anything definite or determinate to be, it would seem that the structure of Being presupposes Being as more nearly basic than itself. Whether or not it is really distinct from beings, the structure of Being is determinate; and as a consequence it is to be contrasted with the beings structured by it. Yet if this structure is determinate, it presupposes Being as the fundamental concept. Being must then be distinguished from the structure of Being, and the identity of Being and structure must be rejected as an explication of the meaning of that concept. Though ontological concepts are universal in their range of reference, they are still less universal than the concept of Being.

In the case of God, emphasis on the concepts of transcendence, ultimacy, and unconditionality effectively negates the claim that God possesses a determinate nature. To the contrary, it would appear that the mystics are to be taken seriously in their insistence that mystery precedes structure in the Being of God.[8] Yet if this is true from the side of God as well as from the side of Being, and indeed, from the standpoint of God as identical with Being, Being and God are presupposed by the structure of Being. This does not mean that the structure of Being is identical with Being as it stands in contrast with beings. For the purposes of that distinction, they appear to have a place within the realm of finite things.

When this point has been reached, it might appear that the dialectic requires us to return to the original dichotomy between Being and beings. It could be maintained that since the structures of Being are determinate, they are either abstract, upper level beings, or abstractable aspects of concrete beings. As abstract or abstractable, they are presupposed by concrete beings; but as presupposed by them, they are not merely concrete things. However, as beings or abstractable aspects of beings, they themselves have Being. Consequently, the structures of Being presuppose the concept of Being as the fundamental concept; and the distinction between Being and beings thereby reemerges as the underlying contrast that we must maintain.

The distinction between Being and the structure of Being that results from the foregoing contrast yields significant consequences. First, the distinction in question suggests that there is mystery in Being and God. As contrasted with structure, Being and God are radically indeterminate; and as indeterminate, they are essentially mysterious. Second, the search for a concept that the domain of determinate beings presupposes finds a termination in the foregoing contrast. If Being and God are determinate, they presuppose Being Itself. However, as determinate themselves, they are presupposed by every being. Finally, the distinction between Being and the structure of Being points to the contrast between the concept of Being and the characteristics that can be ascribed to beings. Being is a Transcendental concept in the medieval sense of the term and is not an ordinary concept that can be predicated of a being. The distinction between Being and the structure of Being preserves and underlies this insight, pointing to the mystery of Being in contrast with the intelligibility of the structures of Being.

Despite the apparent advantages that result from the distinction between Being and structure, and in spite of the mystic's preference for the foregoing view, we must not fail to notice difficulties in it that tend to undermine its value. In fact, critical appraisal of this position leads eventually to the view that we should regard Being as a special kind of being. Once we claim that the structure of Being is finite, the seemingly innocent contrast between Being and beings becomes more problematic than it seemed at the outset. It is one thing to say that God transcends all ordinary things, but quite another to maintain that he transcends the structure of Being as well. The identification of God with Being presupposes that we understand the meaning of those concepts. Yet, as we asked in chapter 8, if Being and God transcend determinate structure, on what basis can this understanding rest?

Were we to suggest that the mystery of its terms mediates the identity in question, mystery would become a form of determination, where all determinations presuppose the concept of Being. As essentially mysterious, Being and God would be determinate, and as determinate, they would presuppose the concept of Being. On the other hand, were we to maintain that mystery is not a determination, how could it provide the attribute with which we are to identify Being and God? As we noticed in our previous analysis, it might seem that reference to the mystery of Being and God points to our inability to speak about them. If this were the case, the attempt to affect the identity in question would be unsuccessful. This attempt seeks to provide an intelligible identification between these concepts, but if mystery signifies an inability to speak intelligibly, and if the affirmation of identity purports to be an instance of intelligible speech, reference to the mystery of Being and God does not provide the identification we seek. As a consequence, it would appear that the position in question fails to provide us with a proper view of God.

We must ask, however, whether the foregoing position points to a view that is more nearly adequate as a way of understanding the issues before us; and does it suggest an alternative that avoids the difficulties mentioned? I believe that we can give an affirmative answer to this question and can label the position to which it points the view that God and Being are determined dialectically. This position emerges from reflection on the inadequacies and insights of the foregoing view.

Reflection on the mystery of Being and God confronts us with a dilemma. Either mystery is a determination, where the concepts of Being and God presuppose Being, or reference to mystery signifies radical indeterminacy by virtue of which we cannot establish a meaningful identification between the concepts themselves. Yet both alternatives are unacceptable: To adopt the former is to surrender the ultimacy of Being and God, and to affirm the latter is to render speech about them ineffective.

On the other hand, it does not follow that every kind of reference to mystery is to be precluded when one speaks about these concepts. Otherwise, we must regard the concepts in question as determinate; and as a consequence, under these conditions, the concepts in question lose their ultimacy. We are also unable to maintain the distinction between the determination of structure and the transcendent role of Being as a concept that produces awe and wonder. It would seem that insight balances inadequacy, and this fact demands a different position.

If Being and God were both determinate and indeterminate, and if we regarded them as a special kind of unity in which we distinguished and mediated aspects corresponding to this contrast, a position might emerge that avoids the foregoing difficulties and incorporates the insights that ought to be preserved. As determinate, we could make intelligible reference to God and Being. As indeterminate, we could include the mystery of both concepts. As dialectically determinate, intelligible speech would be possible and we could maintain the mystery of indetermination.

In the following paragraphs, I will consider this position as an attempt to combine structure with the mystery of indetermination. In the process, I will suggest that we can mediate the distinction between structure and mystery by introducing the concept of power. I will then attempt to hold this triad of aspects together in the unity of a special kind of being. This position purports to combine the structure of structure with the mystery of indetermination; to mediate the distinction between mystery and structure by means of the concept of power; and to unify this triad of dimensions in terms of the concept of a special kind of being. From the standpoint of philosophy, this position represents a view of God and Being as dialectically determinate; and from the standpoint of religion, it involves the belief that Being and God are a trinity.[9]

Before we consider the problem of unity that the concept of a special kind of being provides, we should focus initially on the concept of power as a mediating concept. In this connection, we ought to ask the questions: Why must we include power as an aspect of Being and God, and how does it serve to mediate the distinction between the concepts of mystery and structure? Power must be included as an aspect of unity, since structure and mystery presuppose the concept of power as a precondition. Mystery and structure possess the power of self-manifestation: Mystery appears within the human realm as that aspect of Being and God to which awe and wonder are the appropriate responses, and structure appears as the aspect of God and Being to which the human being responds by means of intelligible speech. In both instances, the self-manifestation of Being and God presupposes power.

In addition, mystery and structure presuppose the concept of power in the guise of the power to be. If structure and mystery are to manifest themselves, they must be and must possess the power to resist non-being. As a consequence, we must not subordinate power to mystery and structure; for they presuppose it as an irreducible aspect of the meaning of Being and God. Finally, we must not only regard power as an aspect of Being and God, but also as a term that mediates the distinction between the concepts of mystery and structure. First, power appears as the ground of the concepts in question, where their common reference to a single term binds them together.

Second, power provides a middle term between mystery and structure and is neither intelligible completely nor wholly indeterminate. On the one hand, power is not identical with an intelligible structure; on the other hand, it is not utterly mysterious. It exhibits at least a minimal structure in the guise of duration and intensity; it participates in both mystery and structure that stand in need of mediation; and it provides them with a common ground, as well as a common point of intersection.

The argument of the earlier paragraphs has indicated that the determinate aspect of Being and God is the structure of being, even though the identification of Being with structure is inadequate, forcing us beyond it to a consideration of mystery. Yet reference to mystery by itself is insufficient as an explication of the meaning of Being and God. As a consequence, we need a richer position in which the concept of power mediates the distinction between the structure of being, on the one hand, and the concept of mystery, on the other.

Before I adopt this position, I must develop it more fully by considering a number of difficulties that pertain to it; one of these difficulties arises from the fact that the structure of Being is determinate. In previous paragraphs, I accepted the identification of determination with finitude. Yet if determination implies finitude, Being and God in their determinate guise are also finite in an aspect of their being. If this is the case, it would appear that even as dialectically determinate, we cannot equate God and Being with ultimate reality as distinct from finite things.

In addition, if the structure of Being is finite, it does not have a privileged place as an aspect of Being and God. At best, it is the highest level of a hierarchy of finite items, all of which are modes of Being. Concrete beings have a place within this finite order. Thus, they also comprise a part of the aspect of Being and God that can be understood as determinate. If this is the case, the question arises even more insistently: "How can Being and God be identified with ultimate reality as distinct from finite things?"

If I am to give a satisfactory answer to this question, I must examine the identification of determination with finitude more carefully. This identification rests on the conviction that "determination" must not be defined as "limitation by negation."[10] Presumably, limitation implies the finitude of what is limited; and as a consequence, the structure of Being is determinate, limited, and finite.

We can find a solution for this difficulty if we consider the customary meaning of finitude as "subject to change and to the loss of being." Ordinary beings that we encounter are finite in this sense. On the other hand, it is evident that the structures of Being are not finite in this way. Both qualitative

change and loss of being presuppose the structure of Being. Individualization and participation, and essence and existence, characterize both change
and diminution. As a consequence, we must not regard the structure of
Being as finite in the ordinary sense.

The structures of being are determinate; but they differ from concrete
beings in being subject neither to change nor to the possible loss of being.
There is thus no reason to include them, together with concrete beings, in a
hierarchy of finite items in the ordinary sense of the term. Though the determinate structures of Being are limited, this implies that structure does not
comprise the totality of Being and God. Yet we have acknowledged this
already by adopting the thesis that the structure of Being is an aspect of a
more inclusive complex. Determination, as limitation by negation, merely
reinforces the need for a richer view of Being and God and does not entail
the finitude of these conceptions in any customary sense. We can then agree
with Plato that the structure of being is both eternal and non-derivative.[11] As
a consequence, we are free to incorporate that structure as a non-derivative
aspect of Being and God without the need to include all finite things.

We have now enriched the account of the determinate aspect of Being
and God by giving it a content that is both eternal and non-derivative. Yet
if one accepts the argument to this effect, further questions arise about the
need for a dialectical position. At this stage, we might claim that we do not
need a triad of aspects, and that we can formulate the meaning of Being by
making an exclusive reference to the *structure*. The earlier objection to the
identification of Being and God with structure rested on the claim that the
structure of Being presupposes Being as the ultimate concept, and we supported that claim by making the assumption that the structures of being
are finite. However, if those structures are eternal and non-derivative, we
might wonder whether they presuppose a notion more nearly basic than
themselves. As non-dependent and not subject to change, they are already
an aspect of Being and God. May we not then eliminate any reference to
mystery and power and return to the identification of Being with structure? Were we to do this, we could claim that the limitation of the structure of Being is present, only when parts of that structure are considered
separately; and when we take them together, we could argue that the structure of Being comprises a complex but unlimited totality. In addition, it
might seem that the exclusive identification of Being with *structure* would
enable us to lay aside the troublesome reference to mystery; and it would
no longer be necessary to undertake the even more difficult task of
attempting to effect a unification of the aspects of *structure*, mystery, and
power. It thus might seem that the demand for a dialectical position is

vacuous and that the structure of Being comprises the exclusive meaning of Being and God.

However, it soon becomes evident that the foregoing problems cannot be laid aside and that the demand for a dialectical view of the concepts of Being and God must be acknowledged. First, the view that God is identical with the structure of Being is itself dialectical. Whether or not the structures of Being are distinct from the world, we can draw a distinction between these structures taken in themselves and structures as they constitute the structure of the finite order. A duality of aspects pertaining to structure arises; and in the process, it generates a demand for an account of their unity.

In addition, we might ask whether the structures of Being have being, either as distinct from the world or in their dependent role as abstractible aspects of the cosmos taken as a whole. Since we are considering the possibility that Being is identical with the structure of Being, the answer to this question would be that the structures of Being presuppose themselves as the meaning of Being. Yet when we give this answer the structure of Being becomes the self-referential structure of itself. This consideration leads to further distinctions. Contrasts emerge between the structure of Being taken in itself, the structure of Being as requiring structure, and the structure of Being as providing the structure for itself. We would then be committed to show that we can unify the terms of these distinctions within a single, concrete notion.

Finally, we must not only confront the demand for dialectical unification in terms of the concept of structure, but the concepts of mystery and power also reemerge as essential components in the discussion of the meaning of Being and God. The need for mystery as an aspect arises in the following way: When the structure of Being presupposes itself as the meaning of Being, either we stop the regress of presupposed to presupposing arbitrarily, and the question of the meaning of the structure of Being is left unanswered; or the regress continues indefinitely, so that mystery appears in the guise of the regress itself. In either case, we cannot understand the meaning of Being by making exclusive reference to the *structure*. In the first case, silence indicates the inadequacy of a reference to structure as an answer to the question before us and points to the mystery of Being. In the second instance, the appearance of an infinite regress shows that reference to the *structure* is not sufficient as an answer. We must give that answer repeatedly; and as a consequence, it does not constitute a terminus. This leads us once again to silence. Repetition of this kind indicates the presence of mystery as a regulative demand; as a consequence, a duality of aspects reemerges, not only between two sides of the *structure* of Being, but also between the *structure* of Being and mystery.

The critic might suggest that we can compress the regress into an internal, circular relationship, which requires a perpetual, infinite vacillation from one aspect of the complex to the other.[12] In this case, the regress would not be linear, but circular; and the model of an infinite regress would be replaced by self-referential circularity. In any case, the transition from one aspect to the other would be dynamic and unending, and it would not terminate in the structure of Being as an unambiguous answer to the question about the meaning of Being and God.

It is a mistake to suggest that a reference to Being and God as identical with even an eternal *logos* is adequate as an account of their nature. The structure of Being does appear as a permanent and non-derivative aspect of Being and God, and it provides an intelligible content for the determinate side of those fundamental notions. However, the identification of Being and God with structure leads to the demand for dialectical unification, issues in the reemergence of mystery, and reinforces a unification between the aspects of structure and mystery, even where the nature of structure is more complex than it appeared at the outset.

I have suggested that even if we regard the *logos* as an eternal aspect of Being and God, mystery reemerges as an irreducible component of both concepts. In addition, we must not forget that power is also an aspect of Being and God, since structure and mystery presuppose it and since it provides a term that mediates between them. In fact, power is a necessary component, even when mystery and structure are understood as eternal and inescapable. The relation among these terms is not temporal, but logical; and in referring to them, we have reached the standpoint of autonomous, self-referential circularity.

We should observe that just as in the case of the structure of Being, power is a dialectical concept. Taken by itself, we should distinguish it from power as embodied in every concrete being; and as a consequence, immanent and transcendent modes of power emerge. In addition, power is related self-referentially to itself. As a consequence, we should ask whether the power of Being has Being, and the answer would involve a reference to the power of Being as a self-transcendent ground.

In addition, power bears the following relations to the other concepts of the triad: first, it presupposes mystery in the manner in which the structure of Being also presupposes it. As before, mystery appears in the arbitrary refusal to continue to ask the question of the meaning of Being with respect to power, or in the need to ask that question repeatedly. Second, power presupposes the *logos* in terms of which we can make its dynamic activity partially intelligible. For this additional reason, we should not exclude *logos* as a necessary aspect of the meaning of Being and God. Finally, *logos* presupposes power, and not simply itself, together with mystery. As the self-referential structure of itself, it must be, in order to be structured. The structure of being thus presupposes the power to be.

In the previous paragraphs, I have not only attempted to exhibit the relations of mutual presupposition among the concepts of mystery, power, and structure, but have also argued that power constitutes a middle term between the other two. It is both a common ground and a common point of intersection between them. In light of these distinctions, we must ask the question: Do the foregoing considerations provide us with a solution for the problem of the meaning and unity of Being and God?

We have claimed that the aspects of Being and God are interrelated as a series of mutual, self-referential presuppositions, and we might suggest that these mutual interrelations provide us with the unity we seek. In addition, as a middle term between the others, power binds them together and provides an additional dimension of the unity in need. Yet before we can consider this suggestion, we should observe an asymmetry in the mutual relations among the aspects of Being and God. I have claimed that power and the *logos* presuppose themselves; that each presupposes the other, and that both presuppose the notion of mystery. In addition, mystery presupposes power in a dual way: It presupposes the power of self-manifestation, and it presupposes the power to be. On the other hand, I have not claimed that mystery presupposes itself, or that it presupposes the structure of being. Rather, it manifests itself as possessing the power of indeterminate existence.

If mystery is indeterminate, and if it fails to presuppose either itself or the structure of Being, it might seem that we cannot integrate the notion in question as an aspect in a larger whole. Mystery is irreducibly transcendent; and though it bears some relations to the other concepts, these relations are always asymmetrical. It would appear that the circularity of the notions of Being and God is thereby called into question. Yet if the concepts of mystery, *logos*, and power fail to form a bounded whole, how can we speak about their unity? It would seem that what unity there is is only partial and that we must construe the concepts of Being and God as open-ended notions. The element of truth in this suggestion is that the notions in question do not comprise a static, stable complex. Rather, their relation to one another is inherently dialectical, and this dialectical relation prevents the unification of its aspects in a bounded whole.

However, the foregoing fact about this relation does not prevent a certain kind of unity. It does not prevent the kind of unity that we can find by analogy in every concrete being. This fact suggests that we may regard the complex of terms before us as a special kind of being, where a being is a structured center of power. Ordinary beings are unified with respect to the past and the present; and the unity in question is dynamic and changing, since these beings face an open-ended future. The unity appropriate to beings is an accomplished fact only with reference to the past, and unity with respect to the future represents a task that they must undertake anew in every changing situation.

By analogy, I suggest that we should understand Being and God as a being, the unity of which must be accomplished repeatedly. In this case, the relations between these pivotal concepts are logical rather than temporal, and the repeated "accomplishment" of *de facto* unity is never problematic as in ordinary cases. This is due to the fact that God and Being always have sufficient power to affect it, though this fact fails to change the fundamental structure of their internal constitution.

The suggestion that we should understand Being and God as a special kind of being might seem to involve a radical mistake, especially in the light of my earlier arguments to show that we must distinguish them from the realm of concrete things. Yet at this stage of the discussion it should be clear that those earlier considerations depended on an inadequate understanding of both concepts. In those earlier arguments, I assumed that the concepts of Being and God are incompatible with the concept of determination. I therefore drew a radical contrast between the concepts of Being and God and the concept of a being. In this final stage of the discussion, I attempted to show that contrary to this assumption, it is possible to incorporate the determinate structure of Being as an aspect of Being and God. The presence of this structure makes possible the truth of the thesis that Being and God are a special kind of being.

One further condition must be fulfilled before the concept of a being can be used to interpret the meaning of Being and God. It is essential that these notions be construed as a series of mutual, self-referential presuppositions in which the concept of power plays a central role. Unless this form of self-reference and mutual presupposition were present, it would be possible to claim that Being and God are identical with a set of abstractions that lack the concreteness necessary for the application of the concept of a being. Self-reference, presupposition, and determination provide a triad of conditions that are necessary for using this concept appropriately. Their presence undermines the rationale on which recognition of the ontological difference (*BT*, 34, 70) depends and makes possible the resolution of the problem of the unity of Being and God.

Chapter 10

Metaphor, Analogy, and the Nature of Truth

In philosophical discussions about the nature of Truth, philosophers often draw a distinction between claims that are true and the meaning of Truth. For those who are familiar with the history of the problem, a further contrast emerges between the meaning of Truth and the concept of the highest Truth. We can therefore distinguish among truths, Truth, and the highest Truth as separate contexts in which the problem of Truth arises for reflective consideration. In light of these distinctions, approaching the problem of Truth also appears to have a threefold focus: At first approximation, truths are the preoccupation of scientific inquiry; the meaning of Truth is the special province of philosophy; and the highest Truth is the subject matter of theological speculation. Thus, just as there are three domains in which the problem of Truth arises, so there are three approaches to the problem as it presents itself within each separate region. These approaches overlap, for every theory of the meaning of Truth purports to be true; most of us wonder whether it is true that there is a highest Truth; and Truth and the highest Truth come together for those views that hold that the nature and existence of the highest being are identical (*ST*, 1:235). If the highest being knows what is true because of its own nature, and if the essence of this being is identical with its existence, then the truth that it knows is the Truth that it is, which we must identify in turn with Truth itself. This is the reason why the identity of Truth and the highest Truth point toward philosophy and religion simultaneously—themes to which we will return at the conclusion of this chapter.

In this final chapter, I will begin with the philosophical concern with the nature of Truth and with the traditional philosophical theories that explicate its meaning. In the process, I will connect these theories with their scientific and theological counterparts, seeking to do justice to the scientific attempt to find the truth and to the theological concern with the highest Truth. However, I will also develop an account of the nature of Truth that is not only related to these other regions, but that will also permit me to explicate it in terms of the role of metaphorical and analogical discourse in human experience. My fundamental purpose is to focus attention on the threefold nature of the problem of Truth and to articulate its significance in metaphorical and analogical terms.

The most familiar place to begin is with the correspondence theory and with the definition of Truth as the adequation of the intellect to the real order. According to the traditional Aristotelian formulation,

> To say of what is that it is not, or of what is not that it is, is false, while to say of what is that it is, and of what is not that it is not, is true; so that he who says of anything that it is, or that it is not, will say either what is true or what is false [. . .].[1]

We can translate the "is" of Aristotle's definition in either existential or predicative terms; and depending on the translation, the real-order correlate of what we think or say can be either a thing or a fact. According to the existential formulation, what is spoken about is "what is," while on the predicative version of the definition, what is thought or said is "what is so."[2] This point is important for our later discussion, for according to most modern versions of the correspondence theory, what corresponds with thoughts or statements is a fact about a thing rather than the thing itself. By contrast, Aristotle's definition leaves open the possibility that the objective term of the correspondence relation can be either a fact or a thing, depending on the philosophical intentions of the one who makes the original statement.

It is also important to notice what is perhaps a less familiar fact: Thomistic versions of the correspondence theory not only emphasize the adequation of intellect and thing, but also the adequation of a thing to its own nature and its adequation to the divine idea in accord with which God creates it.[3] In fact, the order of adequation on the Thomistic theory reverses the directionality of the original Aristotelian definition. According to the Thomistic account, the first level of correspondence is between a thing and an idea; the second is between a thing and its own nature; and the third is between the intellect and the thing as a created being in the real order.

According to this view, to be true is first to correspond with God's ideas; then to correspond to one's own nature; and finally, to be true in the more familiar sense of a correspondence relation between the intellect and the fact or object about which we make judgments.

We must not overlook the fact that philosophers in the modern period cancel this reversal of direction, where the first two senses of correspondence drop away and where the real-order object of correspondence at the third level becomes a fact understood as an object of consciousness. From Descartes onward, with only a few notable exceptions, the objects to which thoughts correspond are facts about those objects, which are in turn modeled after the thoughts that appear within the original correspondence relation.[4] According to this view, it is senseless to say that a judgment corresponds with an object rather than a fact, while it is tempting to assume that the facts to which judgments correspond are pale reflections of the conceptual order in terms of which their structure becomes accessible to the cognitive consciousness. The history of the correspondence theory takes us from the world, to God, to consciousness as the fundamental term in the correspondence relation, which in turn tempts us to embrace the philosophical standpoint of transcendental idealism (*CPR*, 117).

Most contemporary criticisms of the correspondence theory presuppose that the objective pole of the correspondence relation is a fact rather than a thing, but most of them also move beyond their Kantian ancestors by assimilating facts to the linguistic order. For example, in the most well-known debate about the correspondence theory in contemporary philosophy, P. F. Strawson insists that facts are linguistic entities and that their obvious kinship with "that-clauses" is a clear reflection of their linguistic origins.[5] In particular, it is a fact that the "indestructible" Titanic once sank into the ocean; and it is also a fact that its builders and designers were amazed when this occurred. Yet in this case, what they were amazed about was the sad but verifiable truth that the ocean liner sank from view. We can formulate this truth in the statement that the Titanic plunged down into the ocean, and one might wonder what this truth could be other than the true statement that this episode occurred.

The transition from facts to truths by means of "that-clauses," and the transition from a truth to a true statement, would scarcely be plasible unless the transformations precipitated by the transcendental turn (*CPR*, 134) lay behind each step of these transitions. In the final analysis, these transitions occur because of the conviction that only objects are in the world and that our cognitive access to them presupposes that facts lose their existential status and become objects of consciousness.[6] Yet when this occurs, and when we notice the analogy between the fact that S is P and the statement that this is the case, what could be more tempting than to suggest that facts are true statements masquerading as objective entities? The fate of the correspondence theory, with its robust sense of reality in both religious and philosophical contexts, is thus a paradox of transformation. What began as a doctrine about the distinction between the mind and the world, and about the relation between the real and the logical orders, became a domesticated offshoot of the modern triumph of subjectivity.

There was another voice in the contemporary debate about the correspondence theory, and in his paper, "Unfair to Facts," J. L. Austin attempts to demonstrate that facts are not linguistic entities, but are items in the world by analogy with things.[7] He says that just as targets can be what correct signals signal, so facts can be what true statements state. In both cases, Austin claims that the subject term is in the world and that there is no reason to reduce either of them to its linguistic counterpart.[8] However, what Austin overlooks in comparing facts with objects is that we can understand a fact as a true statement in use rather than as a special kind of object. Thus, the contrast between "What we state is always a fact" and "What we state is always a statement" need not point to the distinction between a fact and the corresponding statement that picks it out, but simply to the distinction between a true statement in use and this same statement that we mention. When we state a fact, we make a true statement; and when we "state" a statement, we mention what we might state on another occasion. Yet neither case requires that we refer to facts as objects in the real order.

Austin attempts to buttress his argument by reminding us that the original meaning of the word "fact" connects it with a deed or an action and that there is no etymological justification for assimilating facts to the "that-clauses" that typically express them.[9] However, even if we understand a fact as either an act or a deed, assimilating facts to things or events, the correspondence between fact and statement undermines this reconstruction. The statement that S is P scarcely seems to correspond with a thing or an event, and to reconstrue facts in these terms would seem to deprive the correspondence relation of its objective correlate. Austin says that to deny that facts are in the world is to flirt with idealism, for he sees the implications of the history of the correspondence theory in its modern transformations.[10] However, Austin never considers the possibility that the best way to resist linguistic idealism is not to insist that facts are special kinds of objects or events, but to claim that statements reconstrued as natural objects correspond with them. In this case, structured object would correspond with structured object, and there would no longer be any transcategorial tension in the claim that statements mirror their objective counterparts in the real order.[11]

I will consider how this reconstructed correspondence relation can be obtained at a later stage of my argument; but at this juncture, the important point to notice is that this proposal takes us back to the existential version of Aristotle's original definition of Truth. It also preserves the otherness of the real order, and by implication, calls our attention to the Radical Otherness of God. According to this account of the nature of Truth, the essential mark of Truth is the distinction between the subject and the object; and we must acknowledge this contrast if we are to preserve the correspondence theory of Truth as a way of pointing to a primordial relation. Perhaps a stronger way to make this point is to say that there is no Truth without Radical Otherness and that otherwise, Truth as correspondence would become a pale linguistic surrogate of a real-order relation. However justified the reduction of facts to statements might be, we must acknowledge the otherness of things to prevent Truth from vanishing into a cluster of conceptual relations.

The correspondence theory of Truth lies buried beneath the wreckage wrought by the modern preoccupation with subjectivity. There is no clearer evidence for this than the repudiation of the correspondence theory by other theories of Truth that reject the value of radical externality as a necessary condition for Truth. For example, proponents of the coherence theory turn away from the concept of truth as adequation, claiming that Truth is a relation among epistemic and conceptual elements and that there is no justification for a theory that attempts to bind the real and the logical orders together by a merely external relation. The core of the coherence theory is its commitment to the concept of approximation. However, what is approximated in this case is not an object related externally to a subject, but a system of truths in which every claim to Truth must find its place as a constituent element. As a result, truth ceases to be a relation of adequation and becomes the systematic Whole within which we must include every individual truth. Brand Blanshard formulates the point in *The Nature of Thought*:

> Truth is the approximation of thought to reality. It is thought on its way home. Its measure is the distance thought has traveled, under guidance of its inner compass, toward that intelligible system which unites its ultimate object with its ultimate end. Hence at any given time the degree of truth in our experience as a whole is the degree of system it has achieved. The degree of truth of a particular proposition is to be judged in the first instance by its coherence with experience as a whole, ultimately by its

coherence with that further whole, all-comprehensive and fully articulated, in which thought can come to rest.[12]

In laying the foundation for the pragmatic tradition, Charles Sanders Peirce expresses a similar view about Truth and approximation when he claims that if belief "were to tend indefinitely toward absolute fixity"[13] we would have truth; and when he adds that "the opinion which is fated to be ultimately agreed to by all who investigate, is what we mean by truth."[14] The Peircean pragmatist is not simply an idealist, for he insists that the final opinion is infinitely distant from any finite stage of inquiry and that it displays the externality of a regulative ideal.[15] Nevertheless, both idealism and pragmatism commit themselves to the view that there is a conceptual commensurability between the truth of an individual judgment and a final opinion or a completed system. As a result, both positions maintain that the approximation relation is not merely external, since every judgment is either a partial embodiment of the system it presupposes or related conceptually to the final opinion with which we should compare it. An organic metaphor also lies behind these accounts of approximation, and it replaces the external relation of the correspondence theory with the internal relation among the stages of an unfolding system of Truth or inquiry. As Blanshard suggests in echoing some earlier remarks of Hegel:

> If we want analogies for the relation of our thought to the system that forms its end, we should leave aside such things as mirrors and number systems and their ways of conforming to objects, and think of the relation between seed and flower, or between the sapling and the tree.[16]

In both examples, the seed and the sapling simply are their ends realized imperfectly. Thus, Blanshard suggests that a thought is its object in the organic process of developing toward systematic completion, while Peirce's pragmatic definition implies that thought is the process of inquiry that will always attempt to come to rest in the Truth of a final opinion.

One of the consequences of this organic metaphor and of the theory of approximation that it embodies is that it enables the idealist to repudiate the spatial otherness of the correspondence theory and to transform it into the temporal expectation that Truth will one day appear as a completed system. In this way, the contrast between the subject and the object becomes the distinction between two stages of an unfolding process, the end of which is present at the beginning as an implicit element. The Peircean suggestion that a community of inquirers can approximate the final opinion also permits the pragmatic tradition to accommodate the scientific demand that Truth be achieved within the framework of a philosophical definition of Truth. In this case, the meaning of Truth as a final opinion becomes the goal of the scientific quest for Truth and the foundation for the scientific enterprise that we can understand as a process of inquiry.

The idealistic commitment to a systematic whole in which Truth can be found and the pragmatic suggestion that we can approximate this system only in an indefinite series of stages imply that openness to the process of inquiry is a necessary condition for the emergence of Truth in systematic form. If Radical Otherness is a necessary condition for Truth according to the correspondence theory, and if the coherence and the pragmatic theories transform the spatial otherness of objects into a series of temporal stages that approximates the end of the process progressively, this goal is accessible only if we are open to it in the act of scientific inquiry. As a result, openness to Truth becomes a necessary condition for its complete realization.

However, it is equally important to notice that in transforming the otherness of objects into a sequence of stages that are related internally to the goal of inquiry, the coherence and pragmatic theories also seek to acknowledge the concept of otherness as an element in their unfolding conception of Truth. According to both accounts, the concept of otherness points to the cognitive separation between part and Whole and between beginning and end that makes the process of inquiry necessary, while the concept of openness points to the stages of approximation that make the goal of inquiry accessible to the cognitive consciousness. As a result, both theories involve openness and otherness as necessary conditions under which Truth can emerge in systematic terms.

In a more traditional formulation, I have been suggesting that the "long-run" dimension of the pragmatic theory[17] and the degree of Truth dimension of the coherence theory[18] presuppose the concept of openness, while the separation between the subject and the object of the correspondence theory points to the concept of Radical Otherness. In addition, I have suggested that a transformed conception of otherness is an integral element of the idealistic and pragmatic attempts to understand the nature of Truth and that we must presuppose both openness and otherness if we are to say what is true within the scientific context of cognition. Yet, when we take openness and otherness together, and when we take their nature as epistemic conditions of Truth into account, we must not overlook the fact that the concept of the highest Truth also becomes a crucial element in the attempt to define the nature of Truth. Because they are oriented either toward a larger Whole or toward a final opinion, the idealistic and pragmatic theories point to a highest Truth that we must acknowledge if Truth is to be possible within a finite context.

This highest Truth is not a highest being, but a cognitive ideal that is to be approximated progressively as Truth itself unfolds. However, the definitions of Truth in terms of systematic completeness or of a final opinion are modern ways of identifying the nature of Truth with an ontological condition that we must not reduce to any finite stage in the process of inquiry. The Radical Otherness of the correspondence theory with which we began and the openness and otherness of the idealistic and pragmatic theories toward which we have moved call our attention to an ultimate Truth in terms of which we can appraise particular claims to truth. As a consequence, the otherness of religion and the openness of philosophy begin to have a bearing on one another in our attempt to understand the nature of Truth.

In evaluating these traditional accounts of the nature of Truth, it is important to emphasize the fact that the concepts of openness and otherness are irreducible elements in any attempt to understand the nature of Truth and that we must preserve these concepts if we are to give an adequate account of its nature in philosophical terms. However, it is also clear that these concepts can degenerate easily and can become inadequate modes of access to the Truth they attempt to articulate. We have observed already that according to traditional criticisms of the correspondence theory, the objective pole of the correspondence relation often vanishes into a tissue of linguistic entities. Facts that are first present in the real order collapse into a set of truths about a set of objects; and these truths, in turn, become statements that some philosophers locate in a conceptual domain. In light of criticisms of this kind, it might appear that all that survives of the correspondence relation is an unmediated contrast between a subject and an object that is related only tangentially to the correspondence between statement and fact that proponents of the correspondence theory attempt to articulate. The idealistic theory attempts to remedy this by transforming the Radical Otherness of correspondence into the epistemic otherness of an unfolding sequence of cognitions.

Yet we must also notice that just as an unmediated and unintelligible otherness is all that seems to survive of the correspondence theory, so a dimension of absolute openness that fails to issue in a final Truth is all that remains when we subject the idealistic theory's conception of the Whole to serious scrutiny. We must not identify the Whole with an infinite collection of truths, for such a Whole is self-contradictory; and if we say that the Whole is what allows us to understand a collection of items taken as a whole, the concept of wholeness becomes partially indeterminate. The collection in question is always numerically indefinite, which entails that the concept of the Whole shifts its meaning, depending on the number and the character of the constituents it orders. Yet this means that the Whole is an open-ended context that determinate limits do not bound completely. Other contents can always emerge within any collection that the Whole must then attempt to harmonize, and we can never be certain that the relationships among these elements will not present new configurations that will require holistic modifications. It thus appears that the concept of the Whole explodes into an open-ended context that requires perpetual modification; and as a result, openness alone seems to survive as a mark of that version of the Truth that seeks systematic completion.

Finally, absolute openness and external opposition are all that remain, even when Radical Otherness is taken up into the pragmatic modification of traditional idealistic theories. If Truth is a regulative ideal, as the Peircean pragmatist suggests, and if the end toward which the quest for Truth orients itself exists at an infinite distance from any stage within the quest itself, openness to it becomes the quest for a mystery that the pragmatic journey can never reveal, even in principle. Yet in this case, the quest for Truth as an infinite process is reduced once more to openness, which we cannot distinguish from the mystery of the end toward which the quest for Truth is directed. If we cannot understand the externality of the end that stands in contrast with us as a determinate cluster of truths, but must identify it with a goal that lures the process of inquiry, this goal becomes an external principle that will never be accessible to the finite consciousness. The radical externality between the subject and the object into which the correspondence theory has degenerated is transposed into the dyad of the pragmatic "long-run," and the existential separation between the process and the *telos* of inquiry becomes a chasm that cognitive discourse can never mediate. As a result, even the Peircean pragmatist must face the fact that according to the implications of his own system, there is no Truth, but at best an open-ended framework of otherness that requires specification.

If openness and otherness are necessary conditions for Truth, but if these conditions as the traditional theories of the nature of Truth understand them have degenerated radically, questions arise quite naturally about how we can reinterpret these concepts in order to avoid the defects of the earlier accounts. For example, we might wonder how we can preserve the openness and the otherness characteristic of idealistic and pragmatic theories without reducing them to the mystery of absolute openness, on the one hand, or to the cognitive inaccessibility of a regulative ideal on the other. Furthermore, we might ask how we can recapture the robust sense of reality to which the correspondence theory calls our attention without the subject-object relation that it presupposes degenerating into an unmediated opposition. One way of answering these questions is to transform the openness and the otherness of idealistic and pragmatic theories into a special kind of discourse that exhibits an openness and otherness of its own, understanding the Radical Otherness of the correspondence theory in terms of two kinds of language that transcend literal discourse.

As I have suggested in previous chapters, the open-ended mode of discourse that I have in mind is metaphorical in structure and allows us to preserve the commitments of the idealistic and the pragmatic theories to openness and otherness in intelligible terms. By contrast, the second kind of language involves analogical predication and is an extension of customary theories of analogy, understood as proportions, into a vehicle for the redefinition of Truth in metaphorical and analogical ways. Of course, just what metaphorical and analogical language are, whether they are indeed special or distinct forms of discourse, and if so, how we are to relate these different kinds of language to one another, are difficult questions that we ought to examine in their own right. However, since I cannot deal with all of these questions here, I presuppose a view of metaphor and analogy of the kind that I have used in earlier chapters and that is like that of others who have defended the view that they are autonomous modes of discourse.[19] In what follows I will assume that metaphors and analogies are not reducible to literal statements or to one another; and on this basis, I will attempt to show that both kinds of language have distinct roles to play in giving us access to a conception of Truth that avoids the defects of the earlier accounts.

There are three dimensions of metaphorical discourse that have a bearing on the problem of Truth as we have begun to understand it. First, a metaphor contains structural elements that we can understand as intelligible units and that allow us to identify the metaphor as a whole with a complex interaction of determinate constituents. For example, the "rosy-fingered dawn" contains a set of terms that we can distinguish from one another and that allow us to identify the metaphor in which they occur in terms of an antecedent set of intelligible elements. Second, a metaphor combines its structural elements in a unique and unexpected fashion, generating an open-ended product that can issue in a potentially infinite series of interpretations. As a result, an inherent indeterminacy supplements the structural dimension of a metaphor and allows metaphorical discourse to transcend any finite sequence of determinate responses. Finally, the structural elements of a metaphor stand in tension with one another, and it is this tensional element that accounts for the uniqueness of the metaphor and that drives the process of interpretation forward from stage to stage. To return to our original example, the "rosy-fingered dawn" is not only a unique combination of familiar elements, but is also a tensional unity that can produce an endless cluster of interpretations. Thus, a metaphor is a complex mixture of structural determinations, radical indeterminacy, and a tensional dimension, all appearing in a linguistic expression as a tensional unity.[20]

Though some philosophers assume that we can never relate metaphor and Truth in positive terms, we can bring together the features of metaphorical language that we have just considered into relation with our earlier discussion of the openness and the otherness characteristic of idealistic and pragmatic theories. First, we can correlate the open-ended richness of metaphorical discourse with the temporal openness of idealism and pragmatism, not only because the sequence of interpretations that a metaphor generates constitutes a temporal series of cognitive elements, but also because this sequence can never exhaust the metaphor as a regulative ideal to which we must relate every interpretation of it. In both cases, the indeterminate dimension of a metaphor reflects the inherent indeterminacy of earlier theories, pointing simultaneously to the openness and inexhaustibility of Truth as they appear in these more traditional accounts. Second, the structural dimension of metaphorical discourse serves to give us access to the kind of intelligible content that the quest for Truth attempts to make accessible without suggesting that any finite set of structural determinations can ever exhaust Truth. It is the special merit of idealistic and pragmatic theories that they refuse to reduce the quest for Truth to structural terms, even though neither theory ever succeeds in binding together the determinate and indeterminate dimensions that a metaphor displays as characteristics of its own nature.

The relevance of metaphorical discourse to the problem of Truth emerges from the fact that a metaphor is an intersection of indeterminacy and determination, allowing a metaphor to hold together the open-endedness of the quest for Truth with the structures that the determinate content of Truth requires. The tensional element present in metaphorical discourse reflects the tension displayed in the process of inquiry as it moves from stage to stage within the scientific context of cognition. Even though it is an epistemic process, the stages of the process of inquiry are partially external to one another, and resistance arises as this process unfolds toward the cognitive unity it attempts to achieve. In fact, it is this moment of resistance between stages of the process that allows both idealism and pragmatism to incorporate a dimension of otherness into their conceptions of the meaning of Truth. However, what is most important to notice is that metaphorical discourse not only exhibits this same kind of tension, but it does so in a fashion that allows us to make access to the tension and the structural elements of a metaphor that manifests itself as an open-ended unity. In the end, the superiority of metaphorical discourse as a mode of access to Truth lies in the fact that it can become a microcosm in which determinacy, indeterminacy, and tension exist together as a unified phenomenon. In this way, all the elements that are necessary for Truth as the idealist and pragmatist understand it are present in a metaphor and are accessible to the cognitive consciousness in a tensional unity.

The principle defect of both idealism and pragmatism is that neither theory is able to unify the intelligible structure, the open-endedness, and the dimension of otherness that make Truth accessible within the context of cognitive inquiry. We can see this most clearly from the fact that idealism degenerates easily into absolute openness and that Peircean pragmatism seems to commit itself to an external and unmediated opposition between the end toward which it orients itself and any finite stage in the quest for absolute comprehension. By contrast, I have claimed that metaphorical discourse avoids these degenerations by binding together the openness, the otherness, and the intelligible structure that the quest for Truth presupposes. In fact, we might even argue that both idealism and pragmatism presuppose crucial metaphors, and that in the end, it is these metaphors that make Truth as both a religious and a philosophical phenomenon possible in these more traditional accounts.

The concept of the Whole is a metaphorical extension from finite contexts where bounded totalities occur, and the concept of the pragmatic "long run" is a metaphor for bounded contexts in which we posit a limit in contrast with a determinate sequence of developing stages. In both cases, the strength and suggestiveness of the positions in question depend on the fact that these metaphors unify all the elements necessary for framing an adequate account of the nature of Truth. The corresponding defects of these theories result from the fact that their proponents do not understand these metaphors for what they are, allowing them to degenerate into only one or two of the elements that make Truth possible in metaphorical terms. On the other hand, the strongest claim that we can make for the role of metaphor in giving us access to Truth is that the traditional accounts that we have rejected are theoretical degenerations from the metaphors on which they depend.[21]

The suggestion that both idealism and pragmatism rest on a metaphorical foundation should not be surprising, for the linguistic character of a metaphor is commensurable with the conceptual dimension that dominates both of these traditional accounts. The idealist and the pragmatist attempt to define Truth in conceptual terms, incorporating otherness only in the guise of opposition between one conceptual stage and another or in the contrast between all of these stages and the end toward which the quest for Truth is directed. However, even if the predominance of conceptual elements in these earlier accounts encourages us to reconstruct the positive insights of both theories in metaphorical terms, questions still arise about which metaphors are most fruitful in giving us access to Truth, and about how we can embrace metaphorical discourse without imprisoning ourselves within a linguistic idealism that cuts us off from the real order. Must we not finally face the fact that otherness of a merely intralinguistic kind is not sufficient to anchor our account of the nature of Truth? Formulated in a different way, must we not incorporate a stronger sense of otherness into our discussion if our position is not to degenerate into a tissue of merely linguistic entities? I believe that the answer to these questions is clear and that the only way to avoid linguistic idealism is to return to the positive insight of the correspondence theory about the externality between subject and object, grafting this concept of otherness onto the metaphorical dimension of our constructive account.

As I have indicated already, we can do this by introducing a kind of language that transcends literal discourse but that also stands in contrast with the metaphorical language that lies at the foundation of the idealistic and the pragmatic positions. This mode of discourse is analogical in structure and seeks to do justice to the externality between the subject and the object that the correspondence theory presupposes. We can make the crucial point in the following way: Even if we reduce facts within the world to truths and transform these truths into linguistic entities, it is still possible to claim that we can bind the subject and the object together in a Truth relation by a set of analogies, all of which are elements of the real order. As I suggested in my earlier discussion of Austin, these analogies would hold between utterance and object rather than between statement and fact and would preserve the dimension of difference to which our earlier discussion of the correspondence theory has called our attention. At the same time, the analogies in question would preserve the structural dimension of the relation between structured utterance and the structured object without which Truth would vanish into the unintelligibility of sheer externality. In the following paragraphs, I will elaborate this concept of analogy and attempt to show how I can conjoin it with my earlier discussion of metaphorical discourse to yield a revised conception of the nature of Truth. In the process, I will attempt to show how I can transcend the apparently linguistic character of a metaphor and how I can bring it into an analogical connection with the real order so that I can define Truth in objective terms.

In the previous paragraphs, I have suggested that the use of metaphorical and analogical discourse will allow us to preserve the positive insights of traditional theories of Truth and that both kinds of language have a crucial role to play in giving us access to a revised conception of Truth that avoids the defects of the earlier accounts. The openness and the otherness of idealism and pragmatism are present in the open-ended structure of a metaphor, and we can reinterpret the intelligible otherness of the correspondence relation as an analogical relation between a subject and an object in the real order. However, when we take both considerations into account, two difficulties arise about how we can bring these two different modes of discourse together. On the one hand, as we have noted already, the linguistic character of a metaphor seems to imply that we can understand Truth only in intralinguistic terms and that to move in this direction is to imprison ourselves in a web of words. On the other hand, the characterization of analogy as a real order relation suggests that Truth transcends language and that it has nothing to do with the openness and otherness that metaphorical discourse exemplifies.

In spite of these apparent difficulties, perhaps we should consider the possibility that we can bring the metaphorical dimension of language into an analogical relation with the real order and that we can connect the openness and the otherness of idealism and pragmatism with the more radical conception of otherness characteristic of the correspondence theory. In this way, we can bring a metaphorical utterance into an analogical relation with a structured object, allowing us to bind the openness and the otherness of previous theories together into an intelligible relation. In what follows, I will develop some of the implications of this paradoxical suggestion, attempting to show how we are to understand the object of cognition and the analogical relation in which it stands, and how we must reinterpret analogy if it is to bind a metaphorical utterance and a structured object together in an intelligible relation.

The first step in developing this account of the nature of Truth is to notice that the analogies that bind a subject and an object together are analogies between developing and partially indeterminate contents rather than static substances that merely stand apart in radical opposition. Both the subject and the object of a Truth relation are spatio-temporal entities that are never fully determinate; and as a result, we must understand both the language and the objects of cognition as open-ended contents subject to change and development. However, this point suggests that we must not only use metaphorical discourse to characterize a subject that has a place within a process of inquiry, but must also use the same kind of language to describe the objects of inquiry as present to the cognitive consciousness. There is a sense in which we can find metaphors, not only in language, but also in the world; for as we claimed in our discussion of the nature of Being and God, objects to which metaphorical utterances point are both structured and open-ended by analogy with the metaphors that give us access to them.[22] As I understand the concept, it is the task of analogy to bind these metaphors together and to hold them apart.

Metaphors are in the world in an extended sense of the term; and in this respect, the objective use of "metaphor" is a metaphorical extension of its usual signification. However, this does not cancel the fact that the structured objects to which we can relate metaphorical utterances display a partial indeterminacy that makes them accessible. We can make the crucial point in a more traditional way by claiming that just as there is both an analogy of language and an analogy of being in the philosophical tradition,[23] so the metaphorical dimension of language has its objective counterpart in a metaphor of being. The purpose of this second kind of metaphor is to call our attention to the fact that we can understand objects as metaphorical extensions of the metaphorical language that gives us access to them, even though these objects exist independently of our attempts to know them in metaphorical terms.

The final step in this philosophical reconstruction is to notice that when we reinterpret objects in metaphorical terms, the analogies that connect the utterance and the object will not simply be structural similarities between determinate elements, but analogical relations between contents that are determinate, intelligible, and open-ended. We must therefore reconstrue analogy as a relation between the openness, the otherness, and the intelligibility of objects like Being, God, and finite entities and the corresponding openness, otherness, and intelligibility of the language that we use to make them accessible. The traditional understanding of analogy construes it in mathematical or structural terms, suggesting that analogies obtain only between one set of structures and another that we can bind together in an isomorphic relation. However, the root analogies that make Truth possible are the much richer analogical relations between cognitive contents that display both determinate and indeterminate dimensions.

Formulated in a different way, what we represent in an analogical relation between a subject and an object is not merely lifeless and schematic, but the concrete content of dynamic entities. Metaphorical structures are the living dimension of the contents to which metaphorical discourse gives us access, while the analogies that bind a metaphorical utterance and a "metaphorical" object together point beyond linguistic episodes to which the quest for Truth is relevant. We can summarize the most accurate version of this revised conception of Truth in the following way: Truth is an analogical relation of conformity between a metaphorical utterance and a "metaphorical" content, where the relation in question transcends the usual restriction of analogy to merely structural elements, and where this relation binds the metaphorical dimension of the utterance and the determinate and indeterminate dimensions of the "object" together into an epistemic nexus.

We can express this account of the nature of Truth more concretely in terms of an example. Consider the metaphorical statement, "John is a fox," and the state of affairs to which this statement calls our attention (that John is a fox). If we understand the correspondence relation between these terms in the traditional way, we might reduce the state of affairs that we express in terms of the "that-clauses" to the statement itself; and this statement would reimprison us in the conceptual framework that the idealistic and pragmatic theories have attempted to explicate. However, if the statement "John is a fox" were transformed into the metaphorical utterance "John-the-fox," and if the state of affairs to which this statement calls our attention were transformed into the structured object, John *qua* fox, or John's being a fox, the analogical relation that binds them together would become a real order relation that both preserves the otherness of the object and that also brings it into an intelligible relation with the subject. Thus, the correspondence theory and the otherness to which it points need not degenerate into the kind of linguistic idealism that has often accompanied the reduction of facts to truths and of truths to a tissue of linguistic entities.

Given the account of Truth that I am proposing, both metaphor and analogy are crucial elements for introducing an intelligible dimension into a Truth-context that would otherwise remain opaque. The first of these elements allows us to preserve the openness and the otherness of the coherence and the pragmatic theories; the second permits us to do justice to the more radical concept of otherness that underlies the correspondence theory; and both proposals attempt to accommodate the intelligible dimension to which we must ultimately connect any theory of Truth. The metaphorical dimension of a linguistic utterance allows it to be both determinate and indeterminate and to point to an open-ended set of future interpretations that will serve to develop its cognitive content. In addition, the analogical conformity between utterance and object allows them to maintain their Radical Otherness as they stand together in a relation that is both determinate and indeterminate at the same time.

In developing this account of the nature of Truth in relation to the other theories that I have considered, I should emphasize the fact that analogy as a relation between metaphorical utterance and "metaphorical" object is a way of unifying the spatial and the temporal dimensions of our earlier discussion and a way of holding together the openness and the otherness to which these dimensions call our attention. The openness and otherness of the idealistic and the pragmatic traditions point to the primacy of time as the fundamental condition that allows Truth to emerge, while the Radical Otherness of the correspondence theory suggests that a spatial element is also involved in the cognitive attempt to bring utterance and object together. According to our own account, Truth is a complex interplay of space and time, openness and otherness, structural and non-structural dimensions, and is a way of binding all these elements together into a metaphorical and analogical nexus. Temporality appears on both sides of the subject-object dichotomy as the tensional and open-ended dimension that allows Truth to transcend conceptual obstacles as it unfolds in the process of inquiry. Moreover, space in the traditional sense appears as a relation between utterance and object that allows us to preserve their otherness while we bind their structural dimensions together into an intelligible connection. Finally, analogy as a relation between open-ended and developing contents is the fundamental concept that brings both the determinate and the indeterminate sides of the object into relation with the corresponding sides of the knowing subject. In this respect, this analogical relation between "metaphorical" elements is the locus of Truth; for it is within this context that space and time, determinacy and indeterminacy, and openness and otherness come together at a point beyond the conflict among traditional accounts.

Having begun our discussion by mentioning the relations among the concept of Truth, particular truths, and the concept of the highest Truth, it is now possible to return to these themes and to their religious implications by noticing that the analogical locus that we embrace is not a Place in any ordinary sense, but is the Place of places within which Truth occurs on particular occasions.[24] The Truth of a particular occasion depends on an analogical relation between a "metaphorical" object and a metaphorical utterance, and it is this condition that must obtain if we are to discover truths in the course of scientific inquiry. The claim that this is so is a philosophical thesis, which has as its focus the meaning of Truth rather than the contexts in which we can find particular truths. It is in this sense that the account that I have been developing involves a Place of places, or in philosophical terms, the ground of Truth as we apprehend it on particular occasions.

However, there is also a sense in which we ought to equate the ground of Truth with the religious conception of the highest Truth. The metaphorical and analogical nexus that makes Truth possible is not simply a Transcendental condition for the emergence of Truth, but is also a network of connections between an utterance and an object that actually obtains. It is for this reason that I have not confined my discussion to the distinction between Truth and truths, but have also focused my attention on the concept of the highest Truth. The Place of places is the Truth that makes truths possible, and it is the condition that binds the utterance and object together in every context where truth can be discovered. It is in this sense that the ground of Truth is both the philosophical condition for truths and the highest religious Truth that these contexts presuppose.

In conclusion, we should notice that when we regard the metaphorical and analogical nexus of Truth as the highest Truth, the temptation vanishes to transform the concept of Truth into an overarching unity that subsumes all other truths within itself. The analogical relation between the subject and the object presupposes both the openness and the otherness of its metaphorical terms, but because this relation holds these two dimensions apart, it also preserves its own integrity in contrast with the terms that find a place within it. One way to acknowledge this fact is to insist that the nexus in question is not a Whole, but is the Place in which we can bring a subject and an object together in cognitive and existential interaction. This philosophical Place is as much like the religious concept of the highest Truth as it is like a Transcendental condition, and this fundamental fact undermines the holistic quest for complete comprehension. When the subject and the object stand in contrast with one another, the object moves "metaphorically" from its original determination toward an open-ended future, while the subject moves from its original indeterminacy to a more determinate grasp of the nature of the thing unfolding before it. As we have noticed already, it is this mirror-image relation between them that binds them together and holds them apart and that constitutes the Truth that we can discover in their interaction. Formulated in terms that are both religious and philosophical at once, Truth is a middle ground conception that exists between absolute opacity and absolute completeness; and it is the Place of places where the highest Truth makes the truth of the imagistic relation between one term and another possible on particular occasions.

Notes

Chapter 1

1. Immanuel Kant discusses the forms of intuition in *The Critique of Pure Reason* (trans. Norman Kemp-Smith; New York: St. Martin's, 1965), 198–201. I am supplementing Kant by suggesting that eternity also makes predication possible without being a predicate.
2. This is the position embraced in Aristotle's *Metaphysics* 1003a18–1004a9, 1004a33–1004b17, 1027b18–1028a5, 1028a31–1028b7, in Barnes; see also Pegis 1:42–45, 115–21, 128–30, and 168–73.
3. Hesiod, *Theogony*; see Brown, 56–57.
4. The dialogues I have in mind are the *Parmenides* and the *Sophist* 126a–166c, 216a–268d, in Cooper.
5. Plato expresses his conception of these issues in his discussion of the divided line in the *Republic* 508d–513e, in Cooper.
6. Monroe Beardsley, "The Metaphorical Twist," *Philosophy and Phenomenological Research* 22.3 (1962): 298–307.
7. Carl G. Vaught, "Hegel and the Problem of Difference: A Critique of Dialectical Reflection," in *Hegel and His Critics* (ed. William Desmond; Albany: State University of New York, 1989), 35–48; and idem, "The Quest for Wholeness and Its Crucial Metaphor and Analogy: The Place of Places," *Ultimate Reality and Meaning* 7 (1984): 157–65.
8. Ibid.

Chapter 2

1. This conception is expressed most clearly in Hegel's account of the history of philosophy and in allusions he makes to the place of his own thought in its development. For a general account of this development, see Haldane, 55, 94–110. For Hegel's conception of the role of his own system in this process, see Haldane and Simpson, 545–54.

2. We can find formulations of Hegel's quest for completeness in *PS*, 51–52, 485–93 and *PM*, 302–15. Hegel insists that difference is just as dominant as identity in the development of the Absolute Process. Yet the fact remains that his system displays philosophical progress and that he describes philosophy as a circle where the beginning and the end of the process are the same. For a discussion of the irreducible role of difference in his system, see *SL*, 82–100, and for a statement about philosophical completeness in terms of the metaphor of circularity, see *SL*, 842.

3. It is important to notice that Heidegger's conception of destruction is not altogether negative. Nevertheless, he intended to dismantle the ontological tradition insofar as it had "degenerated" into a representational version of metaphysics. See *BT*, 41–49.

4. In Hegel's account of the history of philosophy, he rarely mentions Augustine, devotes only two pages to Aquinas and Scotus, and discusses Ockham's philosophy only in a cursory way. See Haldane and Simpson, 37, 69, 71–72, 74, 82–84, 291, and 294.

5. Étienne Gilson is the most well known of the scholars I have in mind. See, for example, Étienne Gilson, *The Christian Philosophy of St. Augustine* (trans. L. E. M. Lynch; New York: Random House, 1960).

6. R. G. Collingwood, *The Idea of Nature* (New York: Oxford University Press, 1960), 94–95.

7. Hesiod, *Theogony*, see Brown, 56–57.

8. Secondary substance in the Aristotelian tradition and "second nature" in the medieval tradition are illustrations of the concept understood in this sense.

9. Aristotle, *Metaphysics* 980a22–27, in Barnes.

10. Erich Auerbach, *Mimesis: The Representation of Reality in Western Literature* (trans. William R. Trask; Princeton: Princeton University Press), 1–20.

11. These intentions are expressed in the *Meditations on First Philosophy*. See *The Philosophical Writings of Descartes*, vol. 2 (trans. John Cottingham, Robert Stoothoff, and Dugald Murdoch; Cambridge: Cambridge University Press, 1984), 2–15, and 24–43.

12. Hegel prepares the way for this development in his well-known claim that even animals know that the proper way to deal with sensuous objects is to "fall to without ceremony and eat them up" (*PS*, 65).

13. Karl Marx, *The Economic and Philosophic Manuscripts of 1844* (ed. Dirk M. Struik; trans. Martin Milligan; New York: International Publishers, 1964), 170–93; Herbert Marcuse, *Reason and Revolution: Hegel and the Rise of Social*

Theory (Boston: Beacon Press, 1960); and Jurgen Habermas, *Theory and Practice* (trans. J. Viertel; Boston: Beacon Press, 1973).

14. Though Scotus and Ockham disagree with Aquinas about whether *ens* and *esse* are really distinct, all three thinkers are committed to the thesis that God is really distinct from the world.

15. The concept of a speaking *logos* appears repeatedly in Augustine's *Confessions*, where at one point he says in a citation in book, chapter, and paragraph form, "Say to my soul, I am your salvation" (1.5.5). Yet even in Aquinas, where the Aristotelian commitment to the primacy of vision resurfaces, we find the explicit claim that theology is the highest science and that some truths can only be known through revelation, which is mediated by the concept of speaking. Cf. Pegis, 1:5–7.

16. Aquinas is the clearest example of a medieval thinker who acknowledges the primacy of the judgment of existence. James F. Anderson, *An Introduction to the Metaphysics of St. Thomas Aquinas* (Chicago: Henry Regnery, 1953), 21–23; see also 114–16.

17. *The Collected Papers of Charles Sanders Peirce* (ed. Charles Hartshorne and Paul Weiss; vols. 1–6; Cambridge, Mass.: Harvard University Press, 1931–35), 1.426–40, 1.558, 2.300, 336–37, and 248.

18. I am using the concept of a performative utterance in the same sense in which J. L. Austin first introduced it in his essay, "Performative Utterances," in *Philosophical Papers* (Oxford: The Clarendon Press, 1961), 220–39.

19. It is important to notice that in the original text, the term Moses uses is *hinneni* and the words attributed to God are "*ehyeh asher ehyeh.*" Strictly speaking, the verb "be" is expressed directly only in the second and indirectly in the first. However, this underscores the fact that God's mode of existence is primary and that Moses can exist only as confined to a particular spatial and temporal location.

20. Pegis, 114–16, 118–21, and 126–34.

21. As I have suggested already, Anderson discusses the judgment of existence in *An Introduction to the Metaphysics*, 21–23.

22. For an account of these theories, see Peter Geach, *Reference and Generality: An Examination of Some Medieval and Modern Theories* (Ithaca: Cornell University Press, 1962).

Chapter 3

1. Blaise Pascal, *Pensées* (trans. Honor Levi; Oxford: Oxford University Press, 1995), 50.

2. Plato, *Euthyphro* 10a, in Cooper.

3. Aristotle, *Metaphysics* 1072b15-26, in Barnes.

4. Tertullian, *Apology* (ed. J. E. B. Mayer; Cambridge: Cambridge University Press, 1917), 46.

5. Plato, *Symposium* 203a–203e, in Cooper.

6. Ibid.
7. Ibid., 203a–204c.
8. Ibid., 210e–11a.
9. Søren Kierkegaard, *Fear and Trembling and the Sickness Unto Death* (trans. and ed. Howard V. Hong and Edna H. Hong; Princeton: Princeton University Press, 1983), 70–71; and *Concluding Unscientific Postscript to Philosophical Fragments* (trans. and ed. Howard V. Hong and Edna H. Hong; Princeton: Princeton University Press, 1992), 267–68.
10. G. W. F. Hegel, *Lectures on the Philosophy of Religion*, vol. 2 (ed. Peter C. Hodgson; trans. R. F. Brown, P. C. Hodgson, and J. M. Stewart; Berkley: University of California Press, 1987), 423–54.
11. Ibid.
12. Ibid.
13. Paul Tillich, "Two Types of Philosophy of Religion," in *Theology of Culture* (ed. Robert C. Kimball; New York: Oxford University Press, 1959), 10.
14. One can establish the derivation by consulting a Latin dictionary. There is also an interesting discussion of the point in Thomas R. Martland, *Religion as Art: An Interpretation* (Albany: State University of New York Press, 1981), 15.
15. Numa Denis Fustel de Coulanges, *The Ancient City* (trans. Willard Small; Garden City: Doubleday), 21–33.
16. Aristotle, *Nichomachean Ethics* 1156b6–24, in Barnes.
17. Tillich, "Two Types of Philosophy," 16–18.
18. Pegis, 1:19–20. The context of St. Thomas's remark is his refutation of the thesis that the existence of God is self-evident. Perhaps it would be more accurate to say that God as he is in himself is identical with Truth. But from the standpoint of the finite, knower, he is identical with the Highest Truth. This raises the problem about how the finite knower knows the distinction between God in himself and God for us. And it is a difficult question whether the Thomistic approach to God through the path of remotion solves this problem. Since this issue deserves careful attention in its own right, I will restrict my present point to an epistemic context.
19. Tillich, "Two Types of Philosophy," 16–18.
20. William of Ockham, *Philosophical Writings* (trans. Philotheus Boehner; Toronto: Thomas Nelson and Sons, 1959), 19.
21. Barth, *Epistle to the Romans*, 35.
22. Ibid.
23. *CD* 1:279. I am not endorsing Barth's position. Indeed, I am prepared to defend a modified version of *analogia entis*. However, at this point in the argument, the crucial point is not Barth's rejection of the analogy of being, but his attempt to mediate the contrast between God and the soul through the analogy of faith.
24. Kierkegaard, *Fear and Trembling*, 70-71; Gen 22.8.
25. Carl G. Vaught, "Faith and Philosophy," *The Monist* 75.3 (1992): 327.
26. Aristotle, *Nichomachean Ethics* 1156b6–24, in Barnes.

27. We find an analogy between experience and reflection, first in Augustine (*C*, 7.1.1) and then in Anselm (*P*, 3); and we also find an analogy between Augustine and Anselm in this respect. It is these analogies that move toward identity and difference simultaneously.
28. Paul Tillich moves in a non-verbal direction in "Two Types of Religion," 23–29, but he also builds a theological system in his three volumes of *Systematic Theology*.
29. Pegis, 1:118–19; *ST*, 1:208–10; and Tillich, "Two Types of Religion," 10–11.
30. Vaught, "Faith and Philosophy," 329.
31. Aristotle, *Nichomachean Ethics* 1156b6–24, in Barnes.

Chapter 4

1. Augustine never uses the more familiar Anselmian phrase, *fides quarens intellectum*, to be found in (*P*, Prologue). However, Augustine's motto and Anselm's formula are related closely, not only because Anselm is an Augustinian monk, but also because both thinkers insist that in religious matters faith must always precede understanding (*P*, 1; *OFCW*, 5, 39).
2. Alvin Plantinga, "Augustinian Christian Philosophy," *The Monist* 75 (1992): 291–300. Reprinted in *The Augustian Tradition* (ed. Gareth B. Matthews; Berkeley: University of California Press, 1999), 1–26.
3. Nicholas Wolterstorff, *Reason within the Bounds of Religion* (Grand Rapids: Wm B. Eerdmans, 1976).
4. Ronald Nash, *The Light of the Mind: St. Augustine's Theory of Knowledge* (Lexington: University of Kentucky Press, 1969), 37–38.
5. Plantinga, "Augustinian Christian Philosophy," 18–19.
6. Ibid., 22.
7. Wolterstorff, *Reason within the Bounds*, 94.
8. Ibid.
9. James J. O'Donnell, *Augustine, Confessions. Text and Commentary* (3 vols.; Oxford: Oxford University Press, 1992), 2:14.
10. Aristotle, *Metaphysics* 980a, in Barnes.
11. *PS*, 65.
12. Beardsley, "The Metaphorical Twist," 293–307, 302. See also chapters 6 and 10 of this book.
13. Ibid., 304–5.
14. Ronald Nash, *The Light of the Mind: St. Augustine's Theory of Knowledge* (Lexington: University of Kentucky Press, 1969), 91–93, 107–8.
15. Margaret R. Miles, *Desire and Delight: A New Reading of Augustine's Confessions* (New York: Crossroad, 1992).
16. Augustine does not use these terms in formulating his account of the relation between God and the soul, but his description of this complex relation presupposes the concepts to which they call our attention. It is important to notice that these categories are not imposed on the text, but are ways of pointing to

crucial distinctions that emerge from it. For analogous uses of these distinctions see the works of Søren Kierkegaard, *The Concept of Irony* (trans. and ed. Edna H. Hong and Howard V. Hong; Princeton: Princeton University Press, 1992), 61–62, 74, 156–58; and Reinhold Niebuhr, *The Nature and Destiny of Man*, vol. 1 (New York: Charles Scribner's Sons, 1953), 150, 170–71, 177, and 178–81.

17. Beardsley, "The Metaphorical Twist," 293–307, 304. See also chapters 6 and 10 of this book.

18. We should not reduce metaphors and analogies to identity and difference understood univocally. Quite to the contrary, they have their own autonomy by comparison with *pros hen* predication in Aristotle's *Categories* 1a20–29, in Barnes.

19. Robert J. O'Connell, *St. Augustine's Confessions: The Odyssey of Soul* (New York: Fordham University Press, 1989), 84, 136.

20. The proper understanding of metaphor and analogy does not presuppose that they are functions of identity and difference, but expressions of what might be called "infinite richness" and "irreducible similarity." For an analysis of these conceptions, see Carl G. Vaught, "Participation and Imitation in Plato's *Metaphysics*," in *Contemporary Essays on Greek Ideas: The Kilgore Festschrift* (ed. Robert M. Baird, William F. Cooper, Elmer H. Duncan, and Stuart E. Rosenbaum; Waco: Baylor University Press, 1987), 17–31; and idem, "Categories and the Real Order: Sellar's Interpretation of Aristotle's *Metaphysics*," *The Monist* 66 (1983): 438–49.

21. O'Connell, *Saint Augustine's Confessions: The Odyssey of Soul*, 26, 82–84.

22. Ibid.

23. Plotinus, *The Enneads* (trans. A. H. Armstrong; 5 vols.; Loeb Library edition; Cambridge: Harvard University Press, 1967), 3:385–87, 4:395–421, 5:47–49, 163–69.

24. James F. Anderson, "The Metaphors of St. Thomas," in *Reflections on the Analogy of Being* (The Hague, M. Nijhoff, 1967), 39–43.

25. William of Ockham, *Philosophical Writings* (trans. Philotheus Boehner; Toronto: Thomas Nelson and Sons, 1959), 59–62.

Chapter 5

1. Charles Hartshorne develops this view in *The Logic of Perfection* (LaSalle, Ill.: Open Court Publishing Co., 1962) and *Anselm's Discovery* (LaSalle, Ill.: Open Court Publishing Co., 1965). I must postpone until another occasion the attempt to do full justice to the subtlety of his neoclassical position.

2. Rudolf Otto, *The Idea of the Holy* (trans. J. W. Harvey; New York: Oxford University Press, 1950), 55.

3. Tillich distinguishes these strands in his essay, "Two Types of Philosophy," 10–29. The present chapter bears certain positive relations to Tillich's, though it develops similar themes in more directly experiential terms.

4. This passage reflects a Tillichian perspective as he develops it in *ST*, 1:38–41, and idem, *Dynamics of Faith* (New York: Harper and Row, 1957), 41–54.

5. For a treatment of some of the problems pertaining to this kind of discourse, see James M. Robinson and John B. Cobb, Jr., eds. *The Later Heidegger and Theology* (New York: Harper and Row, 1963).

6. Gilson emphasizes this point in *Christian Philosophy*, 75, 82, 102–3.

7. Compare this with the view of Gareth B. Matthews, *Thought's Ego in Augustine and Descartes* (Ithaca: Cornell University Press, 1992), 49–51, who takes the alternative position.

8. Gilson, *Christian Philosophy*, 48.

9. Plato, *Meno* 82a-86c, in Cooper.

Chapter 6

1. One of the most serious reactions to Hegel was the "positive" philosophy of the late Schelling. Schelling developed this reaction and Kierkegaard accentuated it in some of his most well-known writings. F. W. J. Schelling, *Werke* (ed. M. Schroter; 6 vols; Munich, 1927–28), 1.2:285ff.; 3:46; 5:729–53. See also Kierkegaard, *Concluding Unscientific Postscript*, 267–82.

2. The attack on Hegel from this perspective began with Marx's early writings. Karl Marx, *The Economic and Philosophic Manuscripts of 1844* (ed. Dirk M. Struik; trans. Martin Milligan; New York: International Publishers), 170–93. For discussions of some of the same themes by Marx's successors, see Herbert Marcuse, *Reason and Revolution: Hegel and the Rise of Social Theory* (Boston: Beacon Press, 1960), and Jurgen Habermas, *Theory and Practice* (trans. J. Viertel; Boston: Beacon Press, 1973).

3. The most important contemporary representatives of this perspective are Martin Heidegger and Jacques Derrida. Heidegger, *Identity and Difference* and Derrida, *Margins of Philosophy* (trans. Alan Bass; Chicago: The University of Chicago Press, 1982), 1–27, 69–108.

4. G. W. F. Hegel, *The Logic of Hegel* (2d ed.; trans. William Wallace; Oxford: Oxford University Press, 1892), 215–18.

5. Hesiod, *Theogony*, see Brown, 56–57.

6. I have discussed the concept of analogy and the kind of intelligibility appropriate to it in a variety of contexts: *QW*, 178–97, "Categories and the Real Order, "438–49; "The Quest for Wholeness and Its Crucial Metaphor and Analogy: The Place of Places," *Ultimate Reality and Meaning* 7 (1984): 157–65; "Metaphor, Analogy, and System: A Reply to Burbidge," *Man and World* 18 (1984): 55–63; "Semiotics and the Problem of Analogy: A Critique of Peirce's Theory of Categories," *The Transactions of the Charles S. Peirce Society* 22 (1986): 311–26; "Subject, Object and Representation: A Critique of Hegel's Dialectic of Perception," *International Philosophical Quarterly* 26 (1986): 117–29; "Metaphor, Analogy, and the Nature of Truth," in *New Essays in Metaphysics* (ed. Robert C. Neville; Albany: The State University of New York

Press, 1986), 217–36; "Participation and Imitation," 17–31; and *The Journey Toward God in Augustine's Confessions: Books 1–6* (Albany: The State University of New York Press, 2003). I would like to express my indebtedness to the writings of two of my friends and former students, each of whom has attempted to move beyond dialectical intelligibility. See William Desmond, *Desire, Dialectic, and Otherness: An Essay on Origins* (New Haven: Yale University Press, 1987), and Brian John Martine, *Individuals and Individuality* (Albany: The State University of New York Press, 1984).

Chapter 7

1. Martin Heidegger, *On the Way to Language* (trans. Peter D. Hertz; New York: Harper and Row, 1971), 21–38, 57–61, and 75–76.
2. John Van Buren, *The Young Heidegger: The Rumor of the Hidden King* (Bloomington: Indiana University Press, 1994), 55–56.
3. Aristotle, *Metaphysics* 1003a33–1003b7, in Barnes.
4. Aristotle, *Categories* 1b25, in Barnes.
5. Ibid., 3a5 and Aristotle, *Metaphysics* 1003a34–100b5, in Barnes.
6. Van Buren, *The Young Heidegger*, 59.
7. Ibid.
8. Aristotle, *Metaphysics* 1038b16, in Barnes.
9. Ibid., 1003b24–1003b34.
10. Dasein is not human beings, but the place where they exist.
11. Edmund Husserl, *Logical Investigations* (trans. J. N. Findlay; London: Routledge and Kegan Paul/New York: The Humanities Press, 1970) and idem, *Ideas: General Introduction to Pure Phenomenology* (trans. W. R. Boyce Gibson; London: George Allen and Unwin/New York: The MacMillan Company, 1958), 64.
12. *Philosophical Writings of Descartes*, 1:9ff.
13. According to this reading of the *Meditations*, the *cogito* engages in an act of construction in which both God and the ego are brought into existence.
14. Ibid.; Husserl, *Logical Investigations*, 2:248–52.
15. Ibid., 2:197.
16. The passages in brackets are my insertions.
17. Gillian Rose, *The Broken Middle: Out of Our Ancient Society* (Oxford: Blackwell Publisher, 1992).
18. The concept of Place has a metaphorical dimension that allows the richness and openness of human existence to express themselves. As a consequence, figurative language is an irreducible dimension of philosophical and religious reflection. For a detailed analysis of this issue, see *QW*, 193–97 and chapter 10 of this book.
19. Karl Jaspers, *Philosophy* (trans. E. B. Ashton; 3 vols.; Chicago: The University of Chicago Press, 1971), 3:166.
20. Ibid., 3:124.

21. The openness is metaphorical because it displays mystery, power, and structure in dynamic interactions that develop in time and that cannot be paraphrased. See Beardsley, "The Metaphorical Twist," 293–307, 304–5. In the case of analogical otherness, we stand in an analogical relation with the transcendent ground of our existence. For a further discussion of this issue, see chapter 10 of this book.

Chapter 8

1. *The Quest for Wholeness* is the title of the book in which I develop more fully the themes of this chapter by using concrete reflection to deal with the philosophical problems associated with the quest for wholeness. See *QW*, 9, 193–97.
2. Edmund Husserl, *Ideas: General Introduction to Pure Phenomenology* (trans. W. R. Boyce Gibson; London: George Allen and Unwin/New York: The MacMillan Company, 1958), 64.
3. Plato, *Euthyphro* 16a, in Cooper.
4. Plato, *Symposium* 176c, in Cooper.
5. Plato, *Euthyphro* 2b, 16a, in Cooper.

Chapter 9

1. This has been true since the time of Augustine. See *C*, 7.1.1, 7.4.6, and 10.24.35.
2. The most notable instance of this view is to be found in Anselm (*P*, 1, 7–11, 22–24, 37–41).
3. I rely, at this point, on the writings of Paul Tillich (*ST*, 1:233–35). The chapter as a whole reflects a considerable debt to Tillich. However, I have suppressed a number of expository issues in the attempt to deal more directly with the theological and the philosophical problems that arise.
4. E.g., we find this view in Benedict Spinoza, *Ethics* (trans. R. H. M. Elwes; New York: Dover Publications, 1955), 45.
5. Paul Tillich, *Biblical Religion and the Search for Ultimate Reality* (Chicago: The University of Chicago Press, 1955), 8384.
6. Husserl, *Ideas*, 168–70.
7. Spinoza, *Ethics*, 22.
8. Bernard McGinn, *The Foundations of Mysticism: Origins to the Fifth Century* (New York: Crossroad, 2000), 27–29, 176–78.
9. Augustine, *Confessions* 1.1.1, 7.1.1, 9.10.23, 10.6.8, 10.26.37, and *The Trinity* 1.2.69, 2.1.98–2.2.105, 7.3.224, 12.3.327 (see trans. Edmund Hill; Brooklyn, N.Y.: New City Press, 1991).
10. Spinoza, *Ethics*, 22.
11. Plato, *Republic* 608c–611e, in Cooper.
12. I owe this point to my former colleague at Penn State, Carl R. Hausman, with whom I discussed these issues for many years.

Chapter 10

1. Aristotle, *Metaphysics* 1011b25–28, in Barnes.

2. A. N. Prior, "Correspondence Theory of Truth," in *The Encyclopedia of Philosophy*, vol. 2 (ed. Paul Edwards; New York: Crowell, Collier, and Macmillan, Inc., 1967), 224.

3. St. Thomas Aquinas, *On the Truth of the Catholic Faith, Book 1* (trans. Anton C. Pegis; Garden City: Doubleday and Company, 1955), 204–5, 208.

4. Descartes is responsible for this transformation, identifying Truth with clear and distinct ideas in *Meditation* 3 and implying in *Meditation* 4 that the real-order existence of objects is a matter of probability rather than absolute certainty. The most notable exception to this subjective transformation is John Locke, however much his British successors undermined his position.

5. P. F. Strawson, "Truth," in *Truth* (ed. George Pitcher; Englewood Cliffs: PrenticeHall, 1964), 37–38.

6. Ibid., 36–37.

7. J. L. Austin, "Unfair to Facts," in *Philosophical Papers* (Oxford: Clarendon Press, 1961), 104–5.

8. Ibid., 120–22.

9. Ibid., 111–12.

10. Ibid.

11. Wilfrid Sellars defends a position of this kind in "Truth and Correspondence," in *Science, Perception, and Reality* (New York: The Humanities Press, 1963), 197–224; and in *Science and Metaphysics: Variations on Kantian Themes* (New York: The Humanities Press, 1968), 116–50. The position that I will sketch is a modification of this view in certain important respects.

12. Brand Blanshard, *The Nature of Thought*, vol. 2 (London: George Allen and Unwin/New York: The Macmillan Company, 1939), 264.

13. *Collected Papers of Charles Sanders Peirce*, vol. 5 (ed. Charles Harshorne and Paul Weiss; Cambridge, Mass.: Harvard University Press, 1960), 416.

14. Ibid., 407.

15. Ibid., 408.

16. Blanshard, *Nature of Thought*, 2:273.

17. *Collected Papers of Charles Sanders Peirce*, 5:408–9.

18. Blanshard, *Nature of Thought*, 2:304–11.

19. Max Black, "Metaphor" in *Models and Metaphors* (Ithaca: Cornell University Press, 1962), 219–43; and Paul Ricoeur, *The Rule of Metaphor* (trans. Robert Czerny; Toronto: The University of Toronto Press, 1977), 286–90, 295–313.

20. This view blends the interactionist view Black develops in "Metaphor," 219–43, and Beardsley's defense of the verbal opposition theory in "The Metaphorical Twist," 293–307. Ricoeur approximates this view in *Rule of Metaphor*, 312–13, and my former colleague, Carl R. Hausman, develops it explicitly in *A Discourse on Novelty and Creation* (The Hague: Martinus Nijhoff, 1975), 99–110.

21. For a detailed discussion of the view that root metaphors are the foundations of philosophical theories, see Stephen C. Pepper, *World Hypotheses* (Berkeley: The University of California Press, 1942).
22. Carl G. Vaught, "Categories and the Real Order: Sellar's Interpretation of Aristotle's *Metaphysics*," *The Monist* 63 (1983), 438–49.
23. Aristotle, *Categories* 1a20-29, in Barnes; and Pegis 1:115–21, 128–30.
24. For a more detailed discussion of this concept, see *QW*, 182–97 and chapter 10 of this book.

Index